Healing the Trauma of
PSYCHOLOGICAL ABUSE

A Lived Experience Roadmap to a Mindful Recovery

MARGOT MACCALLUM

BALBOA.
PRESS
A DIVISION OF HAY HOUSE

NIV: Scriptures taken from the Holy Bible, New International Version®, NIV®. Copyright © 1973, 1978, 1984, 2011 by Biblica, Inc.™ Used by permission of Zondervan. All rights reserved worldwide. www.zondervan.com The "NIV" and "New International Version" are trademarks registered in the United States Patent and Trademark Office by Biblica, Inc.

Balboa Press books may be ordered through booksellers or by contacting:

Balboa Press
A Division of Hay House
1663 Liberty Drive
Bloomington, IN 47403
www.balboapress.com.au
1 (877) 407-4847

Because of the dynamic nature of the Internet, any web addresses or links contained in this book may have changed since publication and may no longer be valid. The views expressed in this work are solely those of the author and do not necessarily reflect the views of the publisher, and the publisher hereby disclaims any responsibility for them.

The author of this book does not dispense medical advice or prescribe the use of any technique as a form of treatment for physical, emotional, or medical problems without the advice of a physician, either directly or indirectly. The intent of the author is only to offer information of a general nature to help you in your quest for emotional and spiritual well-being. In the event you use any of the information in this book for yourself, which is your constitutional right, the author and the publisher assume no responsibility for your actions.

Print information available on the last page.

ISBN: 978-1-5043-1532-6 (sc)
ISBN: 978-1-5043-1533-3 (e)

Balboa Press rev. date: 10/22/2018

Contents

To Helen and Jon, who stood by me, shoulder to shoulder, steadfast, loyal, and kind, as I walked through hell and out the other side

Preface

Some people take gratification from destroying other people's lives. Hard to believe, isn't it? It's especially hard to comprehend when it happens to you, when the person you loved so much you would have given your life for him—your soulmate—walks away (or you flee in fear of your sanity), and you realise he has already taken everything. You gave it to him.

You gave him your heart because you trusted he would treat it with care. You gave him entry to your bank accounts, your past, your secrets, your most vulnerable places because you trusted him. You made him the centre of your world because he wanted you; every bit of you. So you gave him everything slowly, bit by bit. You gave up your career, your friends, your home, or your country. Or you made him partner in your business, gave him control. He promised you would never regret it because he would take such good care of you. He convinced you to stretch your moral boundaries, little by little, in the name of compromise, until you forgot how to say no.

He said all the right things, but somehow his actions didn't match up with his words. There was a shallowness, a hollowness about him that you couldn't quite unravel. His seduction had been like no other: euphoric. He said he had never experienced true love like this before. And he had such a sad story. He was handsome, charming, gregarious, glib, and maybe even famous, but he had nothing material. It had all been taken from him by insane, violent, abusive ex-wives and girlfriends. He had given it all to them. That's why he had to keep divorcing, moving, and swapping jobs, social circles, towns, countries. You believed him. You lent him a helping hand, and loved, loved, loved him, for months or years.

Sometimes, he scared you half out of your wits, so you clung to him for the protection he vowed to give. You gave him the benefit of the doubt every time he swore he'd never do that thing again. You forgave him over and over. And with every concession, you felt smaller and smaller, right out of touch with who you used to be, isolated. He kept asking, and you kept giving, in the hope of getting the things he promised in return. But the return never came. Not yet, anyway. A thousand promises kept you focussed on backing him up, being there for him, making his life easier, picking up the tab, doing what your kind, conscientious, generous heart cried out to do for the man you loved.

And right when you were at your most committed, most invested, he pulled the rug out from under you. You blamed yourself. You could have done more or been kinder, more agreeable, more compliant, skinnier. He said you'd done nothing wrong, there was no one else; it just didn't work out. He wanted to go away and work on his legacy to the world, without you. Or he said you were crazy, abusive, impossible, needy. It was as if the vows and promises—the ones he made only yesterday—had never happened. As if he didn't owe you any explanation. As if none of it mattered. As if he didn't care about you or anything else except what he wanted next. You weren't his problem anymore.

When you tried to reason with him, he changed into a man you didn't recognise. As if his mask had dropped. As if aliens had abducted him and returned his body without a heart and soul. As if he were a snake shedding his skin on the rug you carefully chose together. As if he were the wolf emerging from inside his sheep costume, a cold, calculated, emotionless automaton with a grin of satisfaction. Shocking. And the next day, he proclaims his undying love for another woman on Facebook, happy at last.

And slowly, slowly, you come to realise that everything he said right from the very beginning was a lie or lies sandwiched between truths. You have invested everything in his scam. He deliberately broke you. He took everything that was useful to him and left you with nothing, in debt, and with your reputation shredded. Still later, you realise you married a narcissist, sociopath, or psychopath. That grin he wore privately? That was pleasure at causing you pain and confusion, at making you weep, at the power and control he had over your heart, your mind, your life. Just like in the movies.

After he abandons you, he does everything in his power to leave you homeless and broke, your spirit broken, and your character impugned. He steals, lies, slanders, perjures, manipulates with impunity, as if your life were his to rape and plunder, while he convinces everyone he is the blameless victim again, the sweetest, nicest, most harmless guy in the world. You feel like he is trying to drive you insane, to suicide.

And later still, when you can't seem to recover, you realise you have been seriously psychologically and emotionally abused.

To break a woman and call it love
Is nothing short of Evil.

—narcissisticsociopath.net

Introduction

This book is unapologetically written for women.

Around the world in 2018, thousands of women are searching for understanding, support, and help in healing from the soul-shattering betrayal of psychological and emotional abuse by their most loved and trusted other. It is a hidden epidemic and a misunderstood taboo. Women's suffering is minimised and demeaned. Society now understands how sexual assault and physical violence can leave scars that may never heal, especially if they happen in childhood. Western therapists understand that a single life-threatening incident can leave veterans and first responders with post-traumatic stress disorder (PTSD).

What is *not* understood in the mainstream community is just how damaging it is to be forced—usually by our own decency and loyalty—to endure prolonged, apparently minor injuries from a personality disordered other to whom we are bonded. Our culture does not recognise that pathological lying, manipulation, exploitation, character assassination, financial fraud, and callous cruelty—without a single punch thrown—is *abuse*. That such behaviour can break a person's spirit. That a broken spirit is synonymous with a condition known as complex post-traumatic stress disorder (CPTSD), which is not yet recognised by the Western psychological bible, the Diagnostic and Statistical Manual of Mental Disorders.

For these reasons, women who have been suddenly abandoned or find themselves running in fear of their sanity are left out in the cold. Rather than support and understanding in their families and communities, they find mockery, blame, and scorn. Rather than acknowledgement from Western therapists that their trauma—which often resembles the trauma of PTSD—is legitimate, they are frequently misdiagnosed and offered treatment that is entirely inappropriate for their condition.

People want to compare their situation with normal divorces or break-ups. But there is no such comparison to be made when one partner is without conscience, remorse, or empathy, when one partner vengefully seeks to destroy the other by whatever means, whilst appearing innocent and charming, when one partner has a personality disorder.

When we escape our disguised abuser, we are blamed for having abnormal emotional and psychological issues; the cause of our suffering is completely overlooked; we are dismissed as blamers ourselves. Asked to repeat our confusing and complex stories by therapists and lawyers, we are retraumatised over and over until we learn to just shut up about it, hide our suffering, suppress it, pretend we are over it, keep calm and carry on, often from a place of utter devastation, from whence we must rebuild whole lives and selves that have been brutally shattered by the behaviour of our former intimate partner.

Our relief and validation can only be found behind the closed doors of society. We are driven after-hours into online forums, chat groups, and Facebook groups where we find other survivors whose stories all bear the same hallmarks. We slowly unravel the shock, grief, and anger of being psychologically manipulated. It can take years, depending on which healing methods we stumble across, depending on how much support and validation are available to us in our existing circle of friends, and depending on how many more setbacks we encounter in our social, professional, financial, sexual, and emotional lives.

Because we are by nature givers, sharers, people-pleasers, compromisers, cooperators, co-dependents, or compliant easy prey, our damaged energetic wiring can magnetically attract more and more exploiters and manipulators. Our exaggerated emotional reactiveness can create more social and professional damage. We can sustain more and more loss even after our homes, jobs, businesses, family, and friends are long gone. We may feel crazy and look that way at times. Our individual maladaptive coping responses can drive us further and further into isolation, despair, and victimhood.

This book is my gesture from that lived experience. It is not written from the perspective of a therapist who has treated people recovering from psychological abuse. Nor is it written by a mature and experienced Mindfulness teacher. Rather, it is an account of just one woman's journey in the context of one life, one country, one era. It is the result of four years of dedicated research and experimentation of: victim stories; mental health forums; psychology, trauma-recovery, Buddhism, and mindfulness books; workshops and retreats; book study groups; survivor groups; alternative modalities; cognitive behaviour therapy; and daily mindfulness, yoga, and meditation practice. I firmly believe that in every story, there could be a hidden gem that affirms and inspires us. Reading about another person's journey in life can help us on our own journey.

I encourage you to remind yourself as you read this book that it is all just opinion, conjecture, and theory. Ask yourself, "Is this true for me?" You are the only expert in your life. No book, doctrine, theory, or person can rescue you from your own condition. Only we can do that for ourselves. What works for one person will not work for another. As much as this is an obvious truism, it is worth reminding yourself of it. If it works for you, keep it, and if it doesn't, let it go. If it hurts too much to read it, let it go and come back to it later when you're ready. If it makes you too sad, angry, or afraid, let it go because the time is not right to go there. The realities of psychological abuse are brutal.

It is my sincere and heartfelt hope that this book will help you find what you need to know now. I hope it will uplift you, encourage you, and validate you. I hope it will help you find the courage to awaken to your own suffering and recover your own basic decency and your own good heart. I hope it can serve as a useful stepping stone towards taking personal responsibility for your own healing. I pray you will receive the little offerings in these pages as a gift from one survivor to another.

This is what I learnt.

There is a misconception that Buddhism is a
religion, and that you worship Buddha.
Buddhism is a practice, like yoga.
You can be Christian and practice Buddhism.
I met a Catholic priest who lives in a Buddhist monastery in France.
He told me that Buddhism makes him a better Christian.
I love that.

—themindsjournal.com

Author's Note

So what gives me the authority to write a book about recovering from the covert abusive behaviours of narcissists, psychopaths, and sociopaths?

My own route to healing came via a personal quest to uncover the reasons for my own repeated victimisation and methods for changing myself. I took a sociological approach to researching the vast unofficial online community of victims, survivors, bloggers, authors, healers, psychologists, psychiatrists, and trolls of psychological abuse: over four years and across various online platforms, forums, comments sections, and a veritable library of books.

Throughout the book, the masculine pronoun has been used when referring to the psychological abuser. It is not my intention to exclude lesbians who have been abused by female partners. Men experience domestic abuse too, but the statistics reveal a distinctly gendered issue and it is suffering women to whom I address this book. I trust this editorial choice will not unduly offend any such reader.

The words *moral, ethical,* and *virtuous* all carry a lot of baggage in our vernacular, an association with fire, brimstone, and old-fashioned moralism. But finding substitute words like *integrity, right,* and *nice* doesn't really capture their original meaning. They are used in the spirit of modern secular Buddhism, held lightly and with respect.

There is repetition (reinforcement) in the writing. Repetition is an old-fashioned method of adult learning. Real adult learning is in *experiencing*.

Embrace your suffering and let it reveal to you the way to peace.

—narcissisticsociopath.net

Where there is great doubt, there will be great awakening; small doubt, small awakening; no doubt, no awakening.

—narcissisticsociopath.net

Endurance is courage. Perseverance is courage. Sometimes just functioning is courage. Be brave, little one.

—narcissisticsociopath.net

No beauty shines brighter than that of a good heart.

—narcissisticsociopath.net

Chapter 1

WHAT THE HELL JUST HAPPENED?

Have I Really Been Psychologically or Emotionally Abused?

This break-up has left us absolutely depleted, exhausted to the very bottom of our souls. It is as if every ounce of our former get-up-and-go has been sucked out of us, as if a parasite has slowly been sucking our life force, as if he dragged us to the bottom of the ocean and cut our lifeline. Right when all our strength is sapped, we have to muster more of it to swim to the surface to save ourselves or drown in our own confusion and grief.

This is how you know you are (or were) a victim of psychological abuse. This devaluation behaviour starts the moment you are bonded or hooked. Frequently, it's the day after the wedding. Then it escalates.

- The seduction and courtship was like nothing you'd ever experienced before. He seemed like your perfect match, your soulmate. He swept you off your feet, and before you knew it, he'd moved in with you.
- Once he'd gained your commitment, love, and trust, his behaviour at home began to change.
- You start to realise that there is something very wrong with him, but you can't quite put your finger on it, so you dismiss your suspicions as baseless (you enter into denial).

1

- He ignores you in private but plays the adoring husband in public.
- You seem to be the least important person in his life when you feel like you should be the most important (you enter into cognitive dissonance, or holding two conflicting beliefs at the same time: he loves me, he loves me not). Resolving this can keep your mind very busy until the moment he discards you.
- Your wellbeing is the last thing on his list.
- You mutually agree on a compromise plan, and then he behaves as if you never made the agreement and does what he wanted anyway (gaslighting, or an extreme form of "Are you nuts? I never said that.").
- He convinces you to give up more and more of your independence, your social and professional networks, your family and friends.
- At the same time, he seems to be drawing more and more from your financial, social and professional resources.
- The goalposts keep shifting. He doesn't want today what he wanted yesterday.
- He continually makes promises but almost always breaks them.
- You try to discuss things, but he refuses, walks away, leaves the house for days (stonewalling).
- You feel like you give and give and get very little in return.
- You feel him become emotionally distant and cold, with increasing frequency.
- You feel yourself disappearing.
- You feel like you cannot do enough to regain his affection.
- You are afraid of him abandoning you.
- You are constantly forgiving him for his bad behaviour, but he punishes you for upsetting him with your illnesses, sadness, or anxiety.
- You feel like he continually takes advantage of your good nature (your forgiveness, trust, generosity, putting others' needs before your own).
- You think he's lying to you, but if you ask him directly, he tells you you're paranoid.
- You are walking on eggshells in case you use the wrong words or the wrong tone of voice, or look at him (or someone else) the wrong way.
- You feel guilty but don't know why.

- You feel angry but don't know why.
- You feel used, undervalued, ignored, and disempowered (you feel fat, stupid, incompetent, useless).
- You are constantly being made to apologise for things you shouldn't really have to apologise for.
- You feel accountable for his infidelity, his failures, his financial irresponsibility.
- You feel sorry for him when he plays the victim.
- His friends, colleagues, or family treat you with a total lack of respect, suspicion, and contempt (as if he's putting you down to them behind your back).
- He suddenly discards you like a worthless rag. Even if you had a rough patch leading up to this, you didn't see the discard coming. You might have sensed something was up and tried to discuss it. You might have tried couples counselling. He might have reassured you that he loved you and would never leave you. But he had it all planned, right down to the move into the next woman's home.
- He suddenly morphed into a snarling, accusing, aggressive, seething monster, like he had two personalities. Like the mask he had been wearing suddenly dropped to reveal the evil twin inside.

An abuser *takes* from people who give generosity, kindness and love.
And when he has exhausted the giver's emotional,
psychological, financial, professional or social
resources, he *discards* and *destroys* the giver.

—narcissisticsociopath.net

Not a Normal Break-Up

I would have given my life for him.
Then the mask dropped to reveal the most vile human being …
A man who would destroy me in order to save himself.
Using my goodness to do it.

—narcissisticsociopath.net

He has suddenly abandoned us, for no apparent reason, with no warning. It was a huge shock. He had a sudden personality change right before our eyes. His mask dropped. He turned into a cold-blooded monster, just like in the movies. His eyes turned cold and reptilian. His speech turned callous and contemptuous. A cruel grin appeared at leaving us so utterly dependent. He left us carrying the can, big time. So we need to get on with things. Keep calm and carry on. Put on a brave face and get on with it. Just another break-up that we didn't see coming, but we'll never forget that moment when he morphed into a monster. He didn't seem human. He was unrecognisable. It was horrifying. It happened in slow motion, like it wasn't quite real.

The traumatic event has passed, but we still feel as if we're about to die. Logically, we know that the threat has gone, but our bodies are still pumping out fear hormones that will help us fight or run. It's as if a war has started between our logical mind and our instinctual mind, a war between our minds and our bodies.

We often judge ourselves; this is crazy. Nobody should feel this much shock and confusion over a break-up. Break-ups have left us sad in the past, but all we had to do was get through the grieving period, pass through Kübler-Ross's five stages of grief and then get on with life. But shaking hands? Pounding heart? Twisted gut? Brain fog? Terror? Horror? Rage? Not being able to function? Are you kidding? This isn't normal break-up grief here. "When am I going to get back to feeling normal?"

This thing is dragging out way longer than it should and is way worse than it should be: "He didn't hit me. But I'm scared half to death by what he might do to me now he's gone. I'm scared he's going to take all our money out of that bank account he never got around to giving me access to. I'm scared he's going to lie under oath and hide his assets, and the court will give him half of what I haven't already given him. I'm scared he's going to stalk me and threaten me. I'm scared he's going to have someone hurt me. I'm scared he's going to trash my reputation. I must be paranoid. I must have lost my mind. Yesterday, this guy was my husband. I would've given my life for his. I'm a terrible person for having these thoughts. I've gone nuts."

What we don't yet understand is that we've been manipulated, big time, scammed. We believed the lies right up until he discarded us (or we got too frightened and ran). He lied about things that no one should ever lie about, like loving us. That offends not only our egos but also our deeply held core beliefs, our morals. We have sustained a deep moral *injury*.

We weren't just cheated *on*; we were cheated out of whole lives. Somewhere deep inside, we know this, even though the evidence hasn't all come to light yet. We know we invested everything in this relationship; we gave it our all, and only yesterday, we were making big plans for the future. What happened between yesterday and today to make him suddenly abandon the huge investment we made? He made solemn vows. We gave up our careers. We had his baby. We left our family and friends behind and moved to be with him. Our parents gave him a huge dowry. We lent him our life savings. We capitulated to his weird sexual demands. We're really sick and in need of support now more than ever. Whatever. We trusted him with our whole life, and he's gone, leaving us with nothing to hang onto. What the hell?

Our lives aren't just threatened. They've been plundered. Raped. The earth around us is scorched. We trusted him and shared our hearts, our bodies, our social network, our life savings, our business, our home; you name it. We didn't just lose a partner or a future. We lost a life. We let ourselves be convinced to get so far in that there was no way back to independence. We were totally committed, boots and all: more so than ever before. He insisted we go all in. And we did it because we believed he loved us as much as we loved him. A person doesn't just wake up one morning and walk away from all that. No warning. No discussion. No negotiation. No explanation. Just abandonment? WTF? How could anyone do that to someone they say they love?

We reach out for support from friends and family, but they say we have no one to blame but ourselves or claim we're making mountains out of molehills, we're drama queens. Plenty of women get left by their lying, cheating husbands. We must've seen it coming. They could all tell he was a fake. Or they all think he's the most charming guy in the world, so it must be something we did; we just can't admit it. We let ourselves go. We got old and fat. Or because we caught him in a big lie years ago, we should have known he was lying. We should never have invested so much. We have no one to blame but ourselves. Our mental, physical, financial, social health is shot to pieces, and we are being *blamed* for it? WTF is going on here? It feels like we've lost everything and everyone who was dear to us.

This feels like death, or impending death, not a break-up. "I've gotta get a grip!"

Firstly, please give yourself a break if you feel utterly traumatised this time. It's not like you haven't had a break-up before, is it? But this one is different, very, very different. This is not a normal break-up. For a start, the person you loved and trusted most in the world carefully plotted the cruellest and most hurtful way to abandon you. He caught you off-guard and pulled the rug out from under you, just when he had your total commitment to the relationship. He disempowered you psychologically, financially, professionally, and took away any tools you might have had to defend yourself, keeping you from standing on your own two feet and recovering the way you have in previous break-ups.

Your shock, grief, and rage at a time of great loss are normal too. If they feel deeper and more pervasive than before, it is because of the enormous discrepancy between the mutual loving relationship you thought you had and the callous, malevolent hatred you're suddenly faced with. Be kind and gentle towards yourself.

Cultivate patience. Patience is the antidote to anger. Anger is a normal and natural response to grief and betrayal. If you lashed out at your abuser (or others), be patient with yourself. Instead of hating yourself for being angry, remind yourself that this is not who you are. This rage is not a permanent condition; it does not define you. It will pass. It is impermanent, like everything, including your own personality. You are not stuck being an angry, resentful, bitter person for the rest of your life. There is a way out. Take heart. Cultivate patience for yourself first, and your patience for others will grow.

If you always maintained good relationships with your exes in the past and are putting pressure on yourself to forgive your psychological abuser and foster a friendship with him, let it go this time. You may desperately want him to see how badly he has treated you and call him to account for his bad behaviour, but let it go. You may want him to apologise; you may want closure. Let it go; let it go. The longer you stay in contact, the more you open the door to his continued manipulation.

Make more space for forgiveness and understanding of your *own* ordeal. You were effectively brainwashed over a period of time. You were deceived, manipulated, and conditioned to be smaller than you are. Naivety is not a crime. You are not to blame for devaluing yourself or your feelings of helplessness and hopelessness, your weakness and vulnerability. This is conditioning, and it can be changed. You can get back on top of things. You can recover. You are still the beautiful person you were before you were mercilessly discarded by an immoral and ruthless charmer. That will become clear to you soon enough.

Your normal human reward system has taken a severe blow. All the sacrifices you made over time on the basis of his vows to catch you when you jumped have been thwarted. When you jumped, he wasn't there to catch you; he watched you fall, with a grin on his face. He made you feel foolish and gullible for trusting him. And you hid your deep offence at this. You didn't want to be a bad sport. You picked yourself up, dusted yourself off, and carried on regardless.

He didn't leave as a result of your personal failings; he left because he is compelled to treat others inhumanely on his path to self-gratification. You are not to blame.

Your body is low on levels of serotonin, along with other physical responses to betrayal. There are simple, effective, free ways to increase your serotonin: walk in nature; lots of water, water, water, in and around you. Share loving relationships with your children and your pets. Exercise. Sport. Sleep. Rest. Don't punish yourself. Be kind to yourself. Treat yourself as you would your best friend or your child.

If you convince yourself he made a mistake and beg him to come back, that too is normal. It is a normal stage of grief (bargaining) and a normal reaction to the feeling that a part of you is missing. Your oxytocin and vasopressin levels—part of your human bonding system—are shot to pieces. *It's in your body.* Let yourself off the hook. Wanting him back is an illusory response to your drive to restore equilibrium. This chaos is not the new normal. It is not permanent. Restoring the finely tuned balance you managed whilst walking on the eggshells of living with Dr Jekyll and Mr Hyde is definitely not the way to go. You will find balance again, and you can break the ties that bound you to him, even though this break-up feels much worse than others you've had.

You may feel anxious, hyperaroused, constantly on red alert. You got a big shock, after all. You were suddenly abandoned, when you were anticipating a reward of some kind: a new child, or a new life in a new country, or time off supporting him financially so he could support you, or deeper intimacy as a result of being accountable and making compromises. You might feel a bit hysterical. You've never felt this way before. You may have lost the urge to eat or sleep. Your startle response might be exaggerated, and letters, emails, phone calls, and other normal stimuli have become terrifying, unwanted intrusions that fill you with fear and dread. Your stress systems—your fight, flight, or freeze response—are in overdrive. It's in your body. You aren't losing your mind.

You have been betrayed on a grand scale. It's not a normal break-up. Move away from blaming yourself for your own strong emotions, and seek help to deal with them. Not just professional help; be with people who build you up instead of tearing you down, if you can find them. Turn towards your stress symptoms with love, compassion, kindness, and gentleness. They are not here to stay, though if it's PTSD, they might return for years to come. Do your best to face reality. There is nothing normal about this break-up. You can't bury/ignore/be stoic about it this time. Fear demands our immediate attention. And underlying that fear is a huge number of beliefs (attachments), dislikes (aversions), myths, and unknowns (ignorance) that we are compelled to use as fuel for the fire of fear. It is fear itself that is your enemy now. The antidote to fear is courage.

Cultivate courage. Have faith in your deep strength. Start feeding your courage, not your fear.

On top of all that, you might have developed chronic pain or some other condition. If you look back on it, it might have started right when you hooked up with your former partner. Neuroscience is also starting to recognise the link between psychological and physical pain. Alternative Eastern medicine has known about the body-mind connection for centuries, based purely on empirical evidence. You might be experiencing all sorts of aches and pains and illnesses now that your pain systems are also under duress.

Go easy on yourself. Smile at your pain, whether you believe it is psychosomatic or not. And attend to your body with all the loving-kindness you gave to your ex. Nurture yourself with nutritious food, warm baths, sweet aromas, soothing music, gentle words. Take your suffering body-mind in your own loving embrace and heal it, encourage it, reassure it, just as you would a child. And if you haven't tried complementary therapies before, perhaps now is the time to seek them out.

Be careful out there. There are plenty of false prophets promising a whole new you if you fork out a small fortune for a workshop on positive thinking, or spiritual healers promising to suck the pain right out of you. Sounds appealing right at this moment, doesn't it? Someone to come and take the pain away? But that can wait until you've figured things out with your rational mind a bit more. For now, how about you write yourself some affirmations? Just in the meantime, while you need temporary relief. Take breathers from what just happened to you and concentrate hard on words that build you up, remind you of your good heart, and encourage you. Start working as soon as you can, amidst all the confusion, on your own healing.

Traditional Chinese Medicine (TCM), Ayurveda, Qigong, Yoga, Tai Chi and other healing modalities have been around for thousands of years, recognising the mind-body-spirit connection. Secular Buddhism (Insight or Vipassana meditation) teaches specific practices for addressing sickness, despair, dying, and death.

You may have difficulty regulating your emotional systems. You might be trying every trick in the book to calm down; stop losing your rag and telling people to get lost; drag yourself out of this emotional nightmare. Let yourself off the hook. Your distress has a distinct cause. You've been injured. You'll figure out who is responsible for what before too long. Again, this desperate reactive person is not who you are. Don't beat yourself up for being unable to keep it all together.

In fact, if you can let yourself fall apart, your recovery will come quicker than if you push it all down and bury yourself in work or addictions or entertainment or distraction. It sounds counter-intuitive. The very suggestion might make you angry. Our culture of stoicism, our conditioned inner critics, and our friends urge us to do just that. (Run, hide, tell no one, pretend you have everything under control, get drunk, get busy, keep calm, and carry on.)

But instead of a stiff upper lip, what we most need now is balm for our broken spirits. We need compassion, kindness, gentleness, and patience as antidotes to the thoughts and emotions that arise from our wound, over which we have no control.

You might also find, to add insult to injury (and by now you are starting to realise just how deep your injury goes), that your cognitive systems are also up the spout. You are having trouble remembering things, concentrating when people speak to you, paying attention when receiving important information, getting your brain to function the way it always has. This, too, is normal after suffering an abusive or traumatic experience. You can cope with your fuzzy brain. Adjust your habits. Write things down. Keep lists. Express yourself in emails that you send only to yourself, let some time expire, then reread and edit them. No rush. The rush is just another illusion our own minds trick us into feeling. Because we want to escape this pain. Take your time with everything. Everything. Walk slower. Eat slower. Rest more. Let yourself off the hook again. Forgive yourself for having the symptoms you now have. Forgive others (if you can) for not understanding that this time, it's different.

If the trauma has triggered earlier experiences of abuse, you might even be staring down the barrel of complex post-traumatic stress disorder (CPTSD). In this case, patience with your own impaired cognitive function is needed. You might be stuck with it for a while, like any of the human system upsets already described in this chapter. But none of them are permanent.

The people who don't get that you've suffered covert abusive behaviour from your ex may never see it. You might not even get it yet. You just can't reconcile the charming guy you thought you'd married with the callous creature who revealed himself. You think it must have been something you did, but you can't figure out what the deal-breaker was. So you pick apart all your own bad habits and personality flaws to find an explanation. Right when you need to soothe and comfort your grieving self, you pile on the blame (maybe like everybody around you).

Focus on your own healing, your own recovery. Turn your gaze inwards, and let it rest with compassion on the suffering of a lifetime. Suffering is inevitable in the human experience, so don't beat yourself up about it. There is a path out of suffering. Time well spent in recovery will heal your wounds. Self-compassion will heal your wounds. Have patience. Have faith. Have courage. You can depend on your own good heart, your own inner guidance, and your own basic decency to rescue you this time.

The Perfect Storm

> You can't calm the storm
> so stop trying.
> What you can do is calm yourself.
> The storm will pass.
>
> —tinybuddha.com

Sudden abandonment or sudden flight from a psychological abuser is very often the perfect storm. It pulls not just the rug but also the ground right out from under us. On top of the burdens of breaking up, moving house, loss of livelihood, protecting the children and ourselves from further abuse, lengthy and expensive litigation, and possibly degenerative chronic pain, we might have an invisible illness caused by years of storing more and more stress *in our bodies*.

Trauma expert Peter A Levine observes, "We become traumatised when our ability to respond to perceived threat is in some way overwhelmed.

"The capacity to choose, think, behave or feel differently is only possible when our nervous system is in a safe, relaxed and engaged enough state to do so."

You have been convinced that you are unlovable by a man who didn't love you. You have been made to look and feel crazy by the man who drove you there. You have been made to believe you are weak when in fact you are incredibly strong, having borne the weight of your hidden abuse for way too long. You have been devalued and discarded. It is difficult to feel your own worth when someone has treated you as if you are utterly worthless. You may be facing the first enemy you ever had: your own ex-partner. You need the strength of a warrior when you are feeling at your most vulnerable and broken. You can get through this storm. You can do this. You don't know how strong you are until being strong is the only option you have.

The entire relationship was a lie. It is unbearable. But you danced with the devil, and the devil changed you. Courage doesn't mean we don't feel fear. Courage means we don't let the fear stop us. You can deal with this perfect storm by taking one step at a time in the dark. The light will reappear when you regain some faith in yourself. You will heal. He will always be an abuser.

I know. Life is unfair, but this is ridiculous!

I've been there, and if I can do it, you can. Start telling yourself you can do it, and don't stop until the day you realise you've walked out of the storm.

The Four Noble Truths

The lotus is the symbol of enlightenment or spiritual freedom. Its growth is similar to the path we tread in the growth of wisdom. Some people are like tiny buds whose vision is clouded by dark, murky, muddy water. Others are reaching upwards through the gloom. Yet more have breached the water's surface but are still tightly furled buds, not yet ready to bloom. And there are those who are ready to burst into bloom after the long journey into the light.

It is much like the journey a sufferer of traumatic abuse must take in order to move from victim to survivor to thriver.

Buddha, an enlightened being (there are supposedly many around us), taught that to understand the path, we must first understand four fundamental truths of this noble journey:

1. Suffering. It is an inevitable part of human life.
2. The Origin of Suffering. It is our own undisciplined untrained minds that are at the root of our suffering.
3. Cessation of Suffering. By eliminating craving (for things to be different than the way they are), attachment and ignorance (of the way things really are) we can relieve our own suffering.
4. The Noble Eight-Fold Path. The eight mindful steps we must take to reach this goal give us a path out of suffering (outlined in Chapter 6).

Trauma

If ten people are exposed to the same traumatic stimuli, three of them will not be able to shake it off and will be left with enduring symptoms of trauma.

Trauma is something that happens to us, not something we choose to have happen. Healing trauma is not an act of will. Suppressing it or ignoring it is an act of will. But trauma takes hold of the whole being and can leave us feeling as if we have lost our free will. It is something that happens to us, not something we *allow* to happen.

Trauma acts like a vortex, drawing us back into a whirling, swirling sea of incessant, intrusive thoughts and emotions that grab hold. Human responses to traumatic experiences are automatic responses, over which we have no conscious control. Most mammals will shake off the fight, flight or freeze responses to trauma and recover once the traumatic stimulus has gone away.

But some humans will automatically freeze or play dead, and if they never get the opportunity to complete the trauma response by fighting or running, they can remain feeling powerless, helpless, and hopeless for as long as it takes them to find a way to rid themselves of their unique trauma.

The heart knows what the mind will never comprehend. Even when our minds are reeling with trauma, if we can settle into embracing our own good hearts, we have something to hold onto. In the chaos of groundlessness and uncertainty, the goodness in our hearts shines a beam of light through the darkest of times.

The Eight Worldly Concerns

Buddha had a simple equation for the causes of human suffering. Opposing factors keep us trapped in a cycle and prevent us from finding peace. Spiritual enlightenment implies escaping this cycle, but in the meantime, meditation and mindfulness can release us time and again from these attachments (desires) and aversions (dislikes).

Breaking up with a psychological and emotional abuser leaves us battling on all fronts at once. It is not just a life crisis of one kind or another but the perfect storm. It's not just the traumatic events of losing a loved one, betrayal, divorce, losing a job, moving house, being blamed, not being believed, or having our reputations tarnished, but all those traumatic events at once, amplified by the pathological lying and manipulation of our abuser. Understanding our own ordeal by unpacking it into these four sets of opposites (below) can give us a place to start clearing the swirling confusion of trauma.

We can train ourselves to notice when we are clinging or caught in aversion and start to let go; train in mindfulness of our own experience. At no time in our lives are we so close to being aware of all these things as when our world is torn apart by psychological abuse and trauma. When we fall off the hamster wheel and are struggling to get back on, we can fail to notice that being off the hamster wheel is a more peaceful place.

Happiness and Suffering

If we cling to happiness when it arises, we soon lose it. If we keep eating the cake that makes us feel good, we'll soon feel bad again. When suffering arises, we want so badly for it to go away that we make our pain worse by struggling against it. We can convince ourselves that unpleasantness should never happen to us.

Fame and Insignificance

Everyone craves a good reputation, a good Facebook image. This craving creates our own suffering. Fear of insignificance or a bad reputation can cause great pain.

Praise and Blame

We can become addicted to praise. We can strive very hard to be liked, and our fear of not being liked can cause us suffering. We avoid admitting our mistakes or being accountable because blame sucks.

Gain and Loss

We can take delight in wealth, good times, more and more stuff. But the more we get, the more we want, and the more we fear losing it all. That is suffering. We hang on to people, situations, stuff, because we're afraid of the disappointment, anger, humiliation, or grief that is the suffering of loss.

Any of us can be carried away on a constant up-and-down roller coaster of life with these worldly concerns. It is the human condition. Buddha's point is that it is not the pursuit or avoidance of any of these things that brings happiness, but rather our internal state of mind. If we care for ourselves and others, and if we cultivate gratitude, generosity, patience, compassion, and courage, these things will lead us to a peaceful and happy life.

Symptoms of Post-Traumatic Stress Disorder

- intrusive, upsetting memories of events
- flashbacks (acting or feeling like events are happening again)
- anguish
- disbelief
- nightmares (either of the event or of other frightening things)
- having trouble remembering and difficulty processing information
- loss of interest in activities and life in general
- sense of a limited future (you don't expect to live a normal lifespan, get married, have a career)
- difficulty communicating
- difficulty falling or staying asleep
- irritability or outbursts of anger
- difficulty concentrating
- hypervigilance (constantly on red alert)
- feeling jumpy and easily startled
- depression
- hopelessness
- alienation
- guilt, shame, or self-blame
- feelings of mistrust and betrayal
- physical aches and pains

CPTSD is not listed in the diagnostic manual. Many Australian psychiatrists, psychologists, and counsellors think of PTSD as being the result of a physical injury. Oddly, they also recognise that witnesses to physical injury might also suffer PTSD (think war veterans and first responders). But here in Australia, they do not recognise ongoing psychological abuse as cause for a diagnosis of the same moral injury. So if he never laid a finger on us, we'll be labelled with some other malady.

As we progress along the rollercoaster ups-and-downs of recovery—the dance of one step forward and three steps back—we may be labelled with every kind of mental health disorder under the sun, whatever our therapists can remember from training or find in a book. Abusers are frequently misdiagnosed as being on the autism spectrum, and victims are frequently misdiagnosed too. Our patriarchal model of medicine ("Tell me what's wrong, then fix me") can lead us right into the wilderness if we trust the wrong therapist.

All shrinks believe their degrees are worth way more than Dr Google. Fair enough. Rightly so. But my experience through this hell tells me that the universities are not much further ahead in understanding psychological domestic abuse than the average Joe. The concept of PTSD or CPTSD from non-physical abuse is on the periphery of Western psychology. Shannon Thomas, who has counselled victims of hidden abuse for twenty years, acknowledges this gap in the professional counselling community, as does Shahida Arabi, another abuse recovery author. And professional understanding in the United States is way ahead of that in Australia. A recent professional standards survey of Australian psychiatrists found that around 50 percent had "adequate" training in domestic abuse issues (twelve hours) and around 50 percent had "inadequate" training (two hours or less). Enough said.

> The mental health community has been slow to recognize and acknowledge CPTSD, which has led to misdiagnoses of long-standing traumatized individuals with anxiety and depressive disorders, and borderline or dependent personality disorders (Walker, 2013). While Complex PTSD has been discussed in the framework of physical and/or sexual abuse in childhood, it can also be caused by emotional and/or verbal abuse, long-term domestic violence as well as long-term childhood emotional neglect.

—Shahida Arabi, *Power: Surviving and Thriving after Narcissistic Abuse*

Why is naming our experience and our condition so important? Why should we care what it's called? A rose by any other name is still a rose.

Naming our condition (and our abuser's) can be very reassuring. When we know what ails us and can take responsibility for our own healing, we are empowered. Having a cluster of symptoms that has no name can add to our suffering and make us feel alien and alone. Whatever level of trust we place in Western psychologists, there is always room to trust our own inner guidance, our own knowing, and our own wisdom. There is a huge community of people online who relate to a diagnosis of PTSD because they feel an uncanny resonance with the official list of symptoms. I believe them.

Tiny Steps Out of Chaos

In the early aftermath, there are simple practical steps to reduce the feelings of swirling, whirling chaos and work towards restoring a sense of stability.

Make Your Bed
So banal, isn't it? But there is plenty of evidence to suggest this one tiny daily chore is helpful when grappling with anxiety, confusion, or depression.

Instigate a Daily Routine
If you still have a job, you are one of the lucky ones. If you left your job based on his lies and promises, the struggle to find reason to get out of bed each day can be overwhelming. As important as it is to let yourself off the shame hook if you *really* can't make it out of bed, creating a daily routine for yourself is a start to restoring order. Same bedtime, same dinnertime, and so forth set a pattern that is especially useful when brain fog descends. Routine has a stabilising influence.

Try a Little Discipline
Take a walk, go for a jog, do some sit-ups; add whatever floats your boat to your daily routine. Make your choice small and achievable. Refrain from using discipline as punishment. After a week of only ten sit-ups a day, or the like, you'll start to feel a sense of achievement.

Do Chores Mindfully
Start your mindfulness training by concentrating as fully as possible on doing the washing up, ironing, taking a shower. Apply yourself fully, bringing your mind back time and again to the task at hand with as much joyful curiosity as you can muster.

Ground Yourself

Actual contact with the earth, like walking or other outdoor activities, helps lower your centre of gravity. Trauma so easily keeps us stuck in our heads. Having direct mindful contact with nature restores some equilibrium.

Turn Off Your Devices for Regular Periods

Relieving yourself of the shock or horror of unwelcome stimuli is Being Kind to Yourself 101. Of course, if the withdrawal symptoms of leaving phones, Facebook, emails, and text messages cause more pain than respite, then forget this suggestion.

Get a Dog

Dogs are already a recognised form of therapy in some circles for veterans with PTSD, first responders, and at aged care facilities and hospitals. A dog is a big responsibility, but it is also a companion, a teacher, a soother, a giver of unconditional love, and an object for our own love. A mature rescue dog (as opposed to a puppy that might increase anxiety for a time) will provide a reason for the discipline of a daily grounding walk, a routine of feeding and grooming, and a sentient being who instinctively defends and protects us.

It's not just about abandonment.
It's not just about rejection.
It's not just about losing someone you love.
It's not just about losing a future.

It's about being cheated on, lied to, stolen from and slandered.
It's about losing your home, your livelihood, your children, your reputation, your connection to friends, family, community.
It's about loss of innocence.
It's about someone covertly trying to *destroy* you.

—narcissisticsociopath.net

Discovering the Phenomenon of Character Disorders

Trigger Warning: This section may be hard to read. If you find yourself panicking, please put the book down or turn to the next chapter

I have nothing left. To start again.

It's all gone.

Not because I lived beyond my means.

Not because I spent before I saved.

Not because I was lazy or waited for someone else to provide for me.

Not because I made enemies of everyone with my bad behaviour.

But because I trusted a psychopath. A narcissist.

He took it all from me.

All but my courage, my morality, my faith.

That's what I have. To start again.

—narcissisticsociopath.net

There are people amongst us, possibly in leadership positions, positions of power or celebrity, who are charming, intelligent, entertaining, and successful. But there is something that makes these people different from the rest of us. Something we can't see; we can only experience. Even then, not everyone will experience the other side of these people. Frequently, it is only the intimate partners or family members who are exposed to this other, darker side. Their other side—what makes them different—is that they have zero honesty, zero empathy, zero conscience, or zero morality.

Psychologists describe these people as antisocial. This not a word that most of us associate with charm, intelligence, or success. There are now many studies of these people and plenty of statistics. We all love statistics. These people have been written about and described in various guises through the ages and in every culture, by every artist, writer, philosopher, poet, and religion. They are a part of humanity that psychologists are only just coming to understand. Awareness of the psychological damage they do to their intimate partners is exceedingly low; it's not discussed in many quarters. People don't want to know. Even therapists don't much like discussing it. Most often, their victims are not believed. Their sinister behaviour is covert, cleverly disguised, and emphatically denied. The blame is shifted onto the victim.

A bit like autism, the condition has long been mishandled and misunderstood. And like autism, the condition appears in people to a greater or lesser degree, with few people at the extreme end of the spectrum. Like autism, the condition is currently believed to be caused by an abnormality in part of the brain.

Antisocial personality disorder is incurable and very often can only be diagnosed in later life, after habitual patterns of behaviour have been established. This is the new name for people still known as psychopaths, sociopaths, and narcissists; they are often referred to as Dark Triad or Cluster B personalities. The mental health bible, the Diagnostic and Statistical Manual of Mental Disorders 5 (DSM-5), distinguishes between these three types. It can be very confusing trying to work out which one is which. They all share a high degree of narcissism, an extreme lack of empathy, pathological lying, and lack of remorse. They are completely unable to take responsibility for the hurt they cause. These are spectrum disorders. That is, some are a lot worse than others. The worst destroy lives and leave a path of devastation as their legacy. For people who are trusting, highly empathic, sensitive, and honest, the harm these subjects cause can be traumatising.

One person in twenty-five is a psychopath: a wolf in sheep's clothing; a snake in a suit. Then there are malignant narcissists. There is plenty of empirical evidence to suggest that their numbers are growing. For the sake of brevity, I call them narcopaths: narcissistic and pathological. Their abusive behaviours? Narcabuse. There is a condition clearly represented in online recovery forums: narcissistic abuse syndrome.

I am not a clinical psychologist but a lived-experience writer, a researcher, and a student of life. I have teased out the official lists of the personality traits of psychopathy and narcissistic personality disorder for the benefit of those of you who haven't encountered them before:

- glib and superficial charm
- exaggerated estimation of self
- believes he is a legend
- overt or hidden arrogance
- believes in his own extreme entitlement
- constant need for stimulation
- chronic boredom
- pathological liar; will lie and distort facts and change events to suit his own agenda
- cunning
- psychologically manipulative using triangulation (a tactic where he doesn't communicate directly with you, instead using a third person to relay messages) and gaslighting (manipulating you by psychological means into doubting your own sanity)
- shallow affect: limited range of emotions and emotional poverty despite apparent gregariousness
- superficial emotional responsiveness
  - ⇒ emotionally distant and unavailable unless he wants something (or has something to gain)
  - ⇒ passive-aggressive
- callousness and lack of empathy towards those he covertly exploits, disguised cruelty to loved ones or pets
- lacks guilt or remorse (but rather feels disdain and gratification for the suffering he inflicts on others)
- parasitic lifestyle; others supply him with what he wants or needs
- sexually promiscuous
- many short-term marital relationships or a history of past upheavals (many divorces, job changes, location changes, community changes)
- impulsivity; must have what he wants, when he wants it, no matter the cost to others
- irresponsible, extravagant, spends before he saves, unreliable borrower, unreliable period
- lacks realistic long-term goals
  - ⇒ lives in a fantasy world, which may include porn, flirting, affairs, and dreams of unlimited success and fame

- unable to accept responsibility for own actions
- blames his lack of success on others; cannot admit mistakes or having any character flaws whatsoever
- criminal or chameleon versatility (Dr Jekyll and Mr Hyde); acts different in public than in private; two-faced, putting friends and family down behind their backs; says one thing, does the opposite

Not all psychological abusers are narcopaths. But all narcopaths are psychological abusers, manipulative, and exploitative. Abusers don't abuse every day, but their behaviour follows a cycle and shows an overall pattern over time.

The Pattern of Idealise, Devalue, Discard, and Destroy

A narcissistic sociopath lover is a person who:
Vows he loves you,
Rapes your life,
Plunders everything you hold dear,
Discards you,
Leaves you with nothing,
Blames it all on you,
And convinces everyone it is you who is the
lying cheating thieving monster.
Top That!

—narcissisticsociopath.net

Every interpersonal relationship of a narcopath passes through these phases as a *repetition compulsion*. You might have a repeating relationship pattern too and find yourself drawn time and again to similar types. We will examine this a little later in the book.

Narcopaths, by contrast, don't necessarily go for the same physical type but for the person who most represents what he wants right now. Easily bored and extremely impulsive, the narcopath suddenly and unexpectedly switches wives, friends, jobs, states, or countries.

He is unable to bond with his partners or experience emotional intimacy. He is, however, very good at mimicking what he observes in others as good behaviour in a mate or that which he knows his current target is seeking. He is able to tell people exactly what they want to hear. And he can pick a trusting, honest, vulnerable target a mile off. A natural predator, he is a man in a mask, a chameleon. He is the true Dr Jekyll and Mr Hyde character. His is not simply a polite veneer that any of us might adopt in order to succeed socially or professionally. His is a personality disorder, hidden even from himself.

Idealise

This phase is characterised by extreme flattery, validation, and adoption of the new target's home, friends, beliefs, hobbies, habits, likes, and dislikes. The narcopath is so obsessed with obtaining the thing he wants *now* that he can appear deeply compatible and in love; targets believe they have met their soulmate. For a time, she can do no wrong, and the narcopath boasts about his new love very publicly (even if he hasn't closed the book on his previous chapter).

This stage of the narcabuse cycle is commonly referred to as love-bombing.

Devalue

The same things that he once found attractive or desirable, he denigrates, despises, and degrades. Using coercion, bribery, manipulation, or control, he convinces the target to set aside her independence in favour of a mutual shared future until death. Unaware of his psychological manipulation, the target becomes isolated from her support system, is confused and in emotional turmoil, and suffers physical, emotional, financial, and mental degeneration.

Discard

Despite words of undying love, lustful sex, marriage vows, and an extended period of promises, oaths, and agreements, the entire life created by narcopath and target is suddenly and unexpectedly discarded. Homes, children, jobs, countries, social connections, and professional networks are suddenly worthless to the narcopath in favour of the next thing he wants now.

Destroy

Unfathomably vain and with a deep belief in his own specialness, the narcopath will destroy the target rather than be seen to have behaved badly. He will use a deceitful smear campaign to discredit and disempower the woman he has just discarded like a worthless thing. Lacking remorse but gratified by the damage he is able to inflict on someone who loved and trusted him, he wears the appearance of innocent victim himself. He tells the world about his acts of charity, generosity, and altruism, while he covertly annihilates her.

There is a distinct pattern psychological abusers use with the smear campaign too. Again, each story is different, but the broad tactics are the same. We will examine this phenomenon in more detail a little later (there is only so much a koala can bear in one chapter about abusive behaviours).

Hallelujah Moment

Many of us experience a hallelujah moment when we first see the definition of a psychopath, sociopath, or narcissist. The description finally matches the foul human behaviour we have experienced. No conscience. Tick. Flat-lined emotions. Tick. Infuriatingly manipulative. Tick. Charms everybody outside the home. Tick. Suddenly, we are validated. Our instincts, our suspicions, our feelings were correct. Here, this confusing duplicitous man is described in black and white. Hallelujah.

We feel dehumanised, exhausted, discarded like a worthless thing. We feel like we were just the subject of an experiment for the narcopath. It is almost as if he pursued us, married us, had kids with us just to see if he could gain our absolute trust and devotion. Then once he did, he abandoned the whole life created with us because he had *won*, proved his point, used up all our resources, gratified himself, made himself feel powerful.

What takes us longer to discover is that narcopaths typically target people who are nurturers: loving, loyal, compassionate, responsible, successful, and well rounded. Sane.

We can find that person again.

You weren't in a relationship.
You were in a manipulationship.

—Pinterest

Ask the Experts

Thomas, Shannon (2016), *Healing from Hidden Abuse: A Journey through the Stages of Recovery from Psychological Abuse.* MAST Publishing House.

Arabi, Shahida (2017), *Power: Surviving and Thriving after Narcissistic Abuse.* Brooklyn, NY: Thought Catalogue Books.

Levine, Peter A. (2008), *Healing Trauma: A Pioneering Program for Restoring the Wisdom of Your Body.* Boulder, CO: Sounds True.

Walker, Peter (2013), *Complex PTSD: From Surviving to Thriving.* Azure Coyote.

Hare, Dr Robert (1999), *Without Conscience: The Disturbing World of the Psychopaths Among Us.* The Guildford Press.

Chödrön, Pema (2016), *When Things Fall Apart: Heart Advice for Difficult Times* 20th Anniversary Edition). Shambhala Publications, Inc.

Chödrön, Pema (2001), *The Wisdom of No Escape and the Path of Loving-Kindness.* Shambhala Classics.

http://neuroinstincts.com/narcissistic-psychopathic-relationship-abuse/

Chapter 2

INTENSIVE SELF-CARE IN THE EARLY AFTERMATH

Cherish and Honour

Honour the truth of what happened.
Cherish the journey of recovery.

—narcissisticsociopath.net

When we made vows to the narcopath, we promised to cherish and honour him. And we did, while he proceeded to do exactly the opposite for us. Undervalued, undermined, plundered, discarded, and destroyed by our most loved and trusted other? Betrayed in every possible way? It's crazy-making.

So as we work on the seemingly insurmountable task of letting that story go, it is time, right from the moment of abandonment, to cherish and honour ourselves. We have been neglected and psychologically abused for a long time. Now, it is time for intensive self-care. We are embarking on the hero's journey, and we will need every ounce of energy we can muster.

Honour the wounds, and prioritise our healing, starting with simple, practical self-care and progressing to deep spiritual healing for the moral injury that the narcopath inflicted. *Cherish* the ideal of complete recovery from victimisation and the goal of a completely fulfilled life. Honour our own ability to recover and find ways to stand on our own two feet again, even though this seems like Mission Impossible in the aftermath. Cherish our own integrity, honesty, and good heart. Honour our right to self-compassion, self-regeneration, self-sufficiency, and healthy, mutually satisfying relationships. Honour our right to choose our friends, have *no contact* with our former partner (refraining from reaching out to our abuser; discussed in detail in chapter 4), put ourselves back together differently, and construct a whole new life, a whole new self.

Cherish and honour the kindness and generosity of those who step forward to encourage our journey out of the abyss.

Calming

These are tips for soothing, nurturing, or turning your mind away from unbearable emotions:

- watch an uplifting movie
- take a warm, aromatic bath
- get into or close to water, water, water
- listen to uplifting music
- light candles
- turn off your phone, Facebook, and email
- do mindfulness meditation
- lie on the grass or by the water and absorb the beauty of nature
- imagine embracing yourself as a child and as you are now
- do grounding and centring exercises (mindfulness practice)
- practise yoga, trauma yoga, tai chi, or qigong
- start a gratitude journal
- take a nap in the middle of the day
- sleep in
- listen to positive affirmations, aspirations, or guided meditations
- cuddle your children or pets
- repeat simple mantras like "I am safe" as you go about your chores
- do normally mechanical chores (like washing up, vacuuming, or laundry) with full concentration on the chore itself, directing your

mind towards the minutiae of the experience (this is mindfulness in action)

Record your own affirmations on your iPhone, or find them at www. soundstrue.com or www.margotmaccallum.com.

Active
Use the energy of anger, or rouse yourself from feeling frozen and helpless:

- conduct a decluttering session
- pamper your body
- go for a mindful walk, run, or swim
- do a fun workout or take a yoga class
- bounce a tennis ball off the wall with a racquet
- write letters you will never send (or send to yourself)
- make food you love to eat
- dance to loud music
- sing songs, hymns, or mantras over and over until the energy changes
- play with your dog
- do something you've been meaning to get around to
- buy yourself some flowers and arrange them the way you like
- paint a canvas, make a pot, knit a scarf, do something creative you haven't done for a while
- challenge yourself with something you've never done before
- organise your closet
- give some special things to charity (let go)
- tear up old magazines and make a scrapbook of things, ideas, places you like
- write and send someone a thank-you note
- call an old friend and re-establish contact (go easy on explaining your troubles)
- go to a museum, art gallery, show
- do some gardening, planting, cleaning up your outdoor area
- rearrange the furniture or redecorate a little bit
- paint a piece of furniture

Feeling sadness, grief, loss, or compassion for our own suffering is not the same as wallowing in self-pity. Most of us know the difference and can cross the bridge between self-pity and self-compassion once we know how. We can judge ourselves unfairly for our own extreme emotional pain. Our stoic culture, harsh inner critics, or scapegoating friends and family might tell us to stop feeling sorry for ourselves. This can add another layer of shame to our suffering.

Instead of cutting our own suffering off at the knees with culturally imposed thoughts like those, we honour our right to grieve, to feel sadness, to listen to sad country songs: "I lost ma job, ma dog, ma wife, ma kids, and ma house burnt down." Just go with it. It won't last. Cry until there are no more tears to cry. And then cry some more. You wouldn't scold a child for crying a bit longer than a grazed knee really warrants, so refrain from scolding yourself for grieving. Be kind to yourself. When we can be our own kind, compassionate witness, the pain will pass.

Pendulation: A Mindfulness Technique for Acute Distress

> When we are willing to stay even a moment with the
> uncomfortable energy, we gradually learn not to fear it.
>
> —Pema Chödrön, *When Things Fall Apart*

Many narcabuse victims report a time in the aftermath when they felt as if they were going insane. The sensation of falling into the abyss is very frightening. We struggle to regain our normal locus of control, while being dragged back into the vortex of dark thoughts and emotions, like drowning in the undertow.

We cry out, "I just want to stop thinking!" The temptation to dissociate, obliterate ourselves with one drug or another, or throw ourselves in front of a bus suddenly becomes very real. We never thought it would happen to us. But here it is: trauma.

Trying to gain control of our minds in the trauma vortex without formal mindfulness training can just add to the feelings of despair. We desperately want to escape this place, but we don't have the tools for getting out. Pendulation is one of those tools. This (and every other mindfulness practice) begins with centring and grounding ourselves, bringing our awareness home, as one Buddhist master calls it. We focus our awareness on being right here, right now, in this space, at this time, with these aromas, tastes, air temperature, and sounds, near and far. We concentrate the mind on the sensations of the body, inside and out. We can learn to do this anywhere: riding on the bus, doing the washing up, lying in bed.

Pendulation is a technique for handling acute trauma symptoms, when you feel like you just can't contain the overwhelming emotions and thoughts that are driving you insane, when all your bodily systems have gone haywire, and you can't sleep, eat, stop shaking, or escape from your own suffering. You feel like you have completely lost control of your mind and emotions, and they are ruling you, not the other way around. There is so much emotional and psychological pain in your body that you feel like you just can't take any more pain.

Grief, anger, and fear are all strong emotions. But trauma is another beast altogether. They call it the trauma vortex for a reason. Because that is how it behaves. It sucks us back in.

Pendulation: The Practice

Feel the response in your body at this moment. Feel the emotion of anger or hurt or whatever it is (name it if you can), and breathe consciously. Contain the emotion. Tolerate it. Now how does it feel in your body? Where is it? Is it hot, cold, stabbing, numbing, burning, whatever? Is it in your chest, your belly, your solar plexus?

Let the tears come. Go fully into the emotion if you can bear it. When you can no longer bear it, switch your attention back to a part of your body where there is no pain, for example, your elbow.

Concentrate hard on your elbow, and notice your breathing. Notice the momentary relief you feel from focusing on no-pain. Then go back and revisit the strong emotion. You might find that it has shifted and underneath the emotion is another. It might even be in a different part of your body. Find it. Name it. Turn your focus back to the part of your body where there is no-pain again.

Pendulate. Strong emotion to no-pain. Strong emotion to no-pain. Breathe. Before long, the strong emotion should be tolerable, and you will regain some equilibrium.

Tears will give you some relief, and maybe the pendulation will give relief too. Then offer yourself compassion: "I am sorry this is happening to me. I am doing the best I can. This suffering won't last forever." Or braver words: "I've got this. I can cope with this. I am doing really, really well under the circumstances." Soothe yourself. Comfort yourself, just as you would your best friend. No one can see you. Don't be embarrassed about it. Try not to judge yourself. Just soothe and comfort that hurt little person inside you until it feels better.

This practice, over time, will increase your capacity for emotional pain. Later, when you have stabilised enough to heal yourself at a deeper level, your increased tolerance for strong emotions will allow you to stay with them long enough to work through to the other side, to reach insight. Each time you consciously revisit painful emotions, you take the sting out of them a bit. You peel the layers of the onion.

What to Do with Painful Thoughts and Emotions

From the Buddha's *Discourse on the Forms of Thought,* we find this advice about the suffering of painful thoughts and emotions:

Replace negative thoughts with positive ones.
No matter how painful our thoughts and emotions, we put effort into replacing negative thoughts with ones that are more joyous, serene, and happy. It may sound simple, but it's not, especially for those of us who find compartmentalisation difficult. It is about training our minds to shift focus

again and again to things that make us feel good: concentrating on the beautiful bird, the sweet music, the candle flame, the encouraging words of an affirmations soundtrack.

Be clear about what is hurting you.
We think about the origins of our pain. What are the causes and conditions that brought it about? How much of it is the result of our own behaviour? This can be translated as the educational phase of recovery from psychological abuse; working out what the hell just happened. It can take a while to figure all this stuff out. Please take heart that one day, you will.

Take every opportunity—when triggered into fear or anger, when weeping with sadness and grief—to allow the real cause to reveal itself.

Withdraw attention or distract yourself.
It is absolutely okay to find activities that distract us from our own compulsive rumination. Crafts, puzzles, sports and other things that require us to concentrate fully on what we are doing now will give us temporary relief from suffering.

Go to the root; question the way you think.
By developing our observer self, by labelling our thoughts as thinking, we can learn the skill of witnessing our own thoughts, assessing their patterns, and identifying the triggers that give rise to obsessive thinking. With practice, we can see how our minds generate these painful stories and learn to detach from them. (*The Happiness Trap* by Russ Harris offers techniques from a Western psychologist for training in defusing negative intrusive thoughts.)

Clench your teeth and push away disturbing thoughts.
This is incredibly hard to do when traumatised. It is not intended as a long-term coping device but as a short-term remedy for overwhelming emotional pain. It asks us to use our willpower or inner strength to pull our minds away from the trauma vortex that wants to suck us back into the void of distressing thought patterns.

There is profound wisdom in strong emotions. Even anger, with all its sharp edges, can help raise our level of energy and show us what we need to deal with right now. Fear also demands our immediate attention. Mindfulness of emotion can direct us into positive action.

> If you don't have the wound of a broken heart, how can
> you know you're alive? If you have no broken heart, how do
> you know who you are? Have been? Ever have been?
>
> —Edward Albee, *The Play about Baby*

Mindfulness

> A Native American grandfather was speaking to his grandson
> about violence and cruelty in the world and how it comes about.
> He said it was as if two wolves were fighting in his heart. One wolf
> was vengeful and angry, and the other wolf was understanding
> and kind. The young man asked his grandfather which wolf
> would win the fight in his heart. And the grandfather answered,
> "The one that wins will be the one I choose to feed."
>
> —Pema Chödrön, *Feed the Right Wolf*

Mindfulness is not a modern fad. It is an ancient principle that's been practiced by yogis, warriors, and spiritual seekers for over two thousand years. Meditation is about training the mind and has no affiliation with any particular religion. Practicing mindfulness regularly leads us to understand that our thoughts and emotions are neither good nor bad. They just are. This insight leads us into self-acceptance, wisdom, and equanimity. Over time, a dedicated practice helps us create the internal space to bring about lasting change to the mental conditions that arise in response to various stimuli.

> We come to know, unflinchingly, and with great kindness, the
> angry, unforgiving, hostile wolf. Over time, that part of ourselves
> becomes very familiar, but we no longer feed it. Instead, we can

make the choice to nurture openness, intelligence, and warmth.
This choice, and the attitudes and actions that follow from it, are
like a medicine that has the potential to cure all suffering.

—Pema Chödrön, *Feed the Right Wolf*

In the same way that practicing a musical instrument or training our bodies brings about a result, training our mind does too. Just as a sesame seed contains oil, our minds have within them the inherent capacity to habitually generate positive thoughts, no matter what the circumstances. There is nothing miraculous about a state of deep calm and contentment. We have the potential to create this blessed state of mind for ourselves. It is a skill that anybody can learn, even from a place of trauma.

Out of the vortex of our thoughts, first emotions arise, and then
moods and behaviours, and finally habits and traits of character.
What arises spontaneously does not necessarily produce good
results; any more than throwing seeds into the wind produces
good harvests. So we have to behave like good farmers who prepare
their fields before sowing their seeds. For us, this means the most
important task is to attain freedom through mastering our mind.

—Matthieu Ricard, *Why Should I Meditate?*

As rational beings, our natural inclination is to turn the problem over and over in our minds until we understand. This is rumination, not meditation. Meditation is practiced in the paradigm of mindfulness.

There are said to be four foundations to mindfulness: mindfulness of body, mindfulness of feelings, mindfulness of mind, and mindfulness of phenomena.

Mindfulness of Body
Alert awareness of all the sensations of the body (breathing, weight, posture, movement, and so forth) grounds the practitioner to the earth in the present moment, the here and now. Deep contemplation of the body's role in sickness, old age, and death can help us come to terms with these things.

Mindfulness of Feelings

We identify what pleasant, unpleasant, and neutral feelings are present, not only as in emotional feelings but as in every sensation we experience in response to the here and now. We notice how feelings arise and pass away, continually in flux: hot, cold, sad, angry, burning, numb, whatever.

Mindfulness of Mind

We notice thoughts and emotions as they arise and pass away. With time and practice, we learn to notice how our thoughts can come and go without having to follow the story. We train our observer self. We notice our tendency to cling, to crave, to ignore, to suppress, to compartmentalise, to follow thoughts into a downward spiral, to be anxious about survival, whatever. Over time, we learn how our minds work, and learn to tame our minds so as to bring us back, again and again, to the here and now.

Mindfulness of Phenomena

Noticing such phenomena as the vast expanse of the world, human nature and the universe, we come to deeply understand the impermanent nature of existence. We search for the truth of the way things really are - inside ourselves. We gradually see our own biases and negative habits and realise that not only are our bodies and the phenomena around us impermanent, but our very selves or souls are too.

Mindfulness or insight meditation offers not only the benefits of stress and pain relief and relaxation but deep spiritual nourishment. We learn to stop sleepwalking through our days and nights or be pushed around by our out-of-control 'monkey' minds. (The mind is said to have a natural tendency to jump around like a monkey) We are able to make wiser choices. We come to know and love ourselves intimately. And with dedicated regular practice, we learn that mindfulness works to ease our suffering.

> Meditation is not passive sitting in silence. It is sitting in awareness, free from distraction, and realising the clear understanding that arises from concentration.
>
> — Thic Nhat Hahn

Mindful Self-Compassion

This is a moment of suffering.
Suffering is a normal part of life.
May I give myself the comfort I need.

—Kristen Neff, *Mindful Self-Compassion*

A huge craving for kindness can arise in the aftermath of abuse. We suffered incomprehensible psychological and emotional cruelty from our ex-partner (no one else can see it, and we may not yet see it either, caught as we are in love, shock, and denial). Many of us also find that we are faced with the very opposite of kindness from our friends and family, right when we need it the most. This is a sad state of affairs that we will discuss further in the book. Kindness is the antidote to cruelty. And now is the time in our lives when we most need to be kind to ourselves. But some of us find that after a season or a lifetime of giving love to others, we don't quite know how to do that for ourselves. We seek outside ourselves for someone to offer us love, kindness, compassion, and possibly protection, in return for that which we give them, instead of turning inwards to feel the warmth of our own loving hearts.

The practices of Mindful Self-Compassion offer unique and accessible ways for Westerners to gently learn the art of being kind to ourselves. They are, I believe, especially useful for those experiencing trauma, although teachers will give extensive disclaimers about the techniques *not* being a trauma cure. Central to the discipline is learning how to be mindful of our own condition. We learn how to be our own best friend - how to find counter-argument to our harsh inner critics. Along the way, we learn to recognise our own cravings and aversions. After narcabuse, this recognition (which might sound straightforward and obvious to someone in a healthy, stable state) has been severely compromised by months or years of gaslighting and deception by the psychological abuser.

Incorporating the simple practices of Mindful Self Compassion helps us return to our original good heart and basic decency. They also help us welcome up to consciousness those disowned parts of ourselves that the narcopath so ruthlessly victimised in the traumatising discard and destroy phase. Learning the techniques in a group class takes a certain amount of courage and stability, but practicing them at home can be done from within the cotton-wool refuge of our own comfort zones.

The techniques are based on ancient wisdom principles, but are thoroughly Westernised to include modern psychological research and neuroscience to address the commonplace neuroses of low self-worth and a harsh inner critic. They are at the intersection of modern psychology and ancient Buddhism. They are also really useful for people who feel they have tried meditation, it didn't work for them, but they are prepared to try a different way in. Many of the practices are short, concise and easily formed into habit. If the eight-week course (designed specifically around the established timeframe for giving up old habits and acquiring new ones) is not accessible for remote or rural readers then the books and other resources are available online.

http://self-compassion.org/

My own recovery took a giant leap forward after I completed the course, the most useful tool in my recovery toolkit. I learned to have a much healthier relationship with myself. I gained a greater ability to deal with the constant anxiety of acute CPTSD; a deeper love and respect for myself; a firmer belief that recovery is possible; greater discernment and equilibrium; renewed personal agency and purpose. Still practising the techniques now that my symptoms are in full remission, I am my own best friend. I am able to be there for myself in the face of abuse, scorn, aggression or difficulty. And this newfound ability has in turn fuelled my courage and conviction, my acceptance and commitment, my own personal power.

Not everybody is willing to face their own demons. These practices are less about that and more about honouring our own needs. The techniques, when practised long-term, hold the promise of a kind and gentle gradual transformation. They are about shifting the warmth of our own compassion towards our selves before we offer it up to others. They are the oxygen mask we apply before we try to help the person next to us. They are nothing to do with narcissism and everything to do with radical self-care.

There are three keys to mindful self-compassion:

- self-kindness
- common humanity
- mindfulness

We can practice some of these techniques at home without training:

Writing a letter to ourselves from an imaginary compassionate friend
If you are like me, you might squirm with embarrassment when you receive praise or a compliment. We just never learned how to let kind words *in*, yet paradoxically we crave them. In deep calm privacy, we write a letter to ourselves filled with kindness and encouragement. We overcome our squirminess and tell this dear person for whom we wish only the best how much we respect, care for and admire her fine human qualities. We tell her we can see what a hard time she's been having and how diligent she has been in doing her best to do the right thing, to heal, to cope, to rebuild a shattered life.

We literally stroke, soothe, hug, hold ourselves.
In deep calm privacy, we literally take ourselves in our own loving embrace. We stroke our own face or hair. We hold our own hand. We experiment with the way gentleness or firmness makes us feel. We find a gesture (like placing a hand over our heart) that can become our secret message of compassion to ourselves when stress rises in daily life.

Compassionate body scan.
In quiet repose, we mentally scan our bodies. We visit the parts that have physical pain and offer kindness, gentleness, and tenderness to them. We notice the parts that we might dislike and instead of the habitual loathing, we greet them with acceptance and encouragement.

Noting beauty walk.
We take five minutes to walk outside, with no destination in mind. We take note of the beauty that surrounds us: the fallen leaves; the sun shining dappled through a canopy; the sweet little bird flitting from wire to wire; the gentle aroma of petals; the playfulness of a passing dog on a lead; the

hopefulness in a baby's cry. We greet every sense with deliberate positivity. We look for the beauty in everything and let it reach our deep inner places.

This Shouldn't Be Happening to Me

Of all the internal struggles we are faced with in the aftermath of narcabuse, perhaps this is the one that most needs the soothing balm of our own compassion. The resistance to what is actually happening can easily thrust us into the dilemma of suffering over our pain, grief and loss. We may have built our modus operandi on a mantra learned in childhood. "Do unto others as you would have others do unto you." We compromisers might easily have pushed the boundaries of this mantra so that, for us, it has come to mean "*if* you do unto others, then they will do unto you in return", or words to that effect. In other words, we go through life believing that if we are kind, generous, honest and straightforward with people, that they will return the favour. If we make a mistake, apologise and atone, they will forgive us the way we forgive them.

Naïve as this may be, it is not all that uncommon. It most certainly applies for many people in the sphere of intimate relationships. We might believe that quid pro quo is what partnership means: sharing our toys; you scratch my back and I'll scratch yours. We might have had verbal agreements and lengthy discussions with the narcopath along the lines of; "We'll use my savings to secure the deposit on a house, and you can be responsible for a greater portion of the interest payments in return" or "I'll support us both while you complete your degree, then when you get a high-paying job, I can take time off to have our children". We might have had hundreds of such agreements and discussions during the course of our relationship. So it is hardly surprising, when the narcopath abandons the whole complex deal before he ever has to fulfil his part of the bargain, then turns and ruthlessly attacks us that we might get stuck in "this shouldn't be happening".

Getting unstuck from this place means accepting the pain of injustice. It means accepting that things are the way they are. We have a choice: accept the pain of loss and betrayal, or continue to rage against it. Pain is an inevitable part of human life, but suffering is optional. Mindful

Self-Compassion helps us hold our own pain with compassionate non-judgemental awareness. It helps us overcome our incredulity that *anyone* could treat us the way the narcopath has. Once we are able to tolerate, accept, soothe and calm our own pain, it passes. Once we are mindful of our own thoughts and emotions instead of stuck inside the swirling vortex, they shift.

Mindful Self-Compassion teaches us to embrace our pain. "This hurts. This is very hard right now. This anger/jealousy/grief/despair is very difficult to bear. But this suffering is a part of being human. Other people have suffered this and survived. It's okay for me to be having such a hard time. I am not a bad person for having these thoughts and emotions. I am human. Light and dark are a natural part of life. I can get through this. This suffering will not last forever."

Whatever words we choose to accept, soothe and comfort our in-the-moment experience of extreme emotion, we stand side-by-side with ourselves. We are there for ourselves. As much as we can manage it, we don't push the pain away or hang onto the thoughts that feed the painful story. We are right here, right now, offering compassion to our current experience of pain. We give ourselves the kind and comforting words that we most crave to hear right now, right here, the words we craved as a wounded child.

Some of us might never have heard these words before. We might have had stoic parents who told us to "pick ourselves up and get straight back in the saddle" when we took a fall. We might have developed harsh inner critics that scold blame criticise bully us. We might have families or friends who do the same to us because that's what they learned too. We might never have learned the language of kindness. We can now. It is never too late to learn. And aside from the healing we experience when we adopt the practices of Mindful Self-Compassion, we get the bonus of learning a vocabulary that we can share with others in our lives. We learn to spread the love around!

Everything is going to be okay.

> Love and compassion are like seeds within us. Like the seed of
> a tree, these seeds require nurturing so that they can develop.
> We develop the seeds of love and compassion through patience,
> through diligence, and through compassionate action.

— The 17th Karmapa, Tonibernhard.com

Shame

The Second Arrow

A Swedish study in 2017 found that social comparison was the leading underlying cause of suicide in Europe. A new form of suffering can emerge after shock and grief, in the form of rumination on social comparison. We compare our post-abuse scorched-earth landscape with

- our pre-abuse lives,
- our youthful potential,
- our family expectations,
- our dreams, goals, or planned outcomes,
- our friends, neighbours, or contemporaries, and
- people who have suffered overt trauma, like cancer, physical disability, or torture.

We can deny ourselves permission to be traumatised the way we are, judge ourselves as crazy, and feel shame for our own thoughts and emotions. This can fuel an internal struggle of gigantic proportions. Buddhists call this "the second arrow". It is the arrow we shoot at ourselves for having been wounded by the first. For example,

- getting angry because we are suffering anxiety,
- feeling guilty because we felt relief when someone died,
- feeling depressed because we are sick,
- feeling shame because we can't forgive.

If we succumb to maladaptive coping mechanisms or acting out, we can fall into the trap of berating ourselves for being a bad person because we did a bad thing. We can even do this when we are innocent victims, when we were in the wrong place at the wrong time, when we were looking the other way, when we were strapped in and someone else was driving.

The second arrow frequently takes the form of shame. This second arrow aspect of shame is something from which we can find relief by holding our seat, as Pema Chödrön says: opening to the discomfort, recognising it, naming it, embracing it, accepting it, allowing it to just be there. It will soon pass.

Victim Blaming

We are also faced with the phenomenon of victim blaming. What is this weird human conundrum that makes the survivors of combat, domestic abuse, violent assaults, accidents, or rape feel shame? Surely it should be the other way around. The perpetrator should be ashamed for causing so much harm and injury to another. But somehow, that's not how it works. What happens in practice (not theory) is this:

Step 1: People refuse to believe the victim (particularly female victims).
Step 2: People blame victims for bringing it on themselves in some way or for not seeing it coming, accuse them of lying, or blame them for their naivety, stupidity or innocence.
Step 3: People do nothing; they sit on a fence, leaving victims to their own despair and the perpetrator to harm again, or they actively side with the perpetrator.
Step 4: People tell victims they should get over it, suck it up, never mention the hurt or abuse, disguise their symptoms of trauma, and cover up the effects of Steps 1–3. For people who are habituated to receive validation from outside themselves, this pressure can lead to suicidal thoughts.

Suicide is a permanent solution to a temporary problem. But if we are beset by suicidal thoughts, we need to reach out. Make the call. Get the validation we are unable to give ourselves from a trained compassionate non-judgemental helpline worker.

To the untrained, judgemental eye, victims of trauma can look like they deserve the blame that is cast their way. After the fact, they can act out or be angry, resentful, bitter, bad-tempered, illogical, incompetent, or forgetful. We want them to keep calm and carry on, grin and bear it. And when their new behaviour is inappropriate, we say there is something intrinsically wrong with them. They are weak, broken, useless. We assume they just aren't normal, and we can't blame others for dumping them, ignoring them, gossiping about them, and stigmatising them. We judge them by imagining that we would cope with trauma in a much better way. We shame them.

Underlying all this is the false assumption that things are permanent, that the damage is permanent, that leopards don't change their spots, that you can't teach an old dog new tricks, that we will never get over it.

People *do* get over it. They do move on. Recovery is possible. They come out the other side of trauma more resilient, more compassionate, stronger, wiser, braver than they ever imagined. As Shannon Thomas observes, survivors of narcabuse are some of the "sparkliest gems" she has come across. You will emerge from the fire forged into a diamond.

You can take the heat. You can do it.

Mindfulness Practice for Shame

- Pause.
- Make time right now—right while you are triggered into feeling shame—to take five minutes to chip away at it. (Go to the loo if in a public place)
- Sit. Get grounded and centred.
- Breathe consciously, and rest your awareness on what's happening in your body. Where is it tight, painful, hot, cold, and so on? Do a body scan.

- Silently notice and name the sensations and location of the shame in your body (e.g., hot/stabbing/twisting in the solar plexus/ stomach/chest).
- Shift your breathing (by using the imagination) to breathe cleansing air into the part of the body that is most uncomfortable.
- Notice the thoughts that arise when trying to concentrate on your body.
- Contact self-compassion: "This is a moment of shame. Shame is a normal part of life. May I give myself the comfort I need."
- Contact your refuge or feeling of safety; imagine people, places, spiritual figureheads, or concepts like light and warmth that can soothe and calm you.
- Contact self-forgiveness: "I made a mistake. I have an illness. I'm human. I'm not a bad person. I can forgive myself for feeling this way."
- Atone (if necessary): "I'm sorry I did that. I'll take care not to do it again."
- Let yourself off the hook. "I am doing my best. I am not a bad person. I love and nurture the innocence inside me. It's in the past. Right now, I'm okay." Give yourself the words you most want to hear from someone else right now.
- Go back to the day, even if it feels a bit unresolved. It might not be the last time you revisit the same story of shame to chip away at it.
- There is plenty of time. This is what recovery means. It takes time.

Affirmation, Visualisation, and Guided Meditation Tracks

Throughout the book, there are script suggestions for creating your own affirmation, visualisation, or guided meditation tracks. You can do this by recording a voice memo on your mobile phone and playing it back to yourself when the opportunity arises. Some of the phrases will be aspirational (that is, you may not really believe it yet; it may seem like wishful thinking).

If you try this technique and notice that some of the phrases create strong aversions, then re-record the track without those phrases. We are not trying to brainwash or hypnotise ourselves. We are listening for respite from uncomfortable thoughts and emotions. As we gain some benefit from listening to the tracks, we might want to write and record our own scripts. The purpose of listening to these recordings repeatedly is to grow our concentration muscle and to provide the reassuring words we crave to hear, like a child in its mother's arms.

We are listening with the intention of *generating positive mind states*. If you can picture the negative repetitive thought patterns that haunt us as neural pathways or tracks, then the repetitive use of positive affirmations create new neural pathways; new tracks for our minds to follow. Over time, as we carve out more and more positive neural pathways, our recovering minds become like a soundtrack of kind, encouraging, positive melodies that drown out the discordant clanging of the traumatic track. A visual image would be a tapestry of multi-coloured threads woven through and around the single black thread of the traumatic thought.

Allow space and time between each line of dialogue, so that the words have time to resonate (or not) with our unconscious mind. The mind will likely drift away into the trauma vortex and back again, and that's OK. If we fall asleep, great; it's the ultimate relief. Many teachers say that we will hear the things we are ready to hear whether we are awake or not. Studies show that learning can be achieved by playing audio recordings repetitively whilst asleep.

It could be argued that healing from narcabuse is akin to deprogramming from a cult. We have been conditioned to believe a huge number of lies. This practice is a gentle restorative practice to ease our pain and encourage and nurture our fledgling new reality. Do not expect miraculous transformation quickly. Repetition is the key. They are just another tool in our recovery toolkit.

Grounding and Centring

Sit or lie in a comfortable position, where you feel safe.

Close your eyes.

Feel that safety.

Turn your awareness to your surroundings. Become aware of the sounds, the smells, and the other sensations outside your body.

If you need to, readjust your body so that you feel completely comfortable, safe and secure. For a while, you don't have to answer the phone, work at your computer, or speak with anyone. This time is just about you.

Now turn your awareness towards your body.

Notice the breath coming in and going out of your body. You don't need to control it. You can just allow it flow in and then out of your body, and with every breath, a new moment arrives as the old one passes away.

Now relax. Feel the weight of your whole body pressing into the floor, the chair, or the bed. Feel how well you are supported, and give your attention to the parts of your body where you can feel pain, discomfort, or dis-ease. As your breath flows into your body, become aware of that breath bringing nourishment and healing to those parts of your body. Imagine dis-ease collected up into your breath in that moment between the in and out breath, and allow the out breath to carry that dis-ease out of your body with every exhalation.

Relax your face. Feel the tension leave your brow. Feel your eyes sink back into their sockets and your eyelids gently close. Relax your scalp, the back of your head, and the tiny muscles at the back of your neck that do so much work for you.

Relax your cheeks, your lips, and your jaw. Let your tongue rest gently at the back of your upper teeth, and allow your jaw to go slack.

Feel the breath flow easily in and out of your body, bringing nourishment in, and carrying dis-ease out.

Relax your throat and your chest.

Feel the relaxation flow from your head out and down around your shoulders, oozing through the muscles between your shoulder blades, and flowing down your spine.

That same relaxation is flowing into your upper arms, through your elbows, into your forearms, and into your hands.

Feel all the muscles of your hands, fingers, and thumbs relax and let go. The tingling in your fingers is your own pulse, fed by your breath flowing in and out.

Feel the muscles of your chest relax and soften. Do the same for your waist, your hips, your genitals.

Feel the sweet sensation of letting go in your buttocks. Imagine your buttocks spreading out underneath you and the arch in the small of your back softening into nothing.

Feel the letting go in the front of your thighs, your knees, and your lower leg. Notice how the muscles at the back of your thighs relax and soften, and your calf muscles release.

Become aware of all the little bones and muscles in your ankles and feet. Feel the warm relaxation flow in and around them all, relieving them of their important job, for now.

Now let your conscious mind drift, as you listen to these words. There is no right way to do this. Thoughts that come to you are okay. Just let them be there and pass through. Your subconscious mind will hear everything it needs to hear, but for now, just relax. Let your mind drift. There is nothing you need to do, nothing you need to focus on. Give yourself permission to simply be relaxed and calm.

Self-Worth and Body Image Meditation

I am learning a new way of life.
It is safe for me to let go of old habits.
I forgive myself. I let go of the past. All of it. I am letting go and staying open.
I now love and accept myself exactly as I am.
I enjoy my own company.
Within me is a special place of serenity and power.
With every breath, I release the old and receive the new.
I am at peace with myself.
I appreciate who I am.
I value myself as a person.
I am open and willing to change.
As I follow my intuition, creative energy flows through me.

By being myself and doing what I love, I make a significant contribution to life.

I can accept my imperfections.

I free myself from judging my body.

I am okay just the way I am.

I love and accept myself, just the way I am now.

All people have value, and I am a valuable human being.

I deserve to relax.

I deserve to be happy.

I am attractive, desirable, and loveable.

The more I love myself, the more others love me.

I treat myself exactly the way I want to be treated.

When my mood is low, I accept my emotions and recognise that the low mood will pass, and I will be happy again.

I look forward to the good times. My future is bright and positive.

I look forward to the future and enjoy the present.

I release unhappy memories from my past.

I forgive myself for my mistakes.

I forgive myself for my harshness towards myself in the past.

I release my feelings of self-hatred and self-loathing.

I deserve to love and nurture myself.

I have suffered enough. I let myself free.

As I change and learn to love and accept my body and myself, I am gentle with myself.

I am mindful of the pressure that society puts on me about my body and myself, and I lovingly release myself from that pressure.

I am aware of some people's expectations about how I should or shouldn't look, and I let go of my need to fulfil those expectations.

I feel good about who I am today.

I accept the person that I am.

I accept my imperfections. My efforts are good enough, and I'm okay.

No one has to be perfect to be okay. I am fine just the way I am, and I stay away from people who treat me as if I'm not fine. They can think whatever they think about me, but I know that I am fine just as I am.

I enjoy being who I am, and love myself as I am.

I nurture the child within me.

I feel secure in who I am, and do not need to compare myself to others.

I accept myself.

I care for my body and myself.

I am good enough, I am good enough, and I am good enough.

I am my own best friend from now on.

I now love and accept myself exactly as I am.

I enjoy my own company.

Within me is a special place of serenity and strength.

With every breath I release the old and receive the new.

I acknowledge the negative patterns of my past and release them all with forgiveness, kindness and love.

I did the best I could as I was then.

That was then, and this is NOW.

I love myself. I forgive myself. I rejoice in the new me that is growing in strength and joy every day.

Other people's cruelty, nastiness and anger do not affect my love for myself.

I am safe. I am secure. I am fine, even when I make mistakes.

I am loveable. I am good enough. I no longer doubt myself.

I am my own best friend.

I have my inner child for company when I feel lonely.

I have a beautiful, strong, healthy body for the age that I am now.

I am grateful for the support my body has given me over the years.

I accept my body as it is now. I no longer hate any part of my body, even the bits I think are ugly or painful.

My body is fine for me whether I am fat, thin, or pink with purple spots.

I appreciate, love, and respect my body.

I am at peace with myself.

I appreciate who I am.

I value myself as a person.

I can accept my imperfections.

I free myself from judging my body.

I am okay just the way I am.

I love and accept myself, just the way I am now.

I feel good about who I am today.

I accept the person that I am.

I accept my imperfections. My efforts are good enough, and I'm OK.

I appreciate, love, and respect my body.

I am safe. I am secure.

I am loveable. I am good enough. I no longer doubt myself. I no longer hate myself. I no longer hate my body.

I am my own best friend, and I treat myself with loving-kindness.

I am learning a new way of being.

I can accept my imperfections.

I free myself from judging my body.

I am okay just the way I am.

I love and accept myself, just the way I am now.

All people have value, and I am a valuable human being.

I deserve to relax.

I deserve to be happy.

I am at peace with myself.

I appreciate who I am.

I value myself as a person.

I treat myself exactly the way I want to be treated.

My body has been good to me. I lovingly nourish it, exercise it, and groom it.

I dress with care, and when I catch a glimpse of myself in the mirror, I respond with loving-kindness.

As I change and learn to love and accept my body and myself, I am gentle with myself.

I feel good about who I am today.

I accept the person I am.

I accept my imperfections. My efforts are good enough, and I'm okay.

Meet My Own Needs Meditation

I provide myself with the kindness that I need, right now.

I offer myself nurturance, now in this moment and beyond.

I am tender towards myself.

I meet my own needs for fairness and justice.

I recognise and nurture my own sense of accomplishment.

I see myself for who I am.

I know my true intentions come from a place of loving-kindness.

I acknowledge my competence.

I recognise the power at the core of my being.

I am in touch with the true expression of myself when I am in my own company.

I fulfil my own need for companionship.

I fulfil my own need for intimacy.

In my solitude, I know that my presence in this world matters.

I trust that my life has meaning.

I trust that clarity comes to me when I need it most.

I am compassionate towards myself.

I allow myself to grieve for the person I was and the life that didn't happen to me.

I let go of my attachment to visions and dreams for a shared future that will never happen.

I acknowledge myself.

I honour my own values.

I celebrate my unique presence in this world.

I love myself.

I accept myself, and my personality, just as I am.

I know that I am a good person, and I release my attachment to other people's opinions of me.

I am grateful for the love of others, and I send love out to those people who love me and to all sentient beings.

I appreciate all the connections in my life, the good ones and the bad ones, for they are all part of life's rich tapestry.

I value my own contribution to life.

I am my own mother.

I am my own father.

I am my own sister and best friend.

I am easy with myself.

I am honest with myself, without criticism.

I support myself, without judgement.

I trust myself and my own decisions.

I care for my own inner and outer beauty.

Traditional Loving-Kindness Meditation

Let us be composed; sit comfortably in an upright posture with a sense of dignity and grace. Gently close your eyes. Allow your body and mind to relax and be at ease. Sit with the intention that for the next while, you'll be cultivating compassion to benefit yourself as well as all other sentient beings.

As much as you can, free your mind from whatever events have taken place during the day or in the past, or whatever plans you have for the future; just let go of them and dwell in the here and now.

Breathing in, you're aware that you're breathing in. Breathing out, you're aware that you're breathing out. After a few breaths, your mind may wander off. This is quite natural. No need to resist it or resent it. Without sending your mind out to investigate or analyse its content, allow the stray thought to rise and fall on its own. Watch it with clear awareness and then bring back your attention to anchor on your natural breath. In this way, you stabilise your mind.

Think of someone who is close to you, someone you love, a person or an animal. Notice how this love feels in your heart.

Notice the sensations around your heart. Perhaps you feel warmth, openness, or tenderness; now direct your wishes towards this natural object of your love as you inwardly recite:

May you be held in compassion.
May your pain and sorrow be eased.
May you be safe.
May you be at peace.

Now picture yourself with the same feelings of care and love that you have for your loved one. You deserve your compassion as much as anyone else in the world. See yourself as a child or as you are now. Allow your kind attention to rest on your own suffering, and attend to the feelings that arise as you inwardly say:

May I be held in compassion.
May my pain and sorrow be eased.
May I be safe.
May I be at peace.

Now visualise someone you neither like nor dislike, but someone you may see in your everyday life: a bus driver, or a stranger. Although you are not familiar with this person, think of how this person may suffer in his or her own life. This person may have challenges, difficulties, illness, or addiction. Allow your natural feelings of compassion to arise for this person too.

May you be held in compassion.
May your pain and sorrow be eased.
May you be safe.
May you be at peace.

Now visualise a difficult person in your life. Don't feel you have to choose the person who has harmed you terribly; it can be someone less challenging than your abuser. Although you may have negative feelings towards this person, think of how this person has suffered in his or her own life. This person has also had struggles.

May you be held in compassion.
May your pain and sorrow be eased.
May you be safe.
May you be at peace.

As you mentally recite this ancient mantra, let this wholesome energy purify your mind, dispelling your anger, hatred, jealousy, frustration, and depression. Then allow yourself to feel the sense of wellness and the spirit of loving-kindness. Also let this good feeling permeate your body and mind.

Now let's end with a wish for the suffering of all other beings to be relieved. Just as we wish to have peace, experience happiness, and be free from suffering, so do all beings. Allow your feelings of love and compassion to extend out to every being.

May you be held in compassion.
May your pain and sorrow be eased.
May you be safe.
May you be at peace.

Allow yourself to rest in the joy of an open heart as you lightly return to awareness of your surroundings.

(Adapted from Mudita L. S. Yew)

Note: Traditional Eastern Loving-Kindness meditation begins with the self. However, in the West, where low self-worth is such a pervasive problem, teachers have found that many students find it much easier to contact loving feelings for other people than for themselves to begin this meditation. Many students lose concentration, drift off to sleep, or otherwise skip over offering kindness towards themselves. In the beginning of regular practice, I found that I could play this guided meditation on repeat, and my mind would still find ways to skip the bit about goodwill towards myself. If this happens to you, don't worry about it too much. One day, you'll finally hear and feel it.

A Note on Forgiveness

Forgiveness is out of fashion.

A lack of forgiveness can tie us to people. If we can't let them off the hook and cancel out the debt we feel they owe us, it is us who will suffer indefinitely. If we hang on in the hope that the offender will offer an apology or pay off a moral debt, we are making a noose for our own necks. But forgiveness can take a very long time. We need to forgive *ourselves* if there are people we are unable to forgive.

Buddhist forgiveness practice works in much the same way as the compassion and loving-kindness practices. We contemplate forgiveness for a minor offender, then ourselves, and then extend that forgiveness outwards to all humankind. As we repeat the exercise, we will find that our forgiveness muscle is exercised and our good hearts nourished. Over time, we can begin to approach the ten-out-of-ten main offenders in our lives, like our abusers. We can eventually let them off the hook (it might take years).

Then we will be truly free.

In the meantime, here is a forgiveness prayer.

> If I have harmed anyone in any way, either knowingly or
> unknowingly, through my own confusions, I ask their forgiveness.
> If anyone has harmed me in any way, either knowingly or
> unknowingly, through their own confusions, I forgive them.
> And if there is a situation I am not yet ready
> to forgive, I forgive myself for that.
> For all the ways I harm myself; negate, doubt, or belittle myself; or
> be unkind to myself through my own confusions, I forgive myself.

Ask the Experts

Gunaratana, Bhante (2012), *The 4 Foundations of Mindfulness in Plain English*. Wisdom Publications.

Chödrön, Pema (2009), *Taking the Leap*. Boston: Shambhala Publications, Inc.

Ricard, Matthieu (2010), *Why Should I Meditate?*
At: https://www.lionsroar.com/why-meditate-september-2010/

Chödrön, Pema (2017), *Feed the Right Wolf.*
At: https://www.lionsroar.com

Harris, Russ (2013), *The Happiness Trap: How to Stop Struggling and Start Living*. Shambhala Publications.

Neff, Kristen (2011), *Self-Compassion: The Proven Power of Being Kind to Yourself*. William Morrow.

Germer, Chris (2009), *The Mindful Path to Self-Compassion: Freeing Yourself from Destructive Thoughts and Emotions.* Guilford Press.

Welwood, John (2002), *Toward a Psychology of Awakening: Buddhism, Psychotherapy, and the Path of Personal and Spiritual Transformation.* Shambhala.

Dennis, Sandra Lee (2014), *Love and the Mystery of Betrayal: Recovering Your Trust and Faith after Trauma, Deception, and Loss of Love.* West County Press.

Chödrön, Pema (2000), *When Things Fall Apart: Heart Advice for Difficult Times.* Shambhala Classics.

Chödrön, Pema (2013), *Living Beautifully with Uncertainty and Change.* Shambhala.

Kornfield, Jack (2009), *The Wise Heart: A Guide to the Universal Teachings of Buddhist Psychology.* Bantam Books.

Kornfield, Jack (2014), *A Lamp in the Darkness: Illuminating the Path Through Difficult Times.* Boulder, CO: Sounds True.

Brach, Tara (2013), *True Refuge.* Bantam Books.

Kabat-Zinn, Jon (2013), *Full Catastrophe Living.* Bantam Books.

Boorstein, Silvia (2007), *Solid Ground: Buddhist Wisdom for Difficult Times.* Parallax Press.

Boorstein, Silvia (2008), *Happiness Is an Inside Job: Practicing for a Joyful Life.* Ballantine Books.

Courtin, Venerable Robina, et al. (2007), *Dear Lama Zopa: Radical Solutions for Transforming Problems into Happiness.* Wisdom Publications.

Mason-John, Valerie, *A Practice for Developing Kindness toward Yourself.* At: https://www.lionsroar.com/a-practice-for-nourishing-yourself/

Kornfield, Jack, *The Ancient Heart of Forgiveness*.
At: https://www.youtube.com/watch?v=yiRP-Q4mMtk

http://self-compassion.org/

http://www.insightmeditation.org/
http://insightmeditationaustralia.org
http://www.buddhismandpsychotherapy.org/find-a-therapist

On YouTube, search for:

- *When Things Fall Apart*, Pema Chödrön with Oprah
- *Losing It Completely*, Pema Chödrön
- *Working with Difficult Emotions*, Robina Courtin

Chapter 3

THE BRUTAL REALITIES

Manipulative Behaviours

Trigger Warning: Descriptions of the ways we have been manipulated can be extremely distressing to read. If you find yourself panicking, please put the book down or return to the self-care pages.

> So you can see it and nobody else can.
> You're on your own, kid.
> And you can cope.
> You can recover.
> Be brave.
> You are stronger than you think.
> You can do it.
>
> —narcissisticsociopath.net

The sophisticated, shallow, charming persona of the narcopath whitewashes over the sinister tactics that actually operate their day-to-day lives: the covert (some unconscious) manipulation of the truth, the target's emotions, and other people's perceptions of the target and themselves. The things they do for their self- gratification and aggrandisement are counter to what they say to win hearts and minds.

Remember, we are not talking about a macho, aggressive, overtly racist sexist pig here. We are talking about a smooth-talking, glib, easy-going, charming people-magnet. We are talking about behaviour that no one else can see but those they prey on, or those outside the charm circle, and few would believe if they could see it anyway.

Here are some manipulation techniques that fly under the radar for those trusting souls amongst us, listed in order of escalation as the narcopath tightens the screw.

Hypnotic Charm
The most charismatic person in the room, he focuses the spotlight of his full attention on you. With large doses of direct eye contact, he is totally fascinated in whatever you say. If he is a celebrity narcissist, he appears utterly fascinated by the story of how you listened to his music (saw his movie/watched him play footie) when you were a kid, but it will seem as if you were the first person ever to have told him this, and he is utterly flattered and humbled by such a revelation. You walk away, proclaiming, "Wow, he is such a nice, humble, decent, down-to-earth guy," ten minutes after you have met him.

Later in the relationship, you will find that he drops you like a hot cake in order to focus this charm on a total stranger. When there is a new fan to be gained, his loving family become irrelevant and invisible to him.

Love-Bombing Seduction
He gives you excessive attention in the form of emails, texts, letters, flowers, gifts, dinners out, sex, good times, and fun. He has to be with you every minute of every day for the rest of his life. It's like no other seduction you've experienced.

Flattery
He offers extreme validation about your appearance, your personal qualities, your competence, your intelligence, your environment, your professional prowess (the very things he is compelled to undermine and destroy once he has the power to do so).

Mirroring

The coincidences are extraordinary. He professes to share the same beliefs, politics, spirituality, tastes, preferences, likes, and dislikes as you. You were made for each other.

Hurried Intimacy

He progresses the relationship quickly to sharing his innermost insecurities, desires, ambitions, and shame, in an effort to have you reciprocate. When you do, as is natural, he will later use his knowledge of your intimate secrets as a tool to control and manipulate you. He is quick to move into your home, quick to talk about a shared future, quick to propose marriage. It's a whirlwind romance.

Lying

1. Outright lies whilst looking you straight in the eye.
2. Huge omissions that leave holes in the jigsaw. Over time, you will find you have an increasing pile of jigsaw pieces that don't fit into the picture he has painted.
3. Twisted and embellished truths: a tiny truth at the centre of a Russian doll wrapped in layers of lies.

Rationalisation

These are clever and plausible stories to explain why he lied to you. For example, the reason he didn't tell you he was married when he seduced you was that he had found his soulmate in you, and he wanted to leave his wife without causing any moral distress to either of you. (The bare fact that he cheated you both is entirely irrelevant to him and needs no apology.)

Playing the Victim

This is more lying to gain your sympathy and support. For example, he had been loyal to a loveless marriage for years or was the victim of abuse from his mentally unstable wife or had done everything in his power to support his violent, drug-addicted child before it all got too much for him, and he was forced to abandon his family. Crazy exes are *the* go-to victim story for psychological abusers.

Word Play: Empty or Loaded Words

Manipulators are practiced yarn-spinners who know the right words to choose to

- put a convincing argument,
- induce an emotional reaction (flatter, confuse, stifle, insult, defuse, inflame), or
- paint a picture (impress, suggest, plant a seed of doubt, build on commonly-held assumptions).

Telling you exactly what you want to hear, they will make promises, commitments, vows, and oaths they have no intention of fulfilling. "I love you. I've waited my whole life for you. I've finally met my soulmate. I'll never leave you," are uttered easily and frequently (and to many targets over a lifetime). Over time, you will notice that their pledges and self-professed image of themselves don't match up with their actions. They continually break promises, always let you down, and are never there for you when you need them.

Masters of the double-entendre, they occasionally utter words that seem nonsensical or out of place. Because these utterances are so odd, we can let them through to the keeper when in fact they are glimpses of true intention. Expert lie detectors call them "tells". These comments are often in the form of black humour. For example, "We can get married, settle down, have kids, and drive each other nuts," or "Now we are married, darling; it's all downhill from here. Ha ha ha."

Backhanded Compliments

These are barbed comments in which a derogatory observation is disguised within an apparent compliment: "You handled that really well, given that you are so weak and sensitive." "You did a good job on the books, especially when you are so bad with figures." "Doesn't this dress make my wife look slimmer than she is?"

Belittling

This includes behaviour such as rolling eyes, tut-tutting, talking down to you, mocking, scoffing, or teasing. Demeaning the target's opinions, achievements, and abilities in both a private and public context. Induces or increases low self-esteem. Such a common socially acceptable male treatment of women in Aussie culture that it flies under the radar for many of us. We are conditioned to shrug it off.

Intermittent Reinforcement

This is a proven method for increasing trauma bonds with a person or animal and is often used by cult leaders. Rewards for desired behaviours are alternated with punishment for behaviours deemed unacceptable by the manipulator. Experts speak of dosing; that is, providing periods of love-bombing to induce euphoria and bonding in the subject, followed by periods of ignoring, neglecting, or punishing the subject by withdrawal. This creates enormous confusion and co-dependency; that is, the subject's happiness becomes dependent on the positive or negative treatment by the manipulator. An actual physical addiction to the dopamine released in happy times results in a craving to repeat the positive experience during times of neglect. This makes for extremely loyal and obedient dogs and children. It also breaks their spirit.

The Silent Treatment

This is stonewalling, refusing to engage, leaving the room or the home for hours or even days at a time. The target has plenty of time to question what it is they said or did that caused the emotional and physical withdrawal of the manipulator; she becomes conditioned to avoid certain subjects, hide certain emotions, adjust certain behaviour as a result. It becomes patently clear what is off-limits, and important issues slowly become a simmering volcano of unspoken concerns underneath day-to-day life.

Ghosting

This is an extension of the above: ignoring texts, emails, voicemail messages during periods of enforced separation (like work travel) or agreed separation (like family visits). This reinforces your doubts that you just don't matter to him or your fears of abandonment. It creates feelings of insecurity. If, in response, you text or leave an angry voice message, this evidence will then be used to alienate anyone who might be left to support you (triangulation) by him claiming he is the victim of unprovoked abuse (playing the victim).

Goading

This is commonly referred to as pushing someone's buttons: deliberately putting you on the defensive by lying or ignoring, accusing, or belittling you to provoke a reaction. Such goading (or testing your patience) can occur over hours or days. For example, making and breaking promises over and over again; making what should be joint major decisions without consulting you (selling the house, arranging a holiday); meddling with what should be your personal affairs without consultation (changing your passwords, adding himself as signatory to your accounts, taking a loan out in your name); stringing you out by saying one thing overtly and doing another covertly; not turning up at appointments; going AWOL when you need him most, then switching the conversation to phone or email and continuing to ignore increasingly urgent requests for explanation or action (ghosting).

Once it starts, it probably means he has found his new supply, decided to leave, and flip the blame onto you, all the while gathering support and sympathy from the community. He wins. Again. Game over. New chapter begins.

Flipping the Blame

This involves goading you, and then making the story about your bad temper; having an affair, and then making the story about your jealousy or paranoia; triangulating, and then making the story about your low self-esteem; coercing you to stretch a sexual boundary, and then making the story about your prudishness; breaking the law or a moral code, and then making the story about your restrictive religious or ethical sensibilities; coercing you into risky or dangerous situations, and then making the story about your cowardice.

The unconscious process of projecting our own faults onto others is a common human tendency. Then there is the sinister, manipulative increase in shaming and scapegoating used by the narcopath that escalates to the discard and destroy phases.

Triangulation

This technique stimulates uncomfortable interpersonal relations (jealousy, suspicion, or dislike) with another person (friends, family or possible next wife) by defaming that person to you or defaming you to that person, by claiming you or they said or did something neither of you said or did.

Conducted on a broader scale, it can take the form of sly and insidious remarks dropped into public conversations in the form of total fabrications that cast the target in an unflattering light, such that the listener will judge them (or you) harshly or confirm an already-held bias. It relies on our natural tendency to gossip. For example, "I heard from a reliable source that so-and-so is a closet alcoholic/mad bitch/compulsive spender/ adulterer."

Financial Skulduggery (Abuse)

This is hiding his financial situation (or "keeping it private"); denying access to accounts; controlling your earning potential (by suggesting you leave your job so he can support you or you can take care of the kids); justifying his spending decisions and invalidating yours; running up debts; taking loans in joint names without your permission; claiming it was you driving the vehicle when a traffic infraction occurred; borrowing and never repaying; treating lending accounts like a Ponzi scheme (you deposit, he withdraws and lies about where the money came from). A narcopath seems to think that the dollar he brings to the table is worth more than the dollar you do, that his money is his and your money is his too.

Hero Complex

Psychopaths have a very shallow affect (emotional experience); they get a buzz out of risky or dangerous situations. They enjoy instilling fear in those around them so they can observe their discomfort and then present themselves as a rescuing hero.

Machiavellian psychopaths will use this technique with large groups of people. Think of fascist leaders, doomsday cults, Brexit, or the 2016 US presidential campaign.

Gaslighting

This is claiming that a mutual experience didn't happen, such that you begin to doubt your own perceptions. "I never said that. You're imagining things. You're overreacting. It's all in your head. My wife has a very bad memory. Ha ha ha." Gaslighting begins spasmodically and increases in frequency and weight as the relationship progresses. Used with other manipulation tactics, gaslighting has the effect of denying a target's reality. This is deeply damaging over time.

Convenient Memory Loss (Toxic Amnesia)
This is another gaslighting tactic. It's swearing to the fact that he has no memory of a certain event, such that observers must decide who to believe. He forgets agreements, promises, appointments, contracts that were only made to secure your loyalty or trust but are now inconvenient truths. It's not just a lie of omission, but a sworn oath to no memory of a significant truth.

Invalidation
This subtle, covert behaviour indicates a total lack of respect or callous disregard for your rights. Behind-closed-doors behaviour and speech clearly indicate that your ideas, beliefs, boundaries, needs, and goals simply don't matter. He treats you like an inconvenience or a burden.

Humiliation
This is giving others the impression that you are lazy and incompetent and offer nothing to the manipulator but are the beneficiary of tremendous support, kindness, generosity, and loyalty from the abuser.

Shaming and Blaming the Victim
The narcopath holds you responsible for everything that is wrong with the relationship. He can blame his adultery on your unattractiveness or illness; his professional failures on your lack of support; his financial irresponsibility on your being "high maintenance"; his sexual dysfunction on your lack of libido; his stonewalling on your being too demanding or needy, or expecting too much of him; his dishonesty on your suspicion or paranoia; his incompetence on your unrealistic expectations; his alcoholism on your enabling. Over time, this can lead to a victim mentality and deep personal shame in the target.

A narcopath will never admit to any of these behaviours and doesn't see anything wrong with them, anyway. If challenged or held to account, he will accuse *you* of all these foul behaviours. He flips the blame.

You survived all or some of that. Despite being scammed, used, and manipulated, you are still here. Inside you lies the courage to endure, the resilience to overcome, the tenacity to hold on until your journey through hell eventually ends. And it will end. You will emerge into the light wiser, more compassionate, and freer than you ever thought possible. You have been through a trial by fire that not every human being can understand. You will recover. Have faith in yourself. Your beautiful spirit was broken, but you will rise again like the phoenix from the ashes of your previous life. You have everything you need inside of you, even though you may feel weak and exhausted and lost right now. With rest, patience, simplicity, silence, contemplation, self-compassion, discernment, and *no contact*, you will emerge like the lotus from its roots in the mud.

He is not an omnipotent being who has supernatural powers over you. He is a disordered person who has developed this personality strategy of manipulating people to get what he wants out of life; that's all. He wanted you. He got you. He took everything that was useful to him and discarded you, with a callous scorched-earth policy, leaving nothing intact from which you can rebuild. But you will be reborn.

Be strong. Be brave. Be kind to yourself. Wrap yourself in your own tender loving embrace, and nurture the tortured little soul that feels as if it's been thwarted. Take refuge in your own good heart. You will fly again, beautiful soul. Take heart.

> A narcopath *takes* from people who give generosity,
> kindness and love. And when he has exhausted the
> giver's emotional, psychological, financial, professional or
> social resources, he *discards* and *destroys* the giver.

—narcissisticsociopath.net

The Matrix of Psychological Abuse

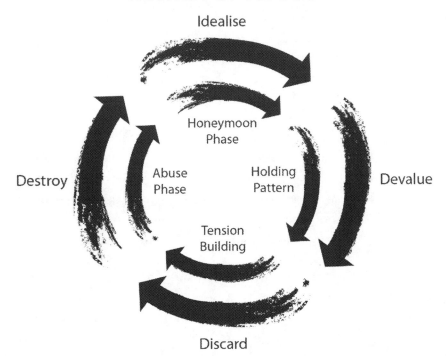

Other people around us in the aftermath, can accuse us of being hysterical, making mountains out of molehills, being drama queens, because the abusive behaviours we try to describe can sound like typical marital disharmony, and no worse. What others can't get is that we have been living inside a matrix of deception and manipulation that *we can't yet see either.* Let alone *articulate.* Psychological abuse is subtle, hidden and easily rationalised.

It can take some of us a long time after the split to realise that what we have experienced is psychological abuse. We have been complicit in our own destruction by being trusting, forgiving, or just cooperative.

Inside the long-term pathological abuse cycle of idealise/devalue/discard/destroy, there is the inner covert cycle of relational abuse. Couples argue. And some of the elements of discord below occur in minor ways in normal relationships. "I never said that" or "I do half the housework" are pretty common delusions. "That whole period of a year where you worked for my business for nothing is all in your head" or "That tree trunk I put in the backyard while you were out has always been there" is gaslighting. That's pathological.

Honeymoon (or Reconciliation) Phase
- He apologises for not being able to cope with her issues, denies the abuse ever happened, says it wasn't as bad as she claims, or subtly blames her for provoking the abuse; he plays the victim.
- She feels compassion and sympathy for him and allows herself to be vulnerable again.
- She absorbs the blame, feels remorseful and guilty, apologises, forgives him, and makes atonement efforts (frequently make-up sex).
- He appears to accept the apology but actually warehouses the incident to be used against her later.
- He promises it will never happen again.
- He love-bombs her again.
- She reciprocates with increased nurturing, loving, care-taking behaviour.

Holding Pattern Phase
- He appears to keep a few promises made during the reconciliation.
- He reverts to a charming, apparently loving partner, especially in public or with an audience.
- He acts like the abuse never happened.
- She hopes the matter is resolved and their bond has grown stronger via managing conflict well. She trusts him again.

Tension-Building Phase
- He starts seething with passive-aggression, getting irritated or angry.
- He belittles, demeans, or accuses her in minor ways.

- Silent treatment. Stonewalling: he refuses to communicate.
- She feels like she is walking on eggshells to avoid conflict.
- He disappears for days on end without communication (ghosting), stays out all night, and lies about his whereabouts.
- His Jekyll/Hyde intermittent reinforcement starts again; he behaves one way in public and another in private, says one thing and does another.
- He humiliates, embarrasses, or invalidates her in public.
- His friends or family embarrass, humiliate, or invalidate her in public (he's actively gossiping and slandering her behind her back again).
- She makes herself more and more available to him, jumps through more and more hoops, and exhausts herself trying to keep track of the shifting goalposts.

Abuse Phase

This hidden abuse convinces women what they experienced isn't really abuse.

Emotional
- goading: testing her patience, pushing her buttons to get a defensive response, then accusing her of being abusive when she reacts
- accusing her of being jealous, paranoid, unfaithful, or mentally unstable; blaming her for everything unsatisfactory in their lives; taking credit for everything positive

Psychological
- gaslighting (denying what happened actually happened; denying what she knows he said or did; moving or tampering with household objects; hiding things, changing passwords, or posting online whilst pretending to be her or someone else)
- triangulation (playing people off against each other with gossip, slander, and lies)

Sexual
- infidelity, withholding sex, extreme porn, failure to notify of sexually transmittable diseases

Financial
- stealing, borrowing, running up debts, gambling, spending joint funds without consultation or lying about where the money came from, over-controlling or limiting partner's access to joint funds, justifying his spending choices whilst attacking hers

Physical
- "accidentally" kicking, punching, or hitting while asleep or drunk; damaging property, pets, or children
- coercive substance abuse

Social
- convincing, encouraging, or coercing her to dump her job, friends, clients, or support networks; leave her home and family; burn her bridges (isolates her so he can control her)
- misrepresenting her behind her back as abusive, violent, drug addicted, financially irresponsible, deceptive, dishonest, crazy

Post-Relationship (An Overlooked Phenomenon)
- after he discards her, the abuse worsens, with smear campaigns, lying under oath, hiding assets, dragging out the legal process. He aims to punish her in whatever way possible, see that she is left with nothing and no support whilst keeping his own hands clean.

So now you've read all that distressing stuff. Good for you. See how brave you are? You are stronger than you think.

Many of us become obsessed with educating ourselves on the phenomenon of narcabuse, in the same way that we keep bothering a mouth ulcer with our tongue. There can be a kind of compulsion to keep picking the scab off the wound, even though we know that it won't heal until we stop picking at it.

If we venture onto the Internet to find some relief, we will find every shade of outrage expressed about narcissists, sociopaths, and psychopaths, and begin to realise at a deep personal level that this is a thing. It's not just me. It's not just the unique Dr Jekyll/Mr Hyde personality of my ex-partner.

Other people have suffered this confusing matrix of abuse. This new awareness can be a double-edged sword. Other people's suffering awakens compassion in us, which can lead to greater sorrow and outrage. But it can also bring comfort, if we let it, in the form of awareness of the shared human condition.

Personally, I don't relate to the expression "You are not alone" that is often reeled out with the good intention of providing comfort. Because we *are* alone. We are more alone than we have ever been in our lives in the aftermath of covert abuse. We are the only person in the world who can find our way out of the abyss. The hero's journey or the warrior's journey is the most solitary journey a person can undertake. We didn't choose this route, but it is the one we are now on. Rather than struggle against it, or drown in the depth of it, we are called upon to ride the waves of it, to learn *how* to ride the waves.

Awakening to narcabuse is ultimately as liberating as it is painful. It is a rite of passage that narcabuse victims must go through. Ouch. Double ouch. But it is not a permanent obsession. There will come a time when the urge to read and understand the shocking behaviours of psychological abusers will pass. We will come to understand and realise we've had enough. Nothing is permanent. This compulsive thinking about it is a temporary phase of abuse recovery. It will pass, just as soon as we feel we've figured out what the Hell Just Happened.

This suffering will end.

There is a fine line between educating ourselves and not taking care of our hyperarousal. Right about now is when mindfulness of our level of arousal becomes really important. We can teach ourselves to notice the racing pulse, beating heart, sweaty palms, shaking knees, knot in the stomach or any other somatic responses. A change of habit is needed. Instead of ignoring our body's warning signals, chastising ourselves for being [insert preferred derogatory term], and applying the habitual stoicism of clamping down on our distress, we stop everything and attend to our suffering.

We take our suffering in our own loving embrace and reach for the new tools in our growing toolbox of self-compassionate behaviours. We take a two-minute self-compassion break. We stop reading and put the book down. We stand up and walk outside to ground and centre ourselves. We write in a journal, send an encouraging email to ourselves, turn inwards to our despair. Be kind to ourselves. We listen to a guided meditation or affirmations, wholeheartedly and with as much concentration as we can manage.

What is important during the education phase of recovery is not to learn more and more about personality disorders as soon as we can, but to assimilate the new information bit by bit. Be really patient with ourselves. Pace ourselves. Nowhere in our past (unless we are trained clinical psychologists) have we been exposed to these brutal truths. We've seen these types in movies. We've read about religious cult leaders and brainwashing. We've admired the sociopathic James Bond and Sherlock Holmes. But we can't reconcile how any of it could happen to *us*. Especially if it has happened before and we thought we had it nailed. We are just ordinary secretaries, nurses, teachers. Not high-flying, go-getting legal combatants or politicians or military personnel who might expect to find themselves fighting evil. We didn't sign up for this. We signed up for a loving relationship and we got a war on our very selves (and a layperson's degree in psychology).

Soon, other big questions arise, like, why did this happen to me? How could I not have noticed? What did I do to deserve this? Is it karma or punishment from God? Why aren't I recovering like I always have with past break-ups? We can start to look inwards, not to offer ourselves kindness and compassion, but to beat ourselves up, blame ourselves, rifle through our personal history looking for all the bad things we did to deserve having our lives ripped apart.

The fact is that a good heart doesn't always see the bad. And when the wicked want to bring down the innocent, they aim for a loving heart.

Did He Ever Love Me? Disenfranchised Grief

A man who lies to himself, and believes his own lies, becomes unable to recognize truth, either in himself or in anyone else,

73

> and he ends up losing respect for himself and for others. When
> he has no respect for anyone, he can no longer love, and in
> him, he yields to his impulses, indulges in the lowest form of
> pleasure, and behaves in the end like an animal in satisfying his
> vices. And it all comes from lying to others and to yourself.

—Fyodor Dostoevsky, *The Brothers Karamazov*

I think it's fair enough to assume, after a number of normal relationships that failed the lifetime compatibility test, that the person who vows he wants to spend the rest of his life with you, at the very least, has your best interests at heart. But a narcopath has nobody's interests but his own in the place where his heart should be. However long you test out the relationship before you convince yourself the love is mutual and enduring, if you marry a narcopath, you will find that everything changes the day after (or the night of) the wedding.

For a start, his natural predatory instincts have assessed you as the thing he most wants next to relieve his chronic boredom. He just *has* to have you, for whatever reason. First up, he likes the town you live in, your house, your cooking, your bank accounts, the lifestyle you can provide for him. Or your looks and style could make you a trophy wife. Bonus. The reasons might include your deep inner qualities, but only because he wants to possess or manipulate them for himself. As jealous as sin, he will set about destroying them rather than have anyone else enjoy them.

He wants your constant adoration, worship, adulation, and praise. He also wants your kindness, generosity, sweetness, humour, honesty, competence, whatever. When he can no longer feel the constant glow of these fine human qualities (because they become hum-drum and boring), he is motivated to destroy them. What he doesn't want is your illness, your sadness, your anger (especially not your anger), your exhaustion, or any other normal human baggage. He'll stick with you until he's got you hooked, reflecting back at you and promising to partner you in all the things you most hope for, crave, or aspire to, morphing himself into everything you ever wanted in a man. Easy. Especially if you give him a list of the things you are looking for (such as on a dating site or a wishful-thinking manifestation chart).

From that moment forth, when he has your total trust, love, and commitment, it'll feel like you're drowning. You are suddenly trapped in a revolving door of episodic kindness and praise, like he used to love-bomb you with, and covert cruel devaluation, ending in dehumanisation and destruction of your life. Just like any old parasite slowly starves and kills its host. Like a frog slowly coming to the boil, you'll fail to notice the rising temperature until you're already cooked. You'll wake up dead.

A narcopath's love is more a combination of greed and contempt than any kind of love. His love is just obsession, a passing fancy. He wants you like he wants a new Ferrari or a holiday on a Greek isle. Once he's got it, the novelty quickly wears off. There are flies. Sure, there are plenty of people like that. What makes the narcopath different from plain old womanisers is that he'll stick around, taking everything he can get, and plotting ways to make it look like you are the reason he was forced to leave. He needs to destroy the evidence rather than risk tarnishing his spotless reputation. He keeps his hands clean, discrediting and disempowering his victims. He *is* the red Ferrari, out of control, without brakes, careering from one reinvention to the next, ploughing remorselessly through lives, leaving a trail of destruction and a pile of bodies.

The narcopath is addicted to continual excitement, and nobody can remain exciting in a committed relationship or excited about their mate. Nobody. But you will find that from the moment he has you hooked, he becomes suddenly and inexplicably bored with you. The excitement was all in the chase. The drive to win at any cost is huge in a narcissist's ego. Once he takes home the prize, the giant stuffed panda (that's you), it gets sat in a corner of the bedroom and thereafter neglected. It's taken out when there's an audience and shown off with pride. Your achievements are claimed as his own, at the same time as he privately belittles them and holds them in contempt. He'll spend your money for you. He'll charm the pants off your friends and family. He'll even do the washing up for you from time to time, or make you breakfast in bed. When there are witnesses. They'll tell you how lucky you are to have such an attentive husband. And when they leave, back in the corner you go.

The thing you imagine you see in him as love is not love. It's excitement. It's gratification at tricking you into loving him, at winning the game. That suspicion you have that his lovemaking is just lust is well-founded. For him, it is simply fulfilling a human need for sex, and no vow or moral boundary is going to prevent him from satisfying that need whenever he wants, with whomever is available. The hypersexuality is not about his love for you; it's just about convenience. The reason he keeps marrying and discarding women is because he likes to have his basic needs for food, shelter, and sex met all the time, and without too much effort. He is lazy. He is always on the lookout for the next thing that might take his fancy. If he senses your imminent withdrawal of any of the things that satisfy his appetites, he'll easily switch to the attentive, adoring man he was before he hooked you. He'll smirk as he sees you take the bait again. Then he'll do exactly the opposite of what he just promised you.

His sense of entitlement is massive. It precludes the possibility of love, since love requires humility, opening up the heart, and allowing another to witness our flaws and trusting them to treat our hearts with respect. Many narcopaths develop very sophisticated stories and word salads (circuitous conversations that always end with you being blamed for everything) to feign humility. They might go to great lengths to prove just how humble they are. People love humility. It garners praise. Anything that garners praise is a worthwhile game. Charity is another. Real charity, real humility don't advertise themselves, but the narcopath can't resist advertising his. He can't resist telling complete strangers what a humble, charitable guy he is, trying to impress them. His flying monkeys will lobby for him, and he'll be showered with accolades or prizes for charitable works that should really go to the little guy out back who's devoted his life to genuinely helping others ("flying monkeys" refers to a narcopath's enablers, derived from the seminal story of the wicked witch in *The Wizard of Oz*, who sent winged monkeys out to do her evil deeds for her). Narcopaths surround themselves with enablers and use them to do their dirty work for them. Keeping their hands clean while they abuse their victims is a hallmark of psychopaths, sociopaths, and narcissists. Once enablers are used (or wake up to his lies), they are discarded too.

The love thing is just another tiny part of his sophisticated personality strategy. If he deems himself naturally superior to others, he must develop the ability to at least appear normal, to fit in. He must climb the social ladder wearing a mask of normalcy, burying the bodies he steps over to advance, to win. With fame or a title appended to his name, even the red Ferrari starts to morph into a Rolls-Royce: the very model of established power and respect. Unquestionable. Now that is success. That is winning, climbing so far up that he is no longer held to account for his actions, beyond reproach. We admire these people in our society. We vote for them. That's the goal. Because there is nothing a narcopath hates more than being challenged in any way. Challenges, queries, being held to account don't fit in with the image he has of himself as Mr Perfect. Most challenges can be swiftly dealt with by using the victim act, anyway: word salads of remorse or regret that flip the blame onto his accuser. He's sorry he couldn't deal with the fact that she's a crazy, lying bitch.

The victim then experiences a more difficult form of grief: disenfranchised grief, genuine grief for something that never existed. Not solid tangible death-type grief, but a grief that belongs nowhere in the psyche, a grief that is more difficult to integrate, precisely because it belongs nowhere. There is grief at losing a home, a future, connections to family and friends, and all the broken promises. But then, there is the disenfranchised grief of loving someone who never existed. Believing ourselves loved by a liar who lied about loving us. It's grief for the death of a loved one who was nothing more than an imaginary friend. That type of grief is crazy making. And I'm sure that many survivors cannot escape their cognitive dissonance in this regard; they continue to struggle for years to understand how such a dream love could result in such a nightmare.

We must face the fact that we were never loved, despite investing everything we had. We face the fact that the love we gave was to an imaginary friend, a spectre. It is this that can make recovery from narcissistic or psychopathic relationships take so very long. We trusted the sheep and were devoured by the wolf. We married Dr Jekyll and were destroyed by Mr Hyde. We grieve the loss of a false persona.

When a liar tells you he loves you, he's lying.

Narcissistic Love
Love is greedy and lustful.
Love is conditional.
It is jealous and envious.
It is boastful.
It is proud and arrogant.
It maligns and slanders.
It serves only itself.
It takes offence easily.
It stores up transgressions to be used later as blame.
It delights in evil and uses truth as a weapon.
It only protects itself,
always uses trust to manipulate,
always looks for greener pastures,
always leaves when there is no more to be taken.

Corinthians 13:4–8
Love is patient,
love is kind.
It does not envy,
it does not boast,
it is not proud.
It does not dishonour others,
it is not self-seeking,
it is not easily angered,
it keeps no record of wrongs.
Love does not delight in evil but rejoices with the truth.
It always protects,
always trusts,
always hopes,
always perseveres.

The Smear Campaign

Rumours are carried by haters, spread by fools, and accepted by idiots.

—Pinterest

Scholarly studies and survivor forums all articulate the phenomenon of the smear campaign that is part of the narcopath's toolkit, his modus operandi. If you're like me, you might have *sensed* that the smear campaign had started because his friends and family treated you with disdain, disrespect, or downright rudeness before he left. After the separation, and once the works of fiction that are his sworn affidavits come through, you will know exactly how he has chosen to smear you; you'll read his character assassination of you with your very own eyes. So will your lawyer (and then begin to doubt you as he or she struggles to be impartial). Mud sticks. The seed of doubt has been planted, and people will search for ways to prove or disprove what they've heard. Usually, they will instantaneously take sides (believe or disbelieve the new information) and then look for ways to prove their decision right, to prove *themselves* right.

"The need to reduce cognitive dissonance also strongly affects our reaction to new information. We like our biases confirmed and we are willing to manipulate and ignore incoming information to bring about that blessed state. This is so regular and strong as to have a name – the confirmation bias. In the words of one British politician, "I will look at any additional evidence to confirm the opinion to (sic) which I have already reached."

"So powerful is our tendency to rationalize that negative evidence is often immediately greeted with criticism, distortion, and dismissal so that not much dissonance need be suffered, nor change of opinion required."

—Robert Trivers, *Deceit and Self-Deceit*

That's when you find out who your friends are. But that's a different story.

Essentially, you can be sure that the narcopath will fall back on an old practice, a habit that has become second nature in his hidden identity as a user, con artist, and predator, a kind of flip side to the mirroring of the idealise phase (the love-bombing phase). This is the exact opposite of pretending to share all your likes, habits, and dislikes. He will describe you and your behaviour by using himself and his foul covert behaviour as a template. The jury is still out on whether it is a conscious process (deliberate lies), or an unconscious one (the result of being amoral and projecting his disowned dark side onto you). It is likely a bit of both. As the jigsaw pieces fall together with uncovering evidence—both legal and anecdotal—and your jaw drops farther and farther at just how deceitful and cruel this man you trusted can be, you can rest assured that he will describe you as a most deplorable human being.

The Smear Campaign. They all do it.

It is the simple manipulation of our human tendency to gossip, criticise, and judge by feeding little or large pieces of misinformation that cast you, his victim, in a negative light and make him out to be a hero in putting up with you. He will twist the truth, exaggerate and maximise any less-than-perfect behaviour that others might have witnessed, leading them to judge you harshly via their own unconscious biases, based on your class, your gender, your profession, your addictions, your weaknesses, your shame. He will invent outright lies to cover his own infidelity, lies, cruelty, and abuse. He will make huge omissions in telling the story of what happened. He will allow Mr Hyde to provide the storyline that Dr Jekyll will tell calmly, politely, gently, as if it were true. It is true for him because he believes his lies a nanosecond after he invents them. He will swear to it, hand on Bible. He is a pathological liar under that charming mask.

Provoking or goading a victim and then videotaping, audio recording, or otherwise saving evidence of an angry, drunken, or distressed response is another tactic used by emotional abusers to blame and shame their targets. Accusing the target of being crazy is the first thing they all reach for in their character assassinations. Maybe this is because they know they have us questioning our own sanity or that their abuse has us traumatised and acting out. Either way, they will use clever methods of entrapment to provoke a reaction that others witness, while hiding or failing to disclose how they provoked us. They will throw a hidden first punch, then cry, "Abuse!" when we retaliate in any way.

This phenomenon, known as reactive abuse, is clearly articulated in the online community. Abusers exert so much emotional pressure on their target by exacting a nightmarish season of appalling behaviour and cruel offensive acts that they finally inflict the proverbial straw that breaks the camel's back, which sends even the most patient and forgiving of souls into a flurry of defensive, angry, hysterical, or frightened expletive-drenched reactiveness. Cruelly deliberate, the blame spotlight is then swiftly refocussed on the reactive abuse from the target, leaving the perpetrator grinning with self-satisfaction at the power and control he has over another, like a man who derives pleasure from prodding a captive bear until it bares its teeth and claws. Bystanders with whom this outburst is shared will then sympathise and side with the perpetrator, leaving the victim to die of shame and humiliation. There are plenty of people out there who believe a woman should never get angry.

And we are utterly powerless to do anything in the face of his smear campaign. By the time he is finally ready to discard us, it is too late to defend ourselves. The damage to our personal relationships has been done, and the seed of doubt has been sown in the minds of those around us. The smear campaign is a grown-up, more sophisticated version of the schoolyard practice of telling tales behind a person's back, yet being perfectly sweet and charming to their face (dosing). When we experience first-hand the pain of the smear campaign, we can develop an acute awareness of just how dangerous gossip can be across a broader horizon than our own little life. And we learn to refrain from it. That is the only empowering act available to us at this stage.

I am aware of the irony contained within the telling of this story. Because describing an experience of a smear campaign by a narcopath looks for all the world like a smear campaign in itself. For many survivors of this kind of abuse, our first impulse was to defend, protect, forgive again, and love our abuser. Keep our vows. Many victims describe ways in which they go half-mad vacillating between believing Dr Jekyll would never do such a cruel thing and realising Mr Hyde has really done it. It is a trap in which many women find themselves and is part answer to the question of why women stay in abusive relationships. We suffer from cognitive dissonance, or holding two conflicting beliefs at the same time, and trauma bonding, or being addicted to our split-personality abuser.

We see the smear campaign played out on a world stage by politicians. We see it in movies, used by unethical corporations against whistle-blowers. We see it used against rape victims in a court system that is ruthlessly archaic. We see it used by preachers accused of sexual misconduct, bent TV cops, or nations accused of genocide. It's falsified negative propaganda, fake news. And now we get to experience its effects for ourselves. They are devastating. Smear campaigns split our world into us and them: those who believe the gossip, and those who stand by us, (and those who, by sitting on the fence, are siding with the perpetrator).

As an empathic, sensitive, generous, honest, and trusting soul (this describes most targets of a narcopath), it might be hard to imagine what dreadful things he could have said about us in order to alienate so many people and convince the courts that it is us who needs to give him the house. The narcopath's vengeful smear campaign is more vile and vicious than anything we could imagine, especially from someone we loved and trusted.

The narcopath will smear you from a long list of bad behaviours that are actually a description of his hidden persona. Normal males will also resort to vicious character assassination, but usually in the confidential court process in an attempt to wrestle custody over children by depicting the woman as an unfit mother. This is borne out by findings in a scholarly survey commissioned by Women's Information Referral Exchange.

That list of accusations is likely to include that you are

- lying about your personal and professional past,
- lying about what happened during the course of your relationship,
- an habitual liar,

- an habitual thief,
- dependent on alcohol or drugs,
- mentally unstable in its myriad possible forms (borderline personality disorder appears to be a favourite accusation),
- financially irresponsible,
- generally deceptive,
- covertly manipulative,
- slanderous,
- turning the children against him,
- an habitual adulterer,
- lazy, having made no financial or other contribution to the marriage, or
- verbally or physically abusive.

The smear campaign doesn't end when he leaves. It escalates. He will use the family legal system to further denigrate, denounce, discredit, and disempower you.

Then you will find that it is not just malicious gossip you are up against but perjury that actually has the power to strip you of your home, your finances, and your children. You will need every ounce of courage, strength, self-love, and self-respect to withstand the bullying metered out to you by him and his lawyers (and possibly your own lawyers, if they cannot recognise the inherent misogyny in the legal system). He will have you over a barrel. It will feel like the lawyers are holding you down while he repeatedly rapes you with a foreign object: the law.

You have a choice. Resort to his and his lawyer's bullying, abusive tactics, or hold the high moral ground and try to fight his lies with the truth. Which kind of person do you want to be?

Are His Friends Narcopaths Too?

Yes. Simple answer. Not all of them, of course. Most narcopaths have an uncanny ability to seduce or coerce the kindest, most empathic, most loyal people who provide a social camouflage. This loyal tribe will forgive and defend the bad behaviour of the narcopath until the cows come home. But people with antisocial personality disorder also tend to hang in like-minded clusters. B-Clusters, especially professionally. People with sociopathic and narcissistic traits understand each other's habits of using and discarding people. They understand preying on vulnerable types. They understand manipulating innocent people. They understand ambition and greed as primary motivating forces. They see people as things to be used, climbed over, stepped on, and treated excessively nicely when they have something the narcopath wants. They compete with each other. They collude with each other. And they support and empower each other.

So if you reach out to his friends who have become your friends (or so you thought) during the course of the relationship, you will come up against a low-empathy brick wall. Either they believe the smear campaign, or they see nothing wrong with their friend dumping his fifth wife when she is of no further use. In short, reaching out to his low-empathy friends in an effort to understand might delay your recovery. They really do live in a world of quid pro quo. Not in terms of kindness, duty, and honour but in terms of "I'll lie for you if you lie for me. I'll break the law if we get to share the spoils. I'll perjure myself if you keep my secret." Narcopaths keep tally of every favour, every dollar, every kindness they do for you, and nothing you can ever do is enough to return the favour. But they will reveal their true nature when in the company of a like-minded individual.

I contend that the reason psychological abusers are never held to account—in addition to their perfect false public persona—is that predatory male behaviour in our patriarchal society is so commonplace it has become invisible. When women such as the #metoo movement hold men to account, a few men may join the chorus, but they are always referring to other men. There is never an imperative for a man to reflect on his own behaviour. Most think the problem is someone else's. As such, the taboo of domestic and psychological abuse is as much an urgent feminist cultural issue as sexual harassment in the workplace.

Let me share an anecdote.

I once heard my narcopath in conversation with his colleague—another narcissistic celebrity—when they both believed I was out of earshot. A good churchgoing pillar of the community, his wife had died, and people were beginning to make enquiries (the way they do) as to whether he had found a new girlfriend (at the age of seventy-three).

He told my narcopath he had found one who was a pretty easy bet. Getting her would be easy, since she was going through a difficult divorce, so all he had to do was be a shoulder for her to cry on. She should do pretty well from her divorce, and she had a good job and a nice house, so she was a good prospect. She had kids, including a nineteen-year-old girl. "I reckon I could've had the nineteen-year-old if I'd wanted. Big fan of the group. But what am I going to do with a nineteen-year-old? Ah ha ha ha ha ha."

Both these men have bullied, manipulated, and exploited the female figurehead of their band for a lifetime, a fact she disguises with public stories of them "brothering" and "fathering" her. They profess a warm familial group dynamic to the press and demean, scapegoat, and mock her behind her back.

I contend that we can all recognise partnerships where one predatory partner is feeding off another. There are partnerships around us where one partner (usually the woman) slowly changes from a vibrant, healthy, slim, attractive, fun-loving, independent extravert to a sick, mousey, insecure, subservient introvert or an angry, dependent pudding or scarecrow, the woman our culture blames as having "let herself go." They are one in four of us (domestic abuse victims). Since the same woman is likely to defend any criticism of her mate and take the blame squarely on her own shoulders (due to her trauma bonding), we overlook the likely abusive causes and conditions happening behind closed doors. Even when a man has married multiple times and reduced multiple women to this condition, we still blame the women.

The Gilead of *The Handmaid's Tale* is not so far off that none of us can imagine it.

Liar's Oath

When I swear she's mentally unstable, what I really
mean is she got upset when I lied to her, cheated on her,
and stole from her. She even cried sometimes.

When I swear she's abusive, what I mean is she got angry when I
gaslighted her, goaded her, humiliated her. She once even swore at me.

When I swear she's alcoholic, what I mean is she never
said no when I poured her a drink every night.

When I swear she's a junkie, what I really mean is
she took the drugs I offered her. Both times.

—narcissisticsociopath.net

Why Me?

Predators choose victims who

- have something they want (sexual allure, a place to live, money, resources, contacts, lifestyle),
- are highly trusting or innocent (perhaps overly trusting and naive),
- tend to look for the good in people,
- are quick to forgive,
- are highly invested in relationships with friends, colleagues, family (loyal to the people around them), and
- are vulnerable to manipulation due to depression, anxiety, low self-esteem, lack of confidence, social isolation, addiction, or earlier abuse or trauma.

Please read that list again. Apart from the last point, they sound like nice people, don't they, these victims? Good people. Kind, competent, responsible, generous, warm-hearted, loyal people. That person is *you*. Remind yourself that this is who you are, not the neurotic mess you now feel like you've become.

You were chosen to support his parasitic lifestyle, not because you are any of the things his smear campaign makes you out to be, but because you are responsible, competent, successful, kind, generous, forgiving, trusting, good-hearted, well-connected, ethical, honest, vulnerable, loyal: an all-round good person. Let yourself read these words; listen to these words. Let them in to your poor, wounded soul. Let yourself weep at how someone you trusted raped your goodness and left you with your own self-belief in pieces, along with the rest of your life.

Somehow, he brainwashed you into believing you are a bad person, worthy of being discarded and destroyed. Right? Now is the time to turn towards that good heart that is still there. Now is the time to become your own best friend, your own firm believer, your own therapist, your own mother, your own authentic powerful self. From this place of brokenness, you can recover.

Narcopath Viewpoint

Kindness = Weakness
Trust invites control
Empathy beckons manipulation
Vulnerabilities urge exploitation
Gentleness invites domination

—Rhonda Freeman, *Huffington Post*

It is possible, nay probable, that we are what shrinks call "other-referencing." That is, we have somehow grown up to put everybody else's needs before our own. Or put another way, we've come to believe that if everyone around us is happy and satisfied, that we will become happy and satisfied too. We find that we cannot rest until everyone around us is comfortable. In so doing, we also have a tendency to ignore our own well-being in the service of others: our parents, partners, children, guests, volunteer groups, work groups. We can reach burnout again and again, and as soon as we regain some energy, we spend it on sorting things out for the people around us.

No, not every woman is like that. It's not just a woman thing, though here in Australia, especially rural Australia, there are plenty of women like that. They'll serve themselves the burnt chop at the barbecue. It's considered polite and virtuous. Mothers, of course, will go hungry to see that their children are fed.

Other-referencing people also need external validation to feel good about themselves. If other people tell us that we are good, kind-hearted, and generous or did a good job, then we can believe it (for a while). Conversely, if others (for example, early caregivers) tell us that we are selfish, ungrateful, stupid, good-for-nothing, or ugly, we can internalise this feedback and develop a harsh inner critic. Many of us grow up in families where the kind of person we are becomes set in stone way before we have formed adult personalities, and we lose the capacity to reference internally, to self-soothe, self-regulate, or self-validate. We are trapped by the way we think others see us, by what others are telling us about ourselves. Our harsh inner critic constantly chastises and denigrates us. That can only be relieved by external validation, by the kindness, flattery, applause, and admiration of others.

So when the narcopath who hooked us with flattery and praise begins to tell us that we are jealous, crazy, ugly, demanding, needy, whatever, we tend to take it on board. Deep inside, we feel offended and so turn inwards, not to offer ourselves compassion and kindness, but to search for all the ways our accuser might be *right* about us. We feel shame for things there is no real cause to be ashamed of. We decide we are bad because he says we did a bad thing. Then we cover over our secret shame by being more and more agreeable and compliant, in the hope of some external praise to compensate for the effects of unfair blame.

This is exactly how a narcopath uses intermittent reinforcement to manipulate us.

We might be fixers, rescuers, and possibly martyrs. We may have a tendency to wade into difficult circumstances, believing we can be the person to set things right, ease the tension, solve the problem. We naturally have empathy for other people's suffering, from the mundane to the extreme. We are quick to pick up on bad vibes or feel other people's sadness, loneliness, or confusion, almost as if it were our own. We might be a Highly Sensitive Person (as defined by Elaine Aron).

When things cannot be sorted, we might have a tendency to take the responsibility onto our own shoulders, blame ourselves for not making enough effort, or feel severely underappreciated, given the effort we make. From there, our mood might descend into any number of pathways, from depression and self-loathing to resentment and aggression at not having the favours returned or our own needs met. We might try to escape by boozing, spending or Facebooking. We might try to punish ourselves by dieting, over-exercising, or botoxing.

It is egocentric but not selfish, the way we tell ourselves it is. That just feeds right back into the never-ending loop of the other-referencing person. It is possible to give ourselves love and nurturance and meet our own needs in a wise, grown-up way. Maybe we just never figured out how that works. We can now. We can learn to become conscious of our own patterns and break these habits. We can move from self-deception to self-awareness, with a new outlook of curious investigation wrapped up in generous doses of loving-kindness towards ourselves.

> "Socially, a potential cost of self-deception is greater manipulation (and deception) by others. If you are unconscious of your actions and others are conscious, they may manipulate your behaviour without you being aware of it."

—Robert Trivers, *Deceit and Self-Deceit*

We may have a deeply entrenched belief that everybody is good on the inside, and we are quick to forgive them or turn the other cheek when we witness bad behaviour. We give people the benefit of the doubt, again and again and again, to the point of finding ourselves exploited, walked over, used as a doormat or a receptacle for everybody else's blame. We never learned how to stop this repeated experience from unfolding and wonder what causes it to happen and what we can change about ourselves to stop it happening over and over.

We might have a very deep need to be liked. Sure. Doesn't everybody?

We may aspire to being virtuous, and we have big, open, generous hearts that we share with anyone who crosses our path. We wear our hearts on our sleeves. Or too many bad experiences have hardened our hearts to protect our vulnerability. Our first instinct may be to trust people. People are innocent until proven guilty, right? And when they betray that trust, take a little bit of advantage, take a mile from the inch we gave them, we'll quickly forgive them, turn the other cheek, give them the benefit of the doubt, and trust them again. We might even think this blind trust is a virtue and therefore unworthy of unpacking by curious self-reflection.

As you read this, can you also see how these things fed into each other, to trap you in a snare set by the untrustworthy fraud who was magnetically attracted to someone they could easily use, lie to, and blame? You weren't to blame for your own exploitation, but you can take some responsibility for tweaking the recipe that makes you tasty prey for predators. You can change the repeating pattern. Take heart.

We are very loyal, and that loyalty even keeps us bound to people we suspect might not have our best interests at heart. We figure if we're more loyal, more trusting, more forgiving, more generous, eventually they'll appreciate it and return the favour. We have high relational investment. Interpersonal relationships are extremely important to us at work, at play, in the home. So we are prepared to exhaust ourselves by investing in these relationships; because we are always the one to ring, the one to have people over, the one to arrange the staff party, the one to clean up when everybody else is too hung over, we may not notice that other people don't give a damn, basically. Soon, other people will come to expect it of us and hold us responsible when things don't happen the way they want. We might ask, "How is this my responsibility?" and fail to recognise that we made it our responsibility ages ago, just by being loyal and people-pleasing.

It is those very aspects of our characters, the very trust, generosity, kindness, loyalty, and investment in being liked, that attracts predators, exploiters, users, and persecutors. A narcopath can pick it up a mile away, and his extraordinary ability to work out how other people tick (whilst being incapable of honest self-reflection) makes us easy prey. Other people can pick it up too. For some people, the urge to exploit kindness, generosity, and gullibility (or weak boundaries) is so great that they simply can't resist the urge to take advantage.

You wouldn't blame an impala for looking like prey to a lion, would you? So don't blame yourself for falling prey to a human predator. You are not to blame. It's not about you. Not right now, anyway. It's about what *happened* to you.

Now is a great time for us to start reassessing and resetting our boundaries, adjusting our blind trust, altering our insane loyalty, reordering our list of relationships that are or aren't worthy of our further investment. Closing doors is a necessary part of any good strategy. Some bridges are well burnt.

We are embarking upon an epic journey. And that journey is the hero's journey. It is essentially a solitary experience of learning and growth. From this trauma, with our lives lying in ruins around us, we get to choose which bricks we pick up to rebuild. And whilst it won't feel like it right now, we find the strength and courage to create better foundations than the ones our childish minds laid down for us. We get to grow up.

Karma, Fatalism, and Free Will

People in the West misunderstand the concept of karma, using the word as meaning "everything that goes around comes around." *Karma* means action and is a much more profound concept than is implied by its use in our vernacular. For a start, it includes the concept of multiple rebirths. What we sow in this life will have far-reaching implications in this or another life. I will leave it to the wise Buddhist scholars to explain in full, but essentially, it is much closer to "as you sow, so shall you reap" from our Christian-derived culture (except this implies a single lifetime or ending

91

up in hell). The hell we ended up in with the narcopath is not necessarily the result of the bad seeds we have sown in this lifetime.

I debated for a long time about my right to discuss an issue that comes up for many survivors of psychological abuse in forums and comment sections online. I am not an accredited philosopher or a Buddhist teacher. I gave myself permission to include a mention of this dilemma, because it is one of the great weights we survivors bear on top of an already devastating trauma. So that's my disclaimer right there. To really understand the teachings on karma, perhaps the Lam Rim from the Tibetan school of Buddhism is the best place to start. We can only find the answers to our questions within ourselves, by contemplating our own lives.

The teachings on karma are profound teachings on cause and effect. We might now struggle to understand what terrible things we did to reap the result of so much pain. Did we tell so many fibs as a child that we are getting lied to, lied about, and not believed on a grand scale? Did our youthful experiments with one-night stands result in being punished by our partner's womanising and adultery? Were we so careless with gossip that we are now the subject of slanderous fake news in our social and professional networks? Is having our life savings or our livelihood stolen from us the result of our adolescent group-pressured attempt at shoplifting? Did we bring this whole disaster on ourselves? Is God punishing us?

What karma is *not* is anything to do with punishment for our sins.

What it also is not is "Everything happens for a reason." That is determinism or fatalism. This now-common platitude rests on the theory that everything that happens in our lives is predetermined. The things we encounter have been scripted by a greater power to teach us a lesson. Whether we use free will or not, the outcome will be the same.

It is *not* the modern New-Age victim-blaming concept of choosing what happens to us, either. (We were victimised because we chose to be born into our family of origin, we chose our psychological abuser, we chose to get cancer, and now we must figure out why we subconsciously made those choices.)

And it is certainly not manifestation, that if we consciously determine what we want from life, we will manifest wealth, fame, or success.

It's strange what we each believe, isn't it? The concept of karma arguably falls midway between all these ideas that have been debated by great thinkers ad infinitum. Karma ripening is about the complex interplay between myriad causes and conditions, some of which we choose and some of which we have no control over. Each thought, act, and deed significantly contributes to our karma, but the results will not necessarily show up in this lifetime. Nor is our current experience necessarily the result of our own bad behaviour in this lifetime.

The main takeaway about karma in recovery from psychological abuse and subsequent victim-blaming is that we hold the steering wheel. We get to choose what kind of person we want to be. Do we want to resort to the cruel tactics of the narcopath in order to satisfy a need for closure or revenge, or do we want to move forward into a life that is filled with love, compassion, kindness, truth, and courage? It's entirely up to us.

> If you are planning revenge
> Be sure to dig two graves.
>
> —Confucius, Pinterest

Is It Contagious? Am I the Narcopath?

> I can explain it for you. But I can't understand it for you.
>
> —T-shirt seen on the street, July 2017

Abandoned victims, already shocked and confused by the double messages and sudden personality change, can really get into a frenzy when they start Googling and get stuck into the education stage of recovery. Many survivors report freaking out over the changes in their own behaviour borne of the need to protect themselves and start to ask, "Is it really *me* who has a character disorder? Is it catching?" These concerns about contagion need to be addressed because they feel real.

Behaviour stemming from the fight, flight, or freeze response to shock is automatic; we have little control over it. With PTSD, we might feel that we don't recognise ourselves. And others—particularly those who are quick to judge or are invested in us being the way we've always been—might not recognise us, either. We all might easily mistake this change in behaviour for the sudden personality change we witnessed in our disordered partner when the mask of the narcopath dropped. It is not. It is trauma behaviour. It is neurosis that can heal, not a character disorder that is incurable.

Self-Centredness

We might go into lockdown, obsessively thinking about the abuse. Or we might reach out to trusted others and try talking it through, oversharing. The preoccupation with our own pain is not narcissism. It is the same instinct that drives a cat or dog to continually lick its wound. It is okay to tend to our own well-being whist under attack or in the aftermath. This form of selfishness is nothing like the narcissistic self-preoccupation and self-referencing of the narcopath. He genuinely believes he is perfect and has likely led us to believe we are deeply flawed over months or years of devaluing cohabitation. Our pain needs our attention. Our trauma symptoms deserve our attention. We need to find a way to silence unfair accusations of selfishness or indulgent self-pity by our internal or external critics. We need to be compassionate with ourselves.

It is not selfish to make our recovery and happiness a priority. It is kindness to ourselves. We are learning to reference internally, a skill we might never have learned before.

Disbelief (Did I Imagine It All?)

The persistent belief that we were more kind, more forgiving, more tolerant, and made more investment in this relationship than any other is not a delusion but likely extremely well founded. Conscientious, vulnerable people capitulate to psychological manipulation with more and more agreeable behaviour in an attempt to restore the homeostasis of the "ideal" union that created the narcopathic bond in the first place, like a beaten dog that comes back wagging its tail.

We are not imagining things. His gaslighting taught us to doubt ourselves. We are *not* lying to ourselves now, even as others doubt us. It is not unreasonable to expect a return on behavioural investment, instead of the callous attack we got. Some relationship experts call this the slot-machine conundrum: investing more and more but never getting a payout. Partnering with someone who coerces us to give up everything so we can be his nothing is not easy to comprehend. We are conditioned to believe, "If you scratch my back, I'll scratch yours." And vice versa. The behaviour is complex and covert. But the proof of the pudding is in the tasting. Accepting this is a big challenge. Believing it really happened to us can take some doing.

We are not the creep his smear campaign makes us out to be. Nor are we the worthless thing he made us come to believe we are. A narcopath can never reciprocate the moral investment his targets make. He is amoral. For someone with a moral conscience, psychopathic behaviour *is* unbelievable until we come to understand and accept it. We danced with the devil, wearing the mask of an angel.

Anger
The anger or rage that might arise from the discard and destroy phases is nothing like the seething passive-aggression or explosive anger of the narcopath. Our betrayal was profound and real, and anger is a natural response to having been scammed. His anger is a response to the smallest insult to his unrealistic conviction that he is so special and different that he must be treated with the reverence and respect of a demigod. We were like a chained animal in a cage responding to being continually poked (or worse). The rage will pass when we have *no contact* and the wound heals.

He promised us a dream and delivered a nightmare. He promised us everything we ever wanted so he could have the satisfaction of taking everything we ever had. Why shouldn't we be angry? We can now learn the art of sitting on a powder keg of rage the best we can, without harming others the way he does.

Difficulty Accepting Blame (There Must Be Two Sides to Every Story)
Our conviction that we were not to blame or did nothing a reasonable person could view as a deal-breaker is not the justification and deflection of the narcopath. Even if we lost our temper or answered back or used the wrong tone of voice (!), the healthy contrition of apology, make-up sex, and atonement are nothing like the cycle of abuse that we endured with the narcopath.

We've had our empathy—our ability to see two sides to every story—twisted around and used against us. Our tendency to turn inwards and blame ourselves can go off the scale after we are discarded. Our cognitive dissonance (holding two conflicting beliefs at the same time) can also go off the scale. When we search inside ourselves to take responsibility for our part in our own demise, we just can't find any real deal-breaker. So we search again. Over and over.

That's just how the narcopath likes it. He has sent us into a spiral of doubt and self-blame, when what we really need to do is let ourselves off the blame hook. Accept that we have been completely used and disposed of, like a thing. Our contrition is genuine. If he bothers with a display of contrition (which is unlikely), it's for the benefit of his fans. But any remorse on his part is just the mimickery of further manipulation, victim-playing, seeing to it that others blame his victim. Nor is he the man he appeared to be at the start or with an audience. We made mistakes, but we are not to blame. We are nothing like him.

Wearing a Mask (I'm as Fake as He Turned out to Be)
Our culture demands that we wear a mask of normality to engage in day-to-day social activity. People don't like it when we express our anguish and despair. It's too challenging, too uncomfortable. So we adapt to the disapproval of others by adopting an inauthentic persona, just to survive. We hide our distress, in the same way an animal hides its limp so as not to appear weak to predators. This inauthenticity is not the same as the mask of a narcopath, which is a cleverly constructed persona designed to hide his predatory nature: Mr Nice Guy, the last person anyone would suspect of being an abuser. He wears his mask, almost permanently, from the

boardroom to the bedroom, until he runs out of puff, until the wearing of it is no longer necessary as he extracts the last drop of usefulness from his prey. The two masks are nothing alike.

The abuse pulls the rug out from under us. We are left groundless. If we choose to fake it till we make it by wearing a phoney, bubbly mask, it's no big deal. It's not a permanent condition. It's a coping mechanism. When we commit to returning to our own good heart, we slowly get closer and closer to our own authentic selves. If there is a hidden gem in the nightmare of narcabuse, it is the strength and authenticity that we find in post-traumatic growth.

Dumping People

Our need to protect ourselves from further hurt by pushing people away is nothing like the callous disregard of the narcopath, who discards people when they are of no further use to him. Break-ups challenge loyalty in our friends and family. They reveal hidden grudges, jealousies, and suspicions in those around us. Finding out who is really on our team and who we can really trust is a part of any break-up. With narcabuse, it's way bigger than ever before.

People-pleasers might easily find that they are surrounded by takers and users. Add to this, the clever impression management and smear campaign of the narcopath, and the recipe for toxicity in our circle is complete. The necessity of avoiding people who have been poisoned by the narcopath's toxicity is a matter of self-preservation. It is real, not imagined. And it is probably better to be safe than sorry. Our trust has been deeply violated and needs room to recover.

The need to interact with people who get it is perfectly understandable. It's absolutely okay to avoid blamers, criticisers, and people with low empathy or compassion. In the aftermath, we need people who are on our team. We need allies, people who don't give up on us, who back us up, lift us up, and acknowledge our trauma, even if they don't understand it. The way a narcopath uses and manipulates loyalty is nothing like our newfound need for a "social stocktake".

Silent Treatment

Setting a boundary with our abuser by going *no contact* is not the same thing as the silent treatment he dished out to us during the devaluation phase. By not returning calls or answering emails from our manipulative ex, we are keeping the wolf at bay. We might feel as if we are being cruel and abusive by stonewalling our persecutors, but we must give ourselves permission to let ourselves off the hook again. We are acting out of healthy self-preservation to prevent ourselves being drawn back into his exploitative, deceptive game. The ghosting, silent treatment, and other withholding behaviours he used were about making us sad, angry, isolated, and confused, or punishing us for questioning him. We go *no contact* to save ourselves from psychological slavery to a man who wants to destroy us: not the same thing at all.

Holding a Grudge

Being unable to forgive is extremely painful, and there is an expectation in our Christian-derived culture that we must do this. We know that even when we tried to mend a rift and offered genuine contrition to our narcopath, he continued to blame us and punish us beyond reason. The inability to forgive we might now struggle with is not the same thing as the ruthless vengefulness of the psychopath. We *want* to forgive but might find we cannot. The narcopath's malicious punishment of us is based in a disordered view of what constitutes an injury to his narcissistic ego. It's a complete invalidation of us as human beings. Therein lies the difference. There can be no mutual acceptance of responsibility or closure from which a healthy friendship might emerge.

It can decades to forgive someone for abuse or betrayal. We need to forgive *ourselves* for not being able to forgive certain people. We know forgiveness relieves the pain in our own hearts, but beating ourselves up for being unable to forgive just adds to our misery. The route to forgiveness can be found through self-compassion. With Mindful Self-Compassion practices, we learn to honour ourselves first and to gradually extend those feelings of goodwill to others. We can let ourselves off the hook of thinking of ourselves as bad people because we are unable to forgive our abuser. In forgiveness contemplation or meditation, we don't go straight to the harshest situations and people, but to the lesser wrongs and betrayals. Gradually, over time, our forgiveness will grow.

Victim Status.
We have been victimised. There are no two ways about it. The feelings of being weak, defeated, and broken are not the result of a personal flaw but of having to bear too great a weight for too long. Read the case studies. This is what malignant narcissists, sociopaths, and psychopaths do to people, particularly women, who continue to love and forgive way longer than they should have (with hindsight). The feeling of being trapped in a snare is the very real result of dealing with a manipulative liar who is exploiting us and our whole lives for his sick gratification. With every day of *no contact*, we move from feeling like a victim to being a survivor.

The narcopath's victim act is just another manipulative weapon to gain support and sympathy in order to shift the blame. People who accuse us of playing the victim are victim-blamers and should be avoided.

Telling People about the Abuse (A Smear Campaign?)
Wanting other people to know the truth of what we've endured, wanting to expose his foul character publicly, and even wanting revenge are natural responses to being bullied or betrayed. We struggle against our darker urges. The narcopath gave in to his a long time ago. When we tell people about his cheating, lying, stealing, and slandering, we are telling the truth.

Some of us never developed a healthy capacity to stand inside our own truth. Self-doubt runs deep in our veins. We have a conditioned *need* to have our truth validated by other people. The narcopath recognised this need and manipulated it. Bringing that truth back inside our core is a big job for some of us. Until we learn this inner strength, we might need to vent about the myriad ways we were deceived and betrayed.

We need to give ourselves time to integrate the truth of what happened.

We know what happened behind closed doors, and one day, the truth will be integrated, whether others believe us or not. We will no longer need their validation. Telling our story is nothing like the narcopath's smear campaign, based on exaggerations, fabrications, and projecting his own behaviour onto us. We want to be heard. He wants to destroy us.

> The truth is still the truth, even if no one believes it.
> A lie is still a lie, even if everyone believes it.

—Pinterest

Retaliation (Am I the Abusive One?)

So we lost it after he left us carrying the can and called the narcopath a liar, a cheat, a thief, or milder stuff like dishonourable or lacking in decency. We threw the second punch. His treatment of us provoked such rage and confusion that we didn't know which way was up anymore. We lost control of our emotions and did or said things we regret. Maybe we stupidly pointed out the fact that we had found his character described in psychology literature and realised he is a narcissist or sociopath. Or our burning compassion for his next victim drove us to reach out and warn her of his pattern of abuse. And he punished us with unfathomable vindictiveness.

Weigh it up. Which is worse: lying or telling a liar he is a liar? Cheating or telling a cheater he is a cheat. Stealing or accusing a thief of thieving? Dishonest character assassination, or revealing secret truths about cruelty and abuse? It's not helpful. It's a tad harmful. But it's not the crime our shame tells us it is. We were the victim of vile and vicious behaviour from someone we loved and trusted. We couldn't handle it with wisdom, patience, grace, and good manners. Of the two sets of behaviours, the lying, cheating, stealing, and slandering are worse, by a long shot.

We are human. We threw the second punch. We made a mistake. We can forgive ourselves for that. We can let ourselves off the shame hook. What we most definitely are not is anything even close to what he is.

And Another Thing …

There is also a deep truth in our questioning itself. If we had a character disorder like his, we would be incapable of questioning ourselves. The fact that we are prepared to turn inwards for an explanation is a testament to our inherent goodness, our basic human decency. We can stop beating ourselves up and blaming ourselves in whatever weird way we can possibly dredge up. We were victimised, not because of our flaws, but because of our goodness.

The aftermath might also include the healthy responses of guilt, regret, remorse, and contrition. Guilt is the honest acknowledgement of our own wrongdoing. Regret is the feeling of sadness that a goal, ambition, or solemn vow wasn't fulfilled. Remorse is the forceful pang of guilt for having hurt others. And contrition is the genuine effort not to make the same mistake again and adjusting behaviour so as to ensure that we don't. (Shame is the oft-unhealthy and unrealistic belief that we are a bad person because we did a bad thing; this is a different story.)

Dark Triad types are incapable of any of this. The character-disordered narcopath is shameless, guiltless, remorseless, and without regret (unless they are exposed); he continues to believe he is essentially a good person, despite all evidence to the contrary. The very definition of evil, a psychopath is without conscience.

> The psychopath carefully plans the most hurtful and heartbreaking way imaginable to abandon you. They want you to self-destruct as they start the grooming of their new host. Destroying you and your reputation reassures them that the next host will be better. They despise your empathy and love – qualities they have learnt to *pretend* to have every day of their lives. This game of repetition temporarily fills the emptiness in their souls.
>
> —Pinterest

The Three Ways Narcopaths Use People

> People were created to be loved.
> Things were created to be used.
> The reason why the world is in chaos is because things
> are being loved and people are being used.
>
> —Dalai Lama, Pinterest

There are essentially three uses a narcopath has for all the people around him.

You were used by a narcopath because you fell into one of these categories:

1. Supply (you have personal, sexual, or professional prowess; financial resources; practical provisions such as a home, car, or tools; friends; or a network that is useful to him)
2. Enabling (your wish to please, keep the peace, avoid conflict, profit or benefit are being used to coerce and manipulate you, vis-á-vis your generosity, kindness, ambition, or greed)
3. Cover (your own reputation, skill, or position in society reflect favourably on the narcopath by association or can be used to deflect blame if he is ever caught)

Narcissists and sociopaths are incapable of bonding. They do not feel the pull of familial and friendship bonds in the same way that you or I do. They do not understand concepts of duty, responsibility, loyalty, or honour, except as those qualities reflect on their public reputation or the way they are perceived. They can only mimic these qualities, if it serves their purposes. People, to them, are highly disposable. Once people fulfil their useful purpose as cover, supply, or enabler, they are discarded. To be fair, narcopaths are being joined in this behaviour all over the world. It is becoming normalised in an increasingly individualistic society. It can make the real narcopaths pretty hard to spot.

Take the analogy of a small child. This child is at the very epicentre of his own universe. He feels *entitled* to have his wants met instantaneously and without compromise. A yellow one simply will not do when it's a red one he wants. And yet he will forfeit the delayed gratification of a pile of red ones if he's satisfied that a single yellow one is the best he can get now. It becomes his primary focus, into which he pours all his energy. He quickly learns that in order to get the yellow one *now*, he must manipulate everyone around him. Some people never deny him anything (enablers); some people have the yellow one (suppliers). He might decide to steal it and blame the theft on someone else (cover). Or he may invite someone who is trustworthy to be complicit in the theft on the promise of sharing the spoils (cover and enabler).

Most of us grow out of this phase of life. We learn that a pile of red ones later on is worth the discipline of waiting or striving. We learn that using and discarding people who enable our journey will cause others to mistrust or disrespect us and that we will wear out our welcome over time (if we stay in the same village). Our conscience grows to prevent us from destroying, defrauding, or stealing from others for our own fleeting gratification, especially if we are likely to get caught.

Narcopaths somehow manage to climb all the ladders of life by using others so skilfully that they rarely slide down any snakes. It is those around them that get the snakes on life's game board. Narcopaths become skilful at having their immediate needs met whilst deflecting blame, coercing others into moral compromise, or disguising their selfishness with loud proclamations of charity and false bravado. Narcopaths are consummate self-publicists and manipulators. And they share with their child counterpart, narcissistic rage. This rage will be expressed by an overt toddler tantrum (violence or verbal abuse), simmering passive-aggression (stonewalling), or sophisticated covert punishment of the perceived offender in the form of triangulation, gaslighting, fraud, mockery and smear campaigns.

A fear even greater than not having his own needs met is that of being uncovered. Intelligent, successful psychopaths skilfully move through life covering their tracks to avoid discovery. Less intelligent, unsuccessful sociopaths end up in gaol. Simple.

So how do we identify these types in our personal landscape? Many theorists suggest that it is nigh on impossible, until the damage has already been done. Whilst we might recognise from the periphery that a friend or work colleague is the object of clever manipulation, it is much harder to identify when we are suffering the same fate. Central to the narcopathic scam is our own trust, respect, and love. We often cannot quite put our finger on why we remain loyal to people or why we don't trust someone. Life gets in the way of continual reassessment of our interpersonal relationships. We just carry on regardless. Why would someone we trust lie to us? Why would someone foster antagonism towards us from our friends, co-workers, and family? Why would someone betray the faith we placed in them after they bent over backwards to prove they were trustworthy?

For most of us, the idea that we are slowly being used and our lives torn apart without our awareness is preposterous. And no one is about to warn us. It's not the done thing to tell a friend her husband is having an affair or share suspicions that his business partner is ripping him off, is it? Well, is it? Hmmmm. Another conundrum. Depends on your friends, I guess.

So narcopaths change locations, jobs, mates, friends, countries, states, towns, homes, or partners with monotonous regularity. Pathological liars, they can only manage their complex personal PR for so long until the various worlds around them collide. This requires more and more thought and energy if they stay in the village. They move through life, exhausting supply after supply, and only take with them those people who are sufficiently unaware as to be useful cover, and those who are sufficiently loyal, ignorant, and trusting as to be useful enablers. These people give them character references, professional success, admiration, and adoration because they have not been used, destroyed, and discarded or because they have not uncovered the true Mr Hyde nature of charming, apparently decent Dr Jekyll. They believe the lies, just like we did. Those most of us would call distant friends, colleagues or even our own families.

By now, most readers will recognise the personality I am describing. They might be as many as one in twenty-five of us, remember. And those of you who haven't been sufficiently wise to avoid such toxic people might wonder how to extricate them from your life. My experience, other than no contact, is to place as much physical distance between yourself and this toxic person as you possibly can, as often as you possibly can. If your own professionalism, loyalty, or compassion prevents you from cutting your ties with such toxicity altogether, then my advice remains the same. Stay away from them as much as possible. Communicate as little as possible.

Remove yourself from their orbit little by little, even though you know their toxicity will fall on someone else. And do whatever is necessary to distance yourself without becoming the target of his toxic rage. Move carefully and cautiously. He is likely as ruthless as he is remorseless. And he does not feel remorse. He *cannot.*

If you recognise yourself as supply, move immediately to protect whatever it is you have that he wants. If you can see that you are cover (your own respectability, trustworthiness, talent, or competency can cover for his lack of these things), examine the complex minutiae of lies and false impressions, untangle them piece by piece, and no longer associate with the parasite. If you see yourself as an enabler of such a person, then set new boundaries: rein in your generosity and kindness, and don't jump so high when he asks you to. If you see that you have been repeatedly used to enable the destruction of others, then stop. You will not be rewarded. You will not be taken along for an exciting and gratifying ride. You will be used, dumped and possibly discredited.

If you can see that you were all these things to a narcopath, then you were the perfect target, the ideal prey. Let go of blaming yourself or absorbing the blame of others. Let go of any concern you have that by removing toxic people from your life, you are behaving just like the narcopath (lots of victims report these concerns). Acting out of self-protection is quite different from acting out of self-gratification and self-aggrandisement. Take your poor wounded soul in your own loving embrace and rest your attention on the courage to overcome that lies buried under a pile of confusion. You can now learn and grow and become courageous and compassionate enough to ensure that you never fall prey to another predator in your life.

A lie doesn't become truth,
wrong doesn't become right,
evil doesn't become good,
just because it is accepted by the majority.

—Pinterest

Empathy Theory, Simplified

Cognitive empathy (highly developed in narcopaths) is the ability to identify and understand another's mental state or perspective.

Narcopaths recognise a number of stimuli that help them predict how another will think or choose to act.

Affective empathy (absent in narcopaths) refers to the feelings and sensations we get in response to someone else's emotions.

Narcopaths do not recognise another person's emotional state or respond with the normal resonance (when others around us are afraid or in despair, we usually begin to feel some of their pain).

So they can tell you exactly what you want to hear, and lie unconscionably, without feeling even slightly uncomfortable emotionally. Narcopaths can learn to fake affective empathy; they're excellent mimics. So they can pretend to share the excitement or sadness that their behaviour has brought about, while getting gratification from their manipulative power and confirmation of their superiority. They are secretly proud of the way they can manipulate other people without anyone noticing they have been used.

Most of the time, they know what they are doing (another big question that arises in the aftermath of psychological abuse).

My own narcopath summed it up beautifully when I tried to appeal to his conscience: "There are people in this world who will climb over the bodies to get to the top, and that is who I am."

Empathic Resonance

In the early days of the aftermath and embarking on recovery, we need to be very careful of other predators. Ever since psychopathy was identified, many studies have shown that people with parasitic behaviour can instantaneously sense vulnerabilities and unmet needs in a person. If you weren't already, you are now a beacon for manipulators and exploiters, even if your public persona says, "I'm fine."

Beware of people you feel an instant connection with, as if you've known each other for years and automatically understand each other. Trust takes time and mutual effort to build. Beware of interactions that make you walk away feeling ten feet tall: confident, validated, kindred spirits with someone who shares your opinions and beliefs on almost every subject. Narcopaths are able to tell you exactly what you want to hear at the very first meeting (including outside of the romantic context).

Take careful note of early boundary violations, such as promises to communicate or commitments to meet that are broken. Notice if you are hoping, wishing, or planning for another interaction with that person, despite a few minor boundary violations. This could be your conditioned attraction towards exploiters and manipulators. Give the new connection space and time, and overcome your natural tendency to be the one who calls. And if you have the opposite problem (a new connection who continually calls, texts, Facebook messages, praises, flatters, follows the story of your daily life), run!

The Law Is No Protection

Note: I am not a lawyer. My understanding of Australian family law is from my own lived experience and may not be accurate. Experience also tells me that most lawyers' understanding of the law differs from one to the next.

A year after our abandonment or flight, just as we are starting to gain some control over our reactivity and find some ground under our feet, a new opportunity for the narcopath to further abuse us presents itself: divorce.

Knowing what to expect in a battle helps us arm ourselves and protect ourselves the best we can. As pacifiers, mediators, compromisers, women, we possibly have underdeveloped skills for standing up for ourselves or fighting back. What we most need now is courage. We can feel the fear and do it anyway. We don't know the law, so how can we instruct our lawyers?

We can arm them with a list of behaviours we anticipate from our abuser. Let them do the advocating for us. With luck, they see this form of abuse all the time and will know how to handle it. Rookie lawyers will make rookie mistakes. The narcopath will manipulate them too.

Right up front, let me say this: If you are now pretty sure he is a narcopath, take him to court. Don't attempt mediation with a skilled manipulator. In court, he will have to balance his perfect public persona with his private abuser persona. His two worlds will collide. Behind closed doors, he holds all the cards. Whilst he will still lie and attack your character, there is more opportunity for a judge to witness his unconscionable behaviour and call him to account.

Whilst divorce laws are different across the globe, the ways in which a narcopath behaves before the law are clearly articulated in the online community. As Shannon Thomas observes, it is as if there is a secret procedure manual from which abusers learn their toxic behaviours. In Australia, which has a "no blame" system (in other words, adultery is no longer grounds for divorce, and alluding to multiple former divorces is forbidden), it is unusual for lawyers to use private investigators.

Forensic accountants might aim to uncover financial abuse, but it is still his word against ours, and he has likely disguised his banking entries with his private secret code as well. The court has no way to compel honest disclosure, other than appealing to a person's conscience. He is a love-fraud, a confidence trickster without conscience. Divorce was always his intention, despite his vows of undying love. It's his trump card. Private investigators might uncover all the other lies. But all these things are expensive and still require having an extremely good lawyer on your case. Extremely good lawyers charge hundreds of thousands of dollars for a divorce case. Many of us will end up with the very antithesis of an extremely good lawyer, or no lawyer at all.

Lawyers are only concerned with what is within the law, as they understand it. They do not concern themselves so much with right and wrong. They are decidedly unimpressed with issues of betrayal or broken promises. They say they just want facts, so if he never hit you, there is no point (at this time in history) arguing psychological abuse. Who would ever think that a woman who can claim physical abuse is better off in a divorce court than one who never suffered it? But that is the way things are.

In any case, any accusation of wrongdoing you make against the narcopath, they will fire back false accusations incalculably worse, designed to discredit and hurt you.

The longer you fight, the more you open yourself up to sustained psychological and emotional torture. But if you don't fight, the court will make a finding based on false evidence, and you'll have to live with this injustice for the rest of your life. You are trapped in the snare of the narcopath until such time as you can remove him from your life. No contact.

Know this about your narcopath, after he discards you (or you escape him):

- His attacks might not occur immediately after he leaves. He might pretend he wants to be amicable via personal communications, while he covertly slanders, smears, steals, spends, manipulates, and hides. He's still got you on the hook. The sooner you accept that all beliefs that he is decent and honourable are false, the better. You are already trying to reconcile your doubts. Do yourself a favour: go with the part of you that suspects he is malicious and vengeful. You will be better armed for what is to come.
- Alternatively, if *you* left *him*, he might start the attack immediately. There are stories of narcopaths taking out apprehended violence orders against their wives by making false accusations to police (and being believed) within days of their seeking refuge with their children, away from his control and manipulation.
- He will spend as much money as he can in the year of separation so that there is nothing in his bank accounts to divvy up when the time comes. He might take a luxury world holiday or buy himself a Lamborghini. In theory, his earnings in the year of separation are still mutual assets, but if the money's spent, it's gone. (There is a legal concept known as wastage, but only the best lawyers can prove it.)

- He will take large sums of money from your joint bank accounts and either spend it or give it to his new victim. These thefts may be disguised by simple entries on the accounts that stipulate payment for professional services. The court will accept that he is within his rights to pay his new lover $40,000, say, for a painting she did of him or $20,000 for photographs she took of him for his professional use. (There is a legal concept called wilful disposal, but only the best lawyers can argue it.) A lawyer cannot advise you to remove money and place it in a separate account yourself in the first year, so use your own ethical judgement here. If you never had access to his accounts, there is nothing you can do to prevent him from draining them.
- He will lie, about everything, under oath, on sworn affidavits, on statutory declarations, whatever. He becomes a lying machine.
- He may agree to mediation, as he wants to appear fair and reasonable publicly. But his intentions are never to do the right thing by you. Don't entertain thoughts that the nice Dr Jekyll you married will surface again. Mr Hyde is running the show from here on in. It will feel like you are now fighting evil itself.
- He will not declare bank accounts or assets that you know exist, and the onus will be on you to prove he has them. (There is, however, a legal concept that if you refer to a secret or hidden fact, and he doesn't refute it, it becomes a real fact for the purposes of proceedings; for example, that he has a new partner, is living somewhere other than his given address, or has a new source of income or an undeclared bank account).
- He will hide assets or convince his mates to hide assets for him. Easy. Men don't like the idea of being taken to the cleaners by women they have already discarded. And he is a master at convincing people to stretch their moral boundaries.
- He will do everything in his power to take everything you have legally, including your children, your home, your superannuation, your savings. The law is now his cover. His lawyers are now his enablers. If he's of retirement age and you aren't, the law wants to give him 70 percent of everything you have. Yes, really.
- He will ignore letters from your lawyers.

- He will not respond to an offer. Do not be misled by your lawyer's letter which stipulates that "your client has until 4 p.m. on Monday 16th to respond." English and legalese are two different languages where common words or phrasing have two different meanings. He is not obliged to respond.

- He will block any attempt to have the value of items in his possession assessed and added to the assets list. He simply has to disagree with any court-approved valuer your team suggest.

- He will try to block your choice of lawyer if you engage one he believes might be smarter than his. He will claim a conflict of interest, whatever.

- He will ignore court orders. He will not supply evidence he is instructed to by the judge until half an hour before the next hearing on the steps of the courthouse, so that your team has no time to assess the evidence and prepare a reasonable argument. (This falls just outside the legal definition of contempt and will not be deemed contemptuous until it has happened over and over).

- He will supply illegible documents, or documents with pages or sections missing, better copies of which have to be sought again and again, at a cost to you, by legal letter. (This is called obfuscation, but you need a good lawyer to argue it.)

- He will volunteer no information whatsoever. In order to get proof of anything, you will be forced to subpoena third parties, for example, his accountant or associates, at a large cost to you for every subpoena (and his associates may provide falsified evidence to protect their own reputations).

- There will be no penalty to him, no slap on the wrist, no authority to punish him for the behaviours above. A judge might acknowledge that he has behaved unconscionably (or might not).

- He will drag the process out by blocking, ignoring, or challenging every move your lawyer makes, in order to force you to spend huge amounts of money on legal fees. The sooner you run out of money, the sooner he wins. If, exhausted and traumatised, you instruct your lawyer to settle even if the outcome is grossly unjust, he will find reason *not* to settle there and then. The experience of making you suffer and manipulating facts and impressions is gratifying to him.

- When a lawyer tells you your next affidavit will be handed to the court, please understand that this means it will be handed to him, so that he can refute, deny, manipulate the facts, discredit, and defame you with impunity in his affidavits.
- He will discredit you by whatever means possible, across the entire landscape of your life. As you suffer extreme anxiety at his attacks from every front and have difficulty maintaining your composure every minute of every day, your own behaviour starts to reinforce the picture he paints of you as a crazy bitch.
- He wants to destroy you, to punish you for your crime of fighting back, after all the kindness and love you gave him over all those years. Please believe this unbelievable point. It's in all the literature, and by now, you are experiencing it. You now have an enemy. You married Dr Jekyll, and now you are divorcing Mr Hyde.

You need to let go of old beliefs you had about good triumphing over evil, truth winning over lies, a court being a place where justice happens. Discovering that these beliefs are unfounded myths can add to your suffering. Your naivety is conditioned, so you can relieve yourself of self-blame for not seeing the world the way it really is until now. Allow yourself to grieve for your loss of innocence.

> When divorcing a narcissist, he completely dismisses any of your needs, or all the years of devotion and support that you built together. For the narcissist, it's all gone, like it never happened. He will undermine you with your friends, your children and steal all your money, all the while looking sincere and generating goodwill among the community.

—Pinterest

Panic Attack Script

This is not a life-threatening situation.
I am safe from harm.
This suffering will pass.

I breathe deeply.

These thoughts and emotions are not at the core of me.

My core is calm, centred, and grounded.

I feel the goodness of my heart.

I smile with compassion at this discomfort I'm feeling.

I can cope with this arousal.

I am in control.

I am safe.

I rest my awareness on my surroundings.

I am not these thoughts and feelings that are flooding my system.

I make room for calm to enter.

There is nothing wrong with me; I'm just anxious.

I can cope.

Life is not all bad.

Good things are going to happen.

I am not what happened to me.

I am what I choose to become.

I rise to the intensity of my feeling and flood my being with positive energy.

My pulse slows, and compassion floods my veins: compassion for myself.

I am grateful for the peace that I know will come.

The struggle I am having now is developing the strength and courage I will have tomorrow.

I rise above fear, anxiety, anger, and intrusive thoughts.

I am my own protector.

It's okay to feel this way. It will pass.

The greater the suffering, the greater the future happiness.

This is uncomfortable, but it is bearable.

I invite more positive thoughts and feelings to come in.

I'm doing the best I can, and I'm okay.

I let go of the need to have repetitive thoughts.

I open the door to happiness.

I am taking care of myself today.

I will survive this, and I will flourish.

I choose to take control now. I'm okay.

Moral Courage Affirmation Script

Grounding and Centring Introduction

This suffering will not last forever.
This anxiety will not last forever.
I shift my focus from my feelings to what needs doing now.
I care for myself.
I protect myself.
A warrior ruthlessly casts off unwanted baggage.
Deciding what to keep and what to cut away is an ongoing process.
The past can be set aside now.
I no longer need false friends.
The right people gather round me.
I concentrate my energies on things that make me stronger.
This is a time for moral courage.
This is a time of renewal.
This is a time for letting go of regret.
I will blossom into a strong, powerful woman.
Being liked is no longer important to me.
What matters is my own behaviour, my own intention, my own heart and mind.
I am an honourable woman.
I am courageous.
I am strong.
I rise like the phoenix from the ashes of my previous life.
I can cope with abuse because I believe in myself absolutely.
I can cope with betrayal because I believe in myself absolutely.
I can see through deception.
I don't have to retreat from difficult situations.
I know when to fight and when to retreat.
I can fight my enemies.
I can cope with this fight.
My public reputation is less important than my own conscience.
What matters is my integrity and the integrity of those around me.
I am strong enough to stand alone.

I believe in myself.

I use my internal strength and willpower to rise above the thoughts pulling me down.

I have learnt how to suffer, and my suffering is much less.

I am gentle with myself.

I am doing the best I can.

The behaviour of others does not destroy my inner peace.

How we walk with the broken speaks louder than how we sit with the great.

I love the person I've become because I fought to become her.

I am taking care of myself today.

Knowledge gives me power, but good character gives me respect.

I am healing, and the damage no longer controls my life.

I am starting over: a new pattern of thoughts, a new wave of emotions, a new connection to the world, a new belief system: in myself.

Each scar serves as a reminder of who I am, who I can become, and who I will never be again.

My life is mine again.

I don't need to have it all figured out to move forward.

I have high standards, and I won't settle for less than I deserve.

In a world full of fear, I am courageous.

In a world full of lies, I am honest.

In a world where few care, I am compassionate.

In a world full of phonies, I am myself.

Sometimes the hardest thing and the right thing are the same.

I am learning how to walk away from situations or people who threaten my peace of mind, self-respect, or self-worth.

I never forget three types of people in my life: those who helped me in difficult times; those who hurt me in difficult times; and those who left me in difficult times.

There is nothing wrong with me.

I am my own hero.

I am a warrior.

I am courageous.

I am strong.

Red Flags

> The Devil doesn't come with a red face and horns.
> He appears as everything you've ever wanted.
>
> —Pinterest

This is not a normal break-up. This is so painful and traumatising that the fear of it happening again can cripple us. Okay, so what are the little things to look out for up front to avoid being scammed by a narcopath in the future? How do you avoid jumping into the lifeboat of another covertly toxic relationship in search of comfort and protection? What are the red flags?

Scientists can give you a list of personality traits, which are helpful in figuring out what the hell just happened to you, in hindsight. Too late. What do the survivors say? There are some weird unscientific foibles that survivors of narcabuse repeatedly report from around the net, the stuff the scientists might scoff at.

- Charm. Obviously. Beware of charming men.
- Flattery. Excessive praise. Watch out for extreme attentiveness and validation.
- Contempt. Every actor instinctively knows that the look of contempt is what separates the villains from the innocents. We all know that look in our fictional baddies. Normal people do not regard others with contempt very often, if at all. Disdain maybe, but not contempt. If you've lived with a narcopath, you'll know that look well, yes? Next time you see it, run.
- Glibness. Superficiality, shallowness, or hollowness; a fake, a show pony, a cardboard man. Inauthentic. Always on stage or on his best behaviour.
- Public displays of affection. Kissing, hand-holding, praising, hugging, chivalrous behaviour and other positive body language when he knows others are watching, but only lustful sex when no one is looking (except himself, admiring his own prowess in the mirror).

- Emotional shallowness. Their emotional response to the information that their shoelace is untied is the same as their response to a terrorist attack. No emotional connection to most stimuli, or a time lapse before they remember to perform the response they have learned is the right one, or to mimic the responses of the empaths around them.

- Moves quickly with vows of undying love, moving into your home, borrowing from you, insinuating himself into every aspect of your life, morphing himself into everything you ever wanted. Sure, we can all obsess about our new loves, but this guy is actually changing his whole life to take over yours. He is a snake shedding his skin.

- Too good to be true. If a small voice inside you muses on this phrase, trust your instincts.

- Hypersexuality. Many women speak of amazing sex or the narcopath being addicted to porn. If he's really good, it could just mean he's had plenty of practice with every conceivable type of woman, not that you are both extraordinarily compatible. Sex creates emotional bonds in women that are not present in males. Beware.

- Reduced need of sleep. Narcopaths reportedly need only three to four hours of sleep a night and are able to stay awake for extended periods of time (with or without the aid of illicit drugs).

- A reduced startle response. Give them a fright, they don't jump.

- A reduced contagious yawn response. Yawn, and they won't catch it (unless they have learned to mimic this odd human foible too).

- Switches attention quickly. Always on the lookout for the next person he can charm; he suddenly drops you mid-sentence to impress the waiter, a stranger, a potentially useful person. It is as if you have just become invisible to him and are no longer even in the room.

- Extremely vain.

- Extremely jealous.

- Cruelty or unkindness towards animals.

- A magnetic quality that attracts people in social situations.

- The psychopathic stare or gaze. Women often describe a hypnotising, mesmerising effect when the psychopath looks directly into their eyes.

- Lack of eye contact the rest of the time. Might resemble shyness. Is actually ingrained duplicity. (Some say the only time he looks directly into your eyes is when he's lying to you.)
- Cheshire cat grin. Not a smile: a self-satisfied grin. It is the grin of duper's delight. They have just fabricated a whole story or wriggled out of a direct challenge by telling a whopping great lie and got away with it.
- Good time Charlie. They just wanna have a good time, all the time. They will be that person who encourages your friend (or you), the recovering alcoholic, to have another drink (or the equivalent). Wicked. They get a buzz out of influencing you to stretch your boundaries. Know the thing? Victims are often left reeling at how they managed to be influenced to be so childish and irresponsible (get so drunk, take the drugs, burn a bridge, resign a job, take out a loan, or spend money on things they couldn't afford).
- Poor impulse control. He sees it, he wants it, he goes for it, whatever the cost to others.
- Unusually easy-going and carefree. Is actually amoral, with callous disregard for others. Does not experience guilt, remorse, or regret for wrongs done to others, and may even boast about getting away with unethical or amoral behavior: lying, cheating, stealing.
- Agrees with everything you say. Never expresses an opinion that differs from yours. Always tells you exactly what you want to hear. Never argues. (Can be seen as agreeable and compatible but is actually warehousing offences against his ego that will later be used against you.)
- Passive-aggressive. May grin and keep a modulated tone of voice whilst he mentally plots your punishment. Takes deep offence at normally excusable human foibles—like interrupting him when he's speaking or joking about his appearance, ego, or reputation— even if done with tact and affection.
- Indian givers. They give something to you, and if you don't use it/ wear it/eat it/thank them adequately, they will take the gift back, either overtly or covertly.
- Vindictive. Needs to punish the waiter, your friends, you if someone fails to acknowledge their specialness and superiority. Because

everything is all about them. This is often done covertly, in the privacy of home, or using other means: taking on fake identities, catfishing (fake online identities), or using enablers so their hands stay clean.

- Many past marriages or a string of wives and girlfriends. All of them were crazy. Odds are it was *they* who housed, fed, and supported him before they were discarded, though he'll try to convince you (or you'll assume) otherwise. Watch for the grin of duper's delight when he shares his life story. Odds are, he's making it up and enjoying watching you fall for it.

- Parasitic lifestyle. Uses you to support him while he works on his no-income artistic career, builds his imaginary business, negotiates the big deal, applies for the status job, puts the band back together, plays video games all day, pretends to look for work.

- Fucked-up families. Kids with big psychological issues, drug problems, other antisocial behaviours. Scientists even report unusual inappropriate relationships with daughters. They treat their daughters more like romantic partners than offspring. A distinct lack of boundaries and lack of emotional maturity in familial relationships. Neglected children. Neglected aged parents.

- Weak family and friendship bonds. Has little contact, little loyalty, little concern for significant others in his past (doesn't seem to know or care if they are dead or alive). The friends you meet don't seem to be all that close, or have only been around on the periphery for a while, or are around because they are necessary or useful in some way. He introduces you to old friends he hasn't seen for years who all seem to know a different story of his life. Easily explained away by the habit of changing jobs, locations, states, or countries often. Can appear adventurous and unattached. No roots.

- Psychological manipulation. This is complicated. If your instincts tell you there is something unusual about this guy but you can't quite put your finger on it, this might be the reason. He somehow makes you feel responsible for everything bad that happens and takes credit for everything good that happens. Weird. This usually begins *after* you are hooked and is deeply damaging over time.

- Sabotages your important occasions. He gets you hopelessly drunk the night before your big interview. He gets really sick and needs you to take him to hospital so you miss your plane (a grey area of responsibility; you could just say no, but a narcopath's powers of coercion and emotional blackmail are phenomenal). He picks a fight or makes a scene at the office celebration of your promotion. You lend him your car, and he returns it too late for you to see the specialist, whose appointment you waited three months for.

A Special Mention: Pathological Lying

There are very good reasons why we were duped, even though we did our due diligence. The principal danger around a narcopath is fake news: pathological lying. His relationships and public image are largely built on compulsive lying.

The thing that makes lies work is having others believe them. That's where the narcopath has it over the rest of us. When he tells a lie, his voice or his pen doesn't waver. His heart rate doesn't rise. He has no pangs of conscience that he has to hide from the world. He has a whole army of fans and enablers who see only the charm and charisma. Being loved is one of the best covers for a liar. He can manipulate anyone who chooses to see the good in people, and that's most of us. If he's a celebrity narcopath, he has a very public billboard of lies woven into a palatable image, a complex fabric with lies as the weft and fact as the warp. It's easy to spread a lie, not so easy to refute it. Lies take root and become myths. Sometimes, they become history. Especially when truth is stranger than fiction.

The first time we hear a lie, the seed of doubt is planted. The next time we hear it, it confirms the slight bias we already hold, and bang: before you know it, a whole bunch of people are proclaiming they know the truth of a big fat lie because they have heard it from different sources. Lazy gossips or journalists get a whiff of a good story and pass on the gossip or publish the lie without checking the facts, or it spreads like wildfire on anti-social media and becomes an alternative fact.

The narcopath is so committed to this public mask that he wears it all the time. He tweets in it at 3 a.m. He wears it in bed, in the shower, in the mirror. The mask is who he thinks he is. The only time he drops it is when someone does a little fact-checking and calls him out. And then all hell breaks loose on the fact-checker. An avalanche of name-calling, smearing, discrediting, character assassination, soul-destroying descends. Where once there was a charming, smooth-talking, soft-spoken lover, there is a cold, snarling, hate-filled monster. This moment when the mask of the psychopath or narcissist drops is one of the most traumatising and talked-about aspects of narcabuse within the online community.

This is how manipulators operate. You were scammed. You were used while you were useful. Your own trust, love, generosity, and kindness were twisted around and used to trap you. You are not crazy. You are beautiful. There are good-hearted people out there. Almost everybody in the orbit of a narcopath gets bent out of shape, one way or another. You can recover from this: by nurturing and protecting the good heart that attracted him.

The wound to your soul is an opportunity to wake up, wise up, grow up, and boost your compassion and love of life. (Sorry if any of these phrases have been used in an accusing way against you. They are said with respect.) Give yourself time, a safe harbour, and lots and lots of self-compassion. Narcopaths prey on the kindest, most open-hearted people. They're the easiest to manipulate. Beware other predators while you are vulnerable. You're temporarily out of order, but you will rebuild yourself, your life, and your relationships. Teach yourself to be your own best friend from now on.

A dog will look down when he's done wrong.
A narcopath will look you right in the eye.

—Pinterest

Growing Pains and Rude Awakenings

If you have ever bought a rare or unusual car, like a Peugeot, you will have experienced something akin to what we now experience, having discovered the phenomenon of character disorders. Until we had our own Peugeot, we never noticed them on the roads before. Now we are driving one, we notice them everywhere.

We start seeing narcopathic traits played out in the world around us, where before we were oblivious. We notice politicians, military men, corporate bosses, corporations, bureaucracies, banks, religious organisations, friends, and colleagues whose behaviour has become normalised but which is actually cruel, callous, and unconscionable. Our newfound awareness can become another huge burden we feel as we try to negotiate our way out of trauma. We can feel overwhelmed at the darkness in the world.

This is where a place of refuge becomes essential. We can start to fear everything and everybody, and we want to go and hide under a rock somewhere. So go hide under a rock. It's okay to feel this way. It's okay to feel confused, to want to backpedal to a safe place of ignorance or denial, to crave kindness, honesty, and decency. This chaos of thought is not going to stain our psyches forever. Our new world view will take time to integrate. And the pendulum of mistrust will eventually swing back to the middle ground. We will develop healthy discernment with this new knowledge. We are experiencing growing pains, that's all. We're starting to sprout our formerly dysfunctional antennae for darkness and the way things really are.

And no, you are not the only one who is concerned that disordered narcissism is creeping into mainstream society at a rapid rate. Many thinkers around the world are trying to pinpoint the moment the gates of hell opened and spilled the inhabitants amongst us. Perhaps the selfie is not so innocuous as it first appears. Perhaps the perceived necessity of each of us having our own personal online billboard to broadcast our ideal selves to the world is fostering an atmosphere that debases our sense of real connection. Perhaps the ease with which we hide behind a text message or tweet is undermining respectful analogue human relationships.

If we can't influence the world to be a kinder, gentler place, we can influence our own little patch. We can refrain, decline, abstain, or withdraw. We can tend our own garden, pull our own weeds, and sow the seeds of our future happiness from this moment forth.

Everything's going to be okay.

Ask the Experts

Simon, George K. (2010), *In Sheep's Clothing.* Parkhurst Brothers Inc.

Birch, Adelyn (2015), *30 Covert Emotional Manipulation Tactics.* Lexington, KY.

Aron, Elaine N. (1997), *The Highly Sensitive Person.* USA: Cliff Harwon.

Chödrön, Thubten, *The Lam Rim, The Gradual Path to Enlightenment.* http://thubtenchodron.org/2001/01/gradual-path-instructions/

https://www.psychologytoday.com/blog/tech-support/201605/13-things-you-must-know-if-you-are-divorcing-narcissist

Chapter 4

NO CONTACT

The bond between a psychological abuser and the people he uses is incrementally traumatic. It slowly drives us crazy and makes us dependent on our abuser by keeping us constantly focussed on how to restore the equilibrium of a normal human relationship. But there is nothing normal about a pathological relationship with a character-disordered other. Intermittent reinforcement and the cycle of abuse create a phenomenon known as trauma bonding. In extreme cases, it leads to Stockholm syndrome. The abusive relationship actually creates abnormal neural pathways and patterns of thinking that make victims love and defend their abusers. There are also endocrine reactions that effectively create addiction. The worse he treats us, the more we crave him treating us well.

It's complicated. Essentially, trauma bonding can induce victims to feel as if they can't survive without their captor, persecutor, or abuser. It's not only about financial dependence, which is all observers seem to care about in the aftermath. "Do you get to keep the house?" It's more like a physical addiction. It's in the body as well as the mind. We become conditioned to the swing between serotonin (the happiness hormone) when he is kind to us and cortisol (the stress hormone) when he withdraws emotionally. Victims can lose the courage and belief in their own ability to walk away, break free, and recover their independence.

It can be part answer to our own and other's indignant retort to realising we have been trapped in an abusive relationship: "Why didn't you just leave?" Of course, there are many other financial, practical, professional, moral, and social bonds that make leaving complicated. But it is the weird physical, emotional, and psychological ties of trauma bonding that are hardest to get over, the bond that we thought was enduring soulmate love in the beginning but morphed into a one-sided, unhealthy, fearful, manipulative bond, steeped in fear of rejection or abandonment.

Survivors in the narcabuse community all seem to agree on one thing: after the split, go *no contact* (or limited contact) as soon as possible. Break free from his manipulation, even though we haven't yet got a clear picture of what he's been doing to us. The fact of psychological abuse only emerges in hindsight. We love and trust Dr Jekyll, and it's very hard to accept the emergence of Mr Hyde in the same person. But we have to stop giving him the benefit of the doubt.

Sure, our ex may never have been diagnosed by a qualified professional as having a personality disorder. And everybody is sceptical of Dr Google. But we are the experts in our own lives. If the descriptions of narcopaths are uncanny depictions of our ex; if the explanations of hidden partner abuse resonate deeply; if we are now experiencing a cluster of symptoms we have never experienced in break-ups before, it's time for us to start referencing internally.

End communications completely, if you can. Resist the urge to bring him to account or seek an apology for his appalling betrayal and deception. Don't keep track of him on Facebook or Google. Don't stalk him. Don't call him out on his lies or remind him of his broken vows and promises. Resist the urge to hurt him back or get revenge in some way. Ignore his texts, emails, posts.

Easier said than done when we are trauma bonded.

Why do survivors in the narcabuse community recommend this? Because the ones who stayed in touch and tried to be friends, call him to account, or get an apology suffered more vicious and vengeful attacks than they could ever have imagined. I can testify to it personally. I made all those mistakes, including trying to warn his next victim. He retaliated with unspeakable lies, theft, slander, and cruelty, an out-and-out attack on every aspect of my life, a full-on scorched-earth policy, an effortless (for him) project of ensuring that I had *nothing* from which to rebuild a life after him.

The literature warned that there is no way to negotiate with a man who has to *win* at all costs, but I was a slow learner. I still credited him with a normal conscience and believed his kind, charming persona would resurface, that he would come to his senses and start atoning for his appalling behaviour. After all, he swore he still loved me. This delay in taking the no-contact advice damaged my finances, my emotional and psychological health, and my social and professional lives.

I had to let go of compassion for the next woman suffering at his hands. I had to let go of the need for closure and my long-held beliefs that truth wins over lies, that good triumphs over evil, that the law would protect the innocent. These injuries to my core moral values magnified the trauma, dragging out injuries from the same source for almost two and a half years until divorce settlement was completed. Even then, right when it was all over, he tried to have his lawyer declare the process null and void so that he could continue to punish me by starting the whole traumatising settlement process over again. He took nearly everything I had—my home, my ability to make a living, my place in the world—but he wanted more. And he wanted the gratification of destroying someone to make himself feel omnipotent. My story is far from unique.

All this stuff can be incredibly hard to do when we are trauma bonded to someone. But here are the reminders as to why it is best all round:

- He gets a buzz out of inflicting pain on you.
- He gets a buzz out of appearing like the sweetest guy in public while he psychologically and emotionally abuses you in private.
- He gets a buzz out of humiliating you.
- He gets a buzz out of saying one thing, doing another, and watching you struggle with confusion.
- He gets a buzz out of slandering you to your friends and family, watching you suffer as they treat you with disdain, suspicion, or disgust.

- He gets a buzz out of seeing or hearing about your despair and anguish.
- He gets a buzz out of destroying your life by legally taking your home, your money, and your children through manipulation of the legal process.
- He gets a buzz out of seeing you beg.
- He gets a buzz out of convincing you to leave your job, burn your bridges, and believe his promises to support you, and then he leaves when you are completely dependent on him.
- He gets a buzz out of seeing others side with him when he tells them you are a liar.
- He gets a buzz out of getting you drunk and then telling everyone he married an alcoholic.
- He gets a buzz out of goading you into a hurt or angry response and then telling everyone you are abusive.
- He gets a buzz out of placing your life in danger with risky situations and watching your fear as it escalates.
- He gets a buzz out of controlling your finances and spending your money in ways you don't agree with.
- He gets a buzz out of tricking you into believing his stories filled with lies that make him look like a poor, hapless victim.
- He gets a buzz out of convincing you to dump your friends, knowing you will have to struggle to cope alone and unsupported after he abandons you.
- He gets a buzz out of convincing others you are a hypochondriac.
- He gets a buzz out of scamming you.
- He gets a buzz out of stroking your dog and then beating it, so it comes back cowering, just like you.
- He gets a buzz out of winning at any cost. In fact, the higher the cost to you, the more fun the game.
- He gets a buzz out of wearing a convincing mask of a kind, gentle, polite, sensitive guy to cover his true hidden nature.
- He gets a buzz out of driving you to suicide: the ultimate power and control.
- He gets a buzz out of tearing your life apart.

And then he calls that love. To break a woman and then call it love is nothing short of evil. This man has demons that are incurable. No amount of love is going to change him.

It's brutal to read, and all the above might not apply in your case, but do you really need more reasons to go *no contact*?

The Grey Rock Method of Limited Contact

After saying all that, it's simply not always possible to go no contact with our psychological abusers. Co-parenting is a classic example, as is co-owning a business or property. Any number of reasons might make it impossible for you. Never fear. It is still possible for you to wriggle your way out of trauma bonding and emotional entanglement that leads to the abuser manipulating your world with power and control.

As you overcome your despair, learn about the personality disorder and methods of psychological abuse, manage your symptoms, and regain control over your emotions, it becomes possible to create a safer distance with your abuser and tighten up those weak boundaries that have been part of your people-pleasing strategy all your life. You can work through the fear of what other people think of you now that your character has been publicly smeared.

For some of us, finding a safe place to lick our wounds might also mean returning to a place with a manipulative narcissist in it: an old familiar one. We are out of the frying pan and into the fire! Grey Rock is useful for staying genuinely safe in the gambit of a family narcissist.

Essentially, it is about changing the nature of your conversations and interactions with the abuser (and other narcissists in your life). You learn to see the manipulative goading that once baited you, and refrain from taking the bait. You learn to see how the narcissist uses your soft spots and loyalty to emotionally blackmail you into doing what they want. Abusers don't abuse every day, after all. That's how intermittent reinforcement works. But instead of playing into their game, you start to withhold, refrain, abstain, decline.

You only discuss the most mundane matters. You stop disagreeing or trying to explain your point of view. You stop defending yourself. You stop hoping or expecting him to be a decent, honourable human being. He is not and never will be. He is not going to wake up and see what an arsehole he is, feel remorse about it, and make amends. Not going to happen.

So you stop asking, "How high?" when he tells you to jump. You stop being agreeable and smoothing things over. You stop sharing your plans, goals, ambitions, hopes (or your fears and insecurities). You don't mention the big event or birthday or job interview he'll ruin for you. You have a Plan B for him ruining the first day of school or graduation day for your kids. You keep your answers clipped, remain polite, and hide your frustration with a smile. You become so boring to him that he no longer looks to you for supply. You become like a boring grey rock. Yes, he'll turn his toxicity onto someone else, but that is not your responsibility. He'll tell the world you're turning the kids against him, whether you try to protect them from seeing his true nature or not. You cannot prevent it with your compassion and empathy. You have to pick your battles.

Meanwhile, you turn inwards and start the climb out of the abyss. Find any method that will work towards your own recovery emotionally, psychologically, physically, spiritually, socially, and financially.

Is He a Narcopath or Just a Garden-Variety Jerk?

Right about now, faced with the prospect of no contact with the person we vowed to love and cherish for the rest of our lives can make us really doubt our experience all over again. He may be hoovering us (making approaches that look like reconciliation or contrition that suck us back into his mind games) or sending his flying monkeys (enablers) to tell us, "He's not really all that bad; it takes two to tango, so half the blame lies with you; he wants to be friends; he wants to settle amicably so you don't need to waste money on a lawyer." It's pretty easy to slip back into denial of his true nature and all the new information about narcabuse we're trying to process, to try and squeeze the abusive behaviours into the mold of normal human behaviour, to believe in a good heart where there is none.

Deceptive and manipulative behaviours are present in some normal break-ups: lying about an affair, planning a departure for a long time beforehand without discussing any dissatisfaction with the spouse, financial abuse. There is even a legal phenomenon that is now recognised in many countries (but not Australia, behind as ever): sudden wife abandonment syndrome.

I've had several friends tell me that they think someone must be a psychopath or narcissist based on several bad behaviours of abusive or manipulative people. And, of course, an official diagnosis of malignant narcissism or psychopathy cannot be made by anyone other than a qualified shrink.

But Dark Triad types make notoriously bad candidates for therapy, are notoriously difficult to diagnose (because they present as Mr Perfect to any audience, including a therapist), and are frequently misdiagnosed as Asperger's due to their profound lack of empathy (and because shrinks are now better educated about the autism spectrum than Cluster B personality disorders).

So if this question is still burning into you after trying to figure out which way is up, deciding if he is or isn't a narcopath, I suggest these are the major differences between a dangerous personality-disordered narcopath and your average garden-variety jerk:

- The jerk has some of the characteristics on the checklist. The narcopath has all of them, in particular, *pathological lying*.
- The entitled sexist jerk occasionally indulges in a few manipulative behaviours. The narcopath uses the whole arsenal with ever-increasing frequency, during the relationship and the divorce process.
- The jerk, suffering a midlife crisis that he believes he can fix by dumping his wife and shacking up with a younger model, just wants to get on with feeling young and virile again, whereas a narcopath additionally wants to destroy you, inflicting as much

emotional, psychological, and financial damage as he possibly can before and after he leaves.

- The jerk may eventually negotiate in good will; bury the hatchet. The narcopath will advertise his generous negotiating skills to the world, whilst blocking, deflecting, stealing, ghosting, stonewalling, triangulating, and dragging the fun out in the mediation process until his wife is completely debilitated.
- The jerk will stop behaving like a jerk when others witness the behaviour or call him to account. The narcopath is too skilful to have anyone recognise his behaviour or suspect him of being guilty of all the things he accuses his wife of being.
- The jerk might eventually admit and apologise for his adultery, deception, or abandonment, whereas a narcopath will never apologise (except for not being able to cope with her issues), never admit to having been in any way at fault, and destroy his wife in order to deflect blame from himself.
- The jerk is acting out from inner pain, grief, and insecurity and isn't aware that he's causing harm. The narcopath is acting from a gratuitous desire to inflict pain, knows precisely just how much he is hurting the target, and gets great satisfaction from doing so. (Does he seem angry, distressed, and anxious, or is he calm, calculated, and charming?)

Finding Peace when the War Is Over

Finding equilibrium while we are trapped in the snare of the narcopath can seem impossible. The education phase of recovery—discovering the disorder, managing trauma symptoms, and travelling through the dark veil—can have us questioning if we will ever recover from the experience. We have notions of being scarred for life, broken, not belonging anywhere; fear of being despised in our community from the smear campaign. We grieve the loss of identity, future, dreams, past achievement, security; and the list goes on. We fear that we will be buried under this avalanche of ugliness for the rest of our miserable lives; it can become a preoccupation. It's heavy shit, man.

Letting go is not an easy thing to do when you don't know how. Our tendency is to hold on for dear life for whatever we can possibly salvage from the annihilation in the aftermath. We can feel like we just can't take any more pain. Perhaps the biggest loss in the discovery phase of the aftermath is our loss of innocence. The feelings of violation are enormous. And we are exhausted from having to defend ourselves against attack from the narcopath and his enablers, and from the second arrows we attack ourselves with.

We just want to go away and hide under a rock somewhere, shut ourselves away, lick our wounds, and start again.

Every one of us was once a child: innocent, hopeful, sweet, open, shining with spirit and curiosity. Along the way, we get all armoured up. We develop a personality strategy to cope with the world and convince ourselves that our armour is who we really are. We needed our armour during the war. But after no contact, we can take a deep breath and lose the armour. We can search for our authentic selves again. And we can find it.

Many survivors speak of the middle and late stages of recovery as being a reawakening, the best thing that ever happened to them. We learn detachment and courage and acceptance, and the power that was stolen from us begins to return. From being victimised, we clawed our way out of that victim place and found a new agency in our lives. We became survivors.

Everything is going to be okay.

Detaching and Letting Go

> Spiritual detachment and equanimity should never be
> equated with indifference or complacent resignation.

—Lama Surya Das, *Letting Go of the Person You Used to Be*

When we are at our most vulnerable and defeated; when we are utterly groundless; when we desperately cling to any part of our comfort zone that can give us the illusion of control; when we are crying out with a primal scream: "why did he do this to me?, why is this happening to me?, I don't deserve this, how am I going to survive this?"; that is exactly when learning the art of letting go will bring us relief.

Letting go is not easy. Some people stay trapped in a prison of their own making, recycling their private stories of pain, betrayal, and injustice for decades. When overwhelmed by the trauma mind, we can feel as if we have no choice to let go, that the capacity to let go has been taken away from us. But the choice is there, hidden deep in our psyches.

The proof of this is in the truth of other people who have learnt to let go and move from victim to survivor to thriver.

Our sense of ourselves has been completely undermined by the shock of sudden abandonment or our flight after deciding we can't take this anymore. What we may not recognise is that this moment holds within it a creative opportunity to let go of things, people, places, ideas, or beliefs that have been holding us back, keeping us prisoner, stopping us from being the person we really want to be. This phenomenon, this state of being where the life we've been living has abruptly ended, is simply no longer available to us, yet the way forward appears as a void of uncertainty, is described in Tibetan Buddhism as Bardo (an intermediate state).

This, the extremely distressing feeling of being entombed, entrapped, or caught in a snare between life and rebirth, is more than just the narcabuse horror of realising that the whole relationship was a lie from the very beginning (which is a slower dawning), but a deep rupture in the fabric of our reality. It is the moment when we have an opportunity to realise— really realise—that the security and control we thought we had over our lives was illusory from the very beginning. It is when we gain the deep personal insight into the nature of impermanence. We finally see that our lives have so far been filled with deaths and rebirths of every kind; that nothing ever belonged to us; that nothing was predestined; that our very selves are constantly changing; that the outcome of everything we ever strove for was never assured. We have been standing on shaky ground all our lives and choosing to ignore this fact.

Now, the value of contriving an ideal self for our egoic self-image is shattered. We realise profoundly that the things we thought of as safe, secure, controllable, reliable, solid, and real were, in fact, in a state of flux. In the case of the narcopath, the truth was buried under a thousand lies and false impressions (including convincing us he loved us, so he could get his hands on what we had). But with the rest of it, it was our own delusions of permanence that gave us a false sense of security. When all pretence and politeness is dropped, life becomes simple, even as we fall, kicking and screaming, into the abyss. There is no need of artifice when we are fighting for our lives. There is just this moment and the inevitable next moment.

This gap, this rip in the fabric of our universe, this void is ripe with creative potential. If we cannot answer now the big questions of "Who am I if I lose my job, my house, my social circle, my life partner, my purpose, my place in the world?" we can tip into the trauma of background anxiety informing everything we do, say, and think. This confusion is totally understandable. But if we dive deeper into the abyss, if we relax and open to the universal truths that lie under all those questions, we will one day become whole. We find the ground of beingness, the ground of the precise nowness and hereness of human existence. We rest in knowing that the confusion we feel now is the very clay from which wisdom will be molded.

We aim to surrender, to relax into not knowing what comes next. There is relief in not having to play by the narcissist's rules anymore. There is relief in not having to fake anything anymore, feeling broken open as we are. There is relief in deciding the time has come to just stop doing and start being. We have nothing left to lose because we feel we have already lost everything. We are like a stone tossed along a riverbed by the current, and that's okay. We can *find a way* to be okay with it.

Letting go is not as easy as it sounds. Knowing we should let go doesn't necessarily mean we know how to do it. We can feel shame because we should let go of the past but can't. Letting go means finding a way to take our focus from the stories of betrayal and injustice and coming to understand that the narcopath's cruel behaviour was really nothing to do with us; it happens to anyone in the intimate life of the perpetrator.

He leaves a string of broken lives in his wake. It's not that we are just a worthless number, but that we are really not responsible for his cruelty towards us. Letting go is not only to do with looking backwards and letting go, but also with embracing change, searching for the good in each thing that happens after world collapse.

It starts with holding less tightly, loosening our attachments, bit by bit.

If you feel you want to talk about all this stuff, and no one gets it when you do, talk to a Buddhist about it.

Here is a visualisation meditation that helped me free up trauma bonds.

Note: This visualisation is adapted from Western psychology (neurolinguistic programming), not traditional Buddhism. When you read this visualisation, you will understand the theory of it: taking thoughts, factual memories, feelings, emotions out of where they are held in your body and choosing a way to create distance between them and you, cutting any attachments that you can. These words might not resonate with you, and you may prefer to find substitute images or words to record your own guided visualisation meditation.

In order to try this visualisation, you will need to suspend your scepticism and take it as your working hypothesis for the duration. Alternatively, you might choose to come back to this when you have trained in mindfulness and tamed your monkey mind a little more.

Letting Go Visualisation Meditation

Grounding and Centring Introduction

Picture the narcopath or an image of what he represents (for example, a demon, a devil, or Darth Vader) in front of you, attached to your belly by an umbilical cord, a rope, a chain, a bond of electrical energy, or any attachment that comes to mind.

Let this image settle in your mind's eye.

Now slowly move him away from you. As he moves away, the ties that bind you become weaker, more brittle, frayed, less and less powerful.

If you are ready, cut that bond between you and let him drift off into eternity, like a helium balloon into space, getting smaller and smaller until you can no longer see him.

Notice your breathing.

Feel the burden of sadness and grief you are left with inside your body. Bundle that burden up and take it outside your body and your heart. See that burden drift away, getting smaller and smaller until you can no longer see it.

Let your attention rest on your breathing.

Feel the burden of all the hollow lies and empty promises, all the betrayals, false accusations, injustices and hurtful words. Bundle them all into a tight, dark mass, and push them out of your body. Watch them drift away from you into the ether.

Follow your breath in and out.

Bundle up the memories of your euphoric seduction and ideal partnership. It was all an illusion, a mirage. That man you married was never real. He was a false persona, an evil twin. Bundle up those memories and see them slowly drift away, like a balloon on a string. If you are unwilling to let them go, then hold less tightly to them. Imagine your attachment to that bundle of memories weakening, and if you can, cut it.

Return to your breath.

Imagine the vision you had of your future together. Gather up all the plans, promises, agreements, and vows in a tight bundle in front of you. Place them all in a coloured balloon and let the string out, bit by bit. If you are able to let go of the string, or cut it, then do. If not, that's okay. Just let it float as far away from you as your mind will let you.

Come back to your breath.

Let go of the hurt of being used and exhausted by someone you loved and trusted. Forgive yourself for being blind to his parasitic ways. Bundle up that whole relationship and all its painful implications, and push it out and away from your body. If you can, drop it and let it all dissolve in a dark puddle at your feet. Then step over it and move forward, and don't look back.

Come back to your breath.

Let go of the anger you feel. You have every right to feel angry, but you can hold less tightly to the anger that is in your body. Let that anger flow through you and pass away, like a red-hot burning cloud, drifting into the distance.

Breathe.

See all the friends or family who left you in your time of trouble. Let yourself feel the sorrow of disappointment or betrayal. Bundle them up, along with your sorrow about how others see you. Push that bundle out of your body, and watch it drift away from you, over the group of people who let you down. See good things happening to them. Send them goodwill if you can.

Now turn your back and walk away.

Let the tears come.

Notice the feelings in your body. Notice any space that has opened up inside you, any pockets of emptiness that have been created. Allow those spaces in your body to be filled with gentle, warm, white light. Feel the comfort and nourishment of that white light. Let the light soothe you.

Let go of the attachment to blaming yourself. Accept that you did the best you could, you tried your hardest, you gave your all, you are not to blame. Let go of blaming yourself.

Let go of the attachment to being believed. You know the truth of what happened, even if you don't quite understand it all yet. Hold less tightly to the need for others to believe you, and hold onto your belief in yourself.

See yourself shrouded in the light of love.

Let go of the need to lean on or depend on someone else. Picture yourself as a strong, beautiful, intelligent woman, independent and warrior-like, able to cope with whatever life throws at you with dignity and grace. Hold less tightly to dependence on others' opinions of you.

Let go of jealousy. See it as a green ball of energy, and let it drift away from you.

Let go of resentment. See it as a blue ball of energy, and let it drift away from you.

Let go of shame. See it as a grey ball of energy, and let it drift away from you.

Let go of fear. See it as a yellow ball of energy, and let it drift away from you.

Go back to your breath.

Let go of the hurt of being ignored, undervalued, or used in your childhood. Send your love and forgiveness back into the past. See the child in you who comes to mind and hug that child. Give that child the feeling of safety and security and love that you have for her in abundance.

Let go of the hurt of not being loved by people who said they loved you. There *are* people who love you. And you will be loved now and in the future. Hold onto your love for yourself, and let go of the hurt of not being loved.

Picture yourself walking towards you, just as you are now.

Embrace yourself, kiss yourself, love yourself, and then let yourself go.

Ask the Experts

Psychopaths and Love, *Red Flags of a Psychopath.* Accessed May 1, 2017. psychopathsandlove.com/red-flags-of-a-psychopath/

Psychopath Free, *30 Red Flags of Manipulative People.* Accessed May 1, 2017. https://www.psychopathfree.com/articles/30-red-flags-of-manipulative-people.212/

Psychopathy Awareness, *Red Flags – How to Identify a Psychopath.* Accessed May 1, 2017.
https://psychopathyawareness.wordpress.com/2011/04/01/red-flags-how-to-identify-a-psychopathic-bond/

Dr George Simon, n.d. *Author, Public Speaker, Consultant, Character Development Coach, Composer.*
https://www.drgeorgesimon.com/

Out of The Fog, n.d. *Helping Family Members & Loved Ones of People Who Suffer From Personality Disorders.*
http://www.outofthefog.org

Chapter 5

COLLATERAL DAMAGE

Nobody Gets It

I know. It sounds like the plaintive cry of teenage angst. But entering through the doorway of trauma from psychological abuse also means entering a world where almost nobody understands what you are going through but other survivors.

Plato supposedly said, "No man is more hated than he who speaks the truth." Trying to talk about the harsh realities of the way things really are can be a minefield of disappointment and misunderstanding.

It is still considered taboo to discuss trauma, mental health issues, or abuse. In some circles, divorce is still frowned upon. Yes, really. If you're someone who normally talks things through with your friends, you can get into big trouble. Honesty won't get you a lot of friends, but it will get you the right ones.

We find ourselves in a double-bind. During the relationship, we were likely loyal and discreet about his financial irresponsibility and other dirty laundry. We had his back. He had us doubting ourselves to our very core. So if we start trying to talk it through after the abandonment, it can sound like we are making excuses. We said we were happy before, and now he's left, we want to heap all the blame onto him? Our bitterness and resentment, spoken with the shrill voice of stress and confusion, make us look exactly like the mentally unstable liar of his smear campaign.

On top of that, if we try to share our pain, we have to deal with the darker side of human nature raising its ugly head in the people around us. Some people don't care or are secretly pleased to see someone fall so far (they may have been secretly jealous or envious): the pecked-chicken phenomenon. Some people will line up to take advantage of a woman who is vulnerable and hanging on for dear life, in case she loses it in public. Being honest about psychological abuse does not always evoke compassion and support from our culture. It often invites derision and isolation.

Nobody can grasp the difference between a normal divorce, where two parties aim for fairness in separating their finances and belongings, and a psychologically abusive one. Taken as single isolated incidents, every complaint just looks like a normal interpersonal tussle. It is impossible for others to grasp the huge matrix of thousands of incidents of deception, trickery, and betrayal. Few can believe that anybody could lie, cheat, plunder, and pillage another person's resources for years without the other person noticing.

Many counsellors and shrinks don't get it. They encounter a sufferer they don't know and assume that the hyper-reactive person before them is who we are. They might even be using their qualifications to take advantage of vulnerable people. I suffered one shrink who advertised a luxury gourmet health retreat with a team of mental health professionals to provide a tailored trauma recovery plan. When in fact, this $1500-a-day establishment turned out to be a three-star renovated garage on a working farm with home cooking and none of the advertised services except a one-hour talk session, a yoga class, and two days of free time, I asserted that this service wasn't value for money. She replied, "You are the kind of person who makes a mountain out of a molehill." No, I'm not. I'm the kind of person who bounces back, who takes responsibility, who faces life with honesty and adversity with dignity. I am traumatised. You don't recognise trauma when it is staring you in the face? Trauma has got a hold of my body and mind, and it won't let go. I'm paying you to help me, not give me free time on your Ma and Pa Kettle farm for $1,500 a day.

Here is my experience of people who will never get it because they think they already know (broadly speaking):

- people who've experienced the trauma of divorce but walked away with a house, a job, or money in the bank (something with which to start a new life)
- people who think they know the charming, easy-going domestic abuser
- people who believe women should know when their husband is lying to them
- people with low empathy
- people who are used to you taking the blame and getting on with it
- people who are totally wrapped up in their own materialism and climb to the top
- people who think the reason their marriage is such a success is that they worked on compromise and stayed together through the hard times (and this is where you failed)
- people who know nothing of character disorders (and that's just about everybody)

These are the people who get it:

- sufferers of PTSD
- some spiritual seekers and teachers
- mature trauma practitioners with knowledge of character disorders
- lived-experience survivors of abuse or other life-changing traumas
- some people who knew your character before you were abused

If you are a talker, not a stuffer, begin your search for a lived-experience support group (or start one yourself). This is pioneering stuff. Search for a book study group of the few authors on psychological abuse out there.

Healing the Trauma of Psychological Abuse Book Study Groups
www.margotmaccallum.com

Healing from Hidden Abuse Book Study Groups
http://healingfromhiddenabuse.com/book-study/

Until we are able to distil our experience of psychological and emotional abuse into two sentences, and speak with a modulated tone devoid of emotion, we might be on our own. "He destroyed my life and broke my spirit. But I'm fine now."

Coercive Persuasion or Coercive Control

People get the idea of coercive control: intimidating, bullying, strong-arming someone into doing what you want them to do. They understand "I forbid you from working" or "No wife of mine is going to do XYZ," spoken in loud, aggressive, domineering tones.

What they don't get is coercive persuasion: manipulating someone into a weak, dependent position where they are in your control. "You should leave that job because you deserve so much better, and I really want to support you financially; we don't need the money; I will take care of you" or "I don't see why you associate with XYZ because that person is just using you, a really bad influence, not your friend," spoken with apparent concern, compassion, and your best interests at heart.

Coercive persuasion is a sinister technique used by so many narcopaths. Online, people use the term brainwashing to describe it, because it requires the trust, love, or respect of the unsuspecting victim in order to work. As one meme puts it:

- Isolate the victim.
- Expose them to inconsistent messages.
- Encourage them to doubt their own experience.
- Wear them down.
- Mix with sleep deprivation or intoxicant abuse, and stir well.

Unfortunately for us, we only recognise the coercive persuasion in hindsight, after the damage has been done, after we left the job; ditched the career; dumped the friends; relocated away from support networks; handed over the car, house, or money; gave the glowing character reference; became complicit in our own demise.

Any of those major life decisions might be fair and reasonable in a fair and reasonable partnership, between two people who have vowed to stick with each other through thick and thin, sickness and health, where there is healthy give and take.

But the narcopath uses the power he is given by someone who loves him as the means by which he gains sadistic pleasure. Using persuasive control, he can convince a trusting, loving, loyal, vulnerable person to go past the point of no return socially, professionally, financially, emotionally, and psychologically. Once that point of no return has been reached, the game is over, and he abandons his victim to the fate he created. It might not be violent in the usual sense of the word, but it is incredibly cruel and abusive.

Very few people, including family, friends, police, lawyers, or shrinks, will understand or acknowledge this kind of cruelty and psychological (rather than physical) domestic abuse. It is covert. Hidden. Secret. Taboo. It escalates incrementally and stealthily, as the victim becomes more and more vulnerable. And articulating it when we are in shock and traumatised is nigh on impossible. If we knew what was happening, we wouldn't have let it happen. Our power was robbed of us, but for a long, long time in the aftermath, we feel like we gave it away willingly. And when the narcopath and others say we have no one to blame but ourselves, it reinforces our own self-blame and papers over the truth of what really happened.

Never wrestle with a pig.
You both get dirty, and the pig likes it.

—George Bernard Shaw, Pinterest

Betrayal Trauma: The Strange Phenomenon of the Pecked-Chicken Chain Reaction

Build others up, because you know what it's like to be torn down.

—narcissisticsociopath.net

"Abandon Hope All Ye Who Enter Here." These are the words over the gate at the entry to hell in Dante's *Inferno*, where betrayers are frozen in ice for all eternity. Not only as punishment for their crimes, but to save others from the suffering they inflict with their compulsive perfidy. Ironically, "frozen in ice" is just one near-adequate description of the profound human suffering that some people go through as a result of a massive betrayal of trust by the person they most trusted and loved. Betrayal trauma is one of the most severe forms of psychological trauma we can undergo, yet it is unacknowledged in popular culture (aside from childhood betrayal). This lack of recognition can lead to those betrayed having their trauma minimised and demeaned, thus leading to secondary trauma. Betrayal is a wound to the soul.

The betrayal of psychological abusers isn't just about the sexual betrayal of infidelity. Psychological abusers betray those in their intimate lives psychologically, emotionally, financially, socially, and professionally. Betrayal by a manipulative, exploitative loved one is unfathomably profound and invisible to most others, except the victim some time later, as the lies come out into the light. Trauma is a whole-of-being experience. The trauma starts with our autonomic nervous system response. Instead of fight or flight, we are trapped in freeze. Our hands are tied by our love bonds to the predator. Unless our first instinct is to fight or run, we get caught in a trauma trap. Psychological abuse can render us powerless, then trauma can render us helpless and hopeless as a result. This particular trauma is caused by targeting and victimisation by one of nature's natural predators, make no mistake. None of us chooses our own victimisation.

Victims of profound betrayal describe their betrayer as "evil," "the devil," "a human parasite," "a vampire," or a "soul thief," having to rely on archaic or mythological concepts to explain the enormity of their grief and anguish; the harm done to them is so great as to almost surpass words. You are not to blame for your anguish and grief, my friends. You are not nuts. You are experiencing betrayal trauma. It's a thing. Hang in there. It will pass.

I think you can see that a dilemma of profound consequences is set up
if the people who are supposed to love and protect us are also the ones
that hurt, humiliate, and violate us. This sets up a double bind that
undermines people's basic sense of self and trust in their own instincts.

—Peter A Levine, *Healing Trauma*

Helplessness and hopelessness—what we in the first world so pejoratively
try to define by the lame term "powerlessness"—are feelings that can break
us down into a hell of frozen time. One profound betrayal so often leads
to more. As the betrayed, we then suffer the pecked-chicken phenomenon:
the strange urge in the human psyche to take advantage of those who are
unable to defend themselves. The rush of criticism, judgement, blame and
out-and-out betrayal that can consume victims of betrayal is a frequently
reported phenomenon in the online psychological abuse community,
minimised again in PTSD recovery literature as lack of support. I can
attest to it personally. Profound betrayal by the person in whom we placed
our deepest trust sets off a chain reaction in the people around us. Other
people begin to treat us as if we are worthless too.

Two days before my husband announced his intention to discard me, I
had a dream and wrote about it on our blackboard, so I could ask him on
his return from a work trip what he thought it meant. As it happened, I
didn't need to ask. "Betrayal most foul, followed by public humiliation".

If you are deeply traumatised after your betrayal by your intimate partner,
let yourself off the hook. Don't join the queue of people who minimise
and demean your experience. Honour it. Don't shame yourself or blame
yourself for it. You are not to blame. This is not a normal break-up,
where 50 percent of the responsibility lies with you. Betrayal trauma—the
trauma of psychological abuse—can be deeper and more profound than
being assaulted or having a car accident or suffering the death of a loved
one. If further betrayal and humiliation doesn't happen to you after your
psychological abuser discards you, you can count yourself amongst the
lucky ones and skip this chapter.

There is a weird phenomenon we all easily identify as that thing that makes us slow down and gawk as we pass a car accident. Or take us into the favelas in Rio or the settlements outside Johannesburg with our cameras cocked to empower ourselves with the knowledge that it is not we who must endure the suffering of poverty, humiliation, or degradation. It is in us. It is in the people around us, the drive to lift ourselves up, to make ourselves feel safe, secure, and powerful by observing the shame and humiliation of those less fortunate than ourselves. It is called schadenfreude.

People blame the victim, pointing out how they brought it on themselves, telling them to get over it. People tell us they don't want to know about our troubles because they have troubles of their own, relieving themselves of their duty as family and friends to support and empower rather than belittle and demean the suffering of their kin.

But there will be those who do not shun us, blame us, or criticise us, do not climb over our shattered beings in their dedicated drive to reach a better place than us. It is those people we most need to find from our place of helplessness and hopelessness after profound (and inevitable) betrayal by a narcopath. And the very first empowering act available to us from that place is to regain some control over our shattered minds and bodies: to control the urge to act out, to lash out with defensive harsh speech, to throw the second punch; to quietly endure the suffering of having our fight, flight, or freeze response stuck on high alert.

Our natural urge is to try to escape the suffering, to latch on to anyone or anything that can drag us out of hell. There is a simple little story that illustrates what we encounter whilst down the abyss.

We are stuck down the abyss, crying for help. Sympathy comes along and peers down the hole. Sympathy says, "Oh, you poor thing, you are so helpless and powerless; how are you ever going to get out of that hole?" And before long, sympathy is down the hole with us. Antipathy comes along and says, "Oh, look at you stuck down that hole. What a lousy position to be in. Glad it's not me. Not my problem," and walks away. Then empathy comes along and, seeing us stuck down a hole, finds a rope, ties it to a tree, and throws it to us so we can drag ourselves out, and sticks around shouting words of encouragement as we embark on our journey skyward.

My point is this: beware of latching on too quickly when empathy appears.

Many people resemble empathy; they will throw you a rope, for a fee. And you will, of course, pay anything for that rope. But instead of tying it to a tree, they tie it to a stick, and it gives way, sending you back down into the abyss when you have barely begun to struggle your way out. (In my case, I found this in expensive mental health retreat scams, wounding healers, and incompetent lawyers who made promises they could not fulfil.)

And there is the person who resembles empathy, who will throw you a rope for no fee and, after you drag yourself up, will then keep you enslaved to the memory of their kindness and use the debt you owe them to control you.

If you are familiar with the story of barnyard chickens, you will know how they will turn on one of their own who is wounded and weak. While the vulnerable chicken is at its weakest, the others will peck it to death. Likewise in human behaviour: betrayal sets off a chain reaction. Once it happens to you, you will start to notice how it happens everywhere.

The dark night of the soul is an experience that has been written about ever since St John of the Cross first described the phenomenon in the Middle Ages. It is a journey through hell, through the underworld. But it *is* a journey. It does lead somewhere, much as it might not feel like it while we are undergoing such a trial by fire. There is light at the end of the tunnel and reason for hope once we glimpse that light. But we must first journey in the dark for some time. I don't say this to invite even more misery and despair in the reader, but as both caution and encouragement to fellow travellers through the dark veil.

Take heart. After finally tying your rescue rope to a strong tree, you will become more empowered, more wise, more brave, more resilient than you ever thought possible. My tree was Buddhist philosophy. I searched for my habitual Christian tree but found no comfort there. It seemed that much of what I had been taught as a Christian—turning the other cheek, forgiveness, choosing to see the good in people—is what got me into so much trouble in the first place. I had to find a new way. Loss of religious faith is another commonly described reaction to betrayal trauma.

I found no one and nothing could save me but myself, and practitioners of Buddhism have walked that path to redemption and awakening for thousands of years. I began a search for people who have walked that road-less-travelled out of betrayal trauma. Embarking on this path, observing a few simple vows (before I was even certain that they would work) to relieve my suffering and the suffering of those around me, was the best thing that ever happened to me. I took hold of a rope that was tied to diligence, generosity, equanimity, and loving-kindness. That rope and that tree were solid, which is why I now write with such evangelical fervor, emerging from the fire with buckets of water for those still in it.

These words might sound moralistic, but for me, they were a simple practical rope to grasp to drag myself out of the abyss. A moral injury requires a moral antidote.

> This shocking wound will heal.
> Cultivate patience.
> Your mind will heal.
> Cultivate deep calm.
> Your body will heal.
> Cultivate tolerance.
> May your tears water the seeds of your future happiness.

> —narcissisticsociopath.net

Turning Isolation, Being Blamed, and Lack of Support into a Positive

> You don't need to be accepted by others.
> You need to accept yourself.

> —Pinterest

For other-referencing people, learning to prioritise our own healing and recovery can be a daunting prospect, something we don't know how to do because we were conditioned to overlook it. We learnt to please other people, to automatically forgive the things we didn't like in others in the pursuit of having them like (or love) us. We habitually put our own health and wellbeing last on our list, and for a long period during our devaluation by a narcopath, we were last on the list for our intimate other as well. By the time we were discarded, we might have come to the conclusion that being ignored, lied to, criticised and blamed was all we deserved. The shake-up of trauma is the perfect lifetime opportunity to change all that.

Whilst we all have some friends who share our values and virtues, we also attract people who somehow suck all the energy out of us, people to whom we give but get back very little in return. These people bask in our vibrancy or our generosity but are quick to blame, judge, criticise, mock, and humiliate when they don't get what they want out of the relationship.

You know what I'm talking about, right? You can recognise these people in your own life? These are not the kind of people we want around us when we are traumatised. Our unconscious self-protective mechanisms know this, and we start pushing people away. We can compound our own trauma and shame by doing this in a very unskilful way. By telling people to fuck off and leave me alone. If someone keeps approaching us to kindly "help" us by telling us what they think is wrong and why they think we should blame ourselves or get over it, how do we tell that person we'd rather not have that kind of help thank you?

Learning how to receive criticism (fair or unfair) and blame (reasonable or unreasonable) is a mature skill that eludes a lot of people. Not throwing the second punch is a response that requires patience and wisdom. Not retaliating with harsh speech that escalates the situation is a life skill that must be practiced. Learning to say, "Thank you for your opinion," instead of "Fuck off," "You might be right" instead of defensively improvising all the reasons they're wrong or aggressively attacking the messenger; learning to detach from the harmful, hurtful speech and actions of others, to intercept our own habitual knee-jerk reaction and respond differently; these are grown-up skills.

The anonymity of an online identity has driven an exponential increase in nasty reactive knee-jerk responses. Online comments are now filled with sarcasm (the lowest form of wit), bile and personal insult. Even our leaders are not immune, with their Twitter accounts. Nasty has become the new normal. There's something to avoid right there. Refrain. Abstain. Decline. Delete.

Being highly reactive is a common trauma symptom. So now we're more likely than ever to blurt out something we'll later regret. We have an opportunity (more like a pressing need) to learn and practice non-reactivity more than ever before.

The mindful approach is very simple, not unlike what our primary school teacher or our grandparents might have taught us (or tried to teach us). It's the very first moment that's the hardest bit. That is, catching ourselves the moment we are hooked, the moment the righteous indignation at wrongful blame, or the anger at criticism, or the humiliation of unkind gossip arises in our being. Catch that moment when we suddenly feel a verbal or physical response to unwanted stimuli. Catch the need to retaliate.

Patience Is the Antidote to Anger

Pause
That is, take a breath. Stop. Breathe. Count to ten. This skill is essential. Without this pause, this momentary do-nothing, we have no room to intercept our habitual reaction and change our habitual response.

From there, in terms of speech, there is a simple teaching:
Is it helpful?
Is it kind?
Is it necessary?

Say Nothing

In short, learning to say nothing at all is Do-No-Harm 101. We can learn not to open our mouths and scream, "You done me wrong!" The feeling of needing to do it doesn't go away. We're stuck with that feeling for a while, until it passes, until the anger or righteous indignation stop flooding our system, on top of the trauma that's already drowning us. But by saying nothing, by doing nothing, by refraining, abstaining, declining, waiting, pausing, being still, keeping schtum instead of acting out from our hurt, we throw water on the fire. We don't make things worse than they already are.

Write It Down

Then if the habit to express our opinion or have the final say is so great, then writing it all out is a commonly recommended antidote. Just not on Facebook and not in an accusing, angry email that we hastily post. Write the angry email if you must, but then send it to yourself. Refrain from pressing Send to the subject of your anger. Wait. Pause. Contain yourself again. For a longer period this time. For a couple of days. Longer. Rewrite it. Over and again. Send it to yourself over and again for editing, or until you have fully expressed yourself and are ready to delete it.

It can feel really uncomfortable. It can feel like we're sitting on a powder keg of emotion. We can feel justified in responding to a hurt or insult with more hurt and insult. We may judge ourselves as weak and not standing up for ourselves when we start to practice non-violence.

Journaling is another antidote. Journaling can help us let some steam out of the bottle. Journaling helps us process a lifetime of losses, including the most recent. There are advanced tantric practices of getting it all out until you are exhausted, and then seeing who you are under all that, a bit like the peace that descends after the catharsis of a good cry. If primal therapy isn't for you, journaling can fulfil this role. We can address our journal entry to our adult or child self, to the people who betrayed us, to our abuser, to an imaginary compassionate confidante, to God, to the front page of the newspaper, or to the world at large. We can allow ourselves the time for some personal reflection; give ourselves permission away from the to-do list. We centre ourselves, ground ourselves, breathe deeply and slowly if we can, and tune in to our wounded self, our kind self, our despairing self. We ask the questions we want to ask and wait for an answer. Or accept that the answer may come much later. We acknowledge what we have experienced and reveal our true feelings to ourselves.

Once we have done this, we have an opportunity to revisit the lists of losses and complaints and reframe them. Revisiting the journal some months later, we might notice how the sting has gone out of some things. We might see how, in fact, some of the pain and loss has given us greater strength, space or opportunity. At the very least, we might notice how our trauma symptoms have eased and the extent to which we have made some progress in letting go and moving on.

Shrinks call telling your story to just anyone "clienting." It is surprising how badly some of us want to tell people how cruelly we've been treated when we are traumatised. We need to be heard. But most people don't want to know.

Seek Refuge
The importance of a safe place to recover can never be underestimated. Only we can know what, who and where makes us feel safe. We need to honour that frightened inner voice and do whatever we can to get to a safe place and stay there for a time if we can. For many of us, it is people that now freak us out the most but people we need the most: another conundrum to deal with.

Some people will be kind enough to let us open up, express our jumbled emotions, tell our ugly story of cruelty and abuse, share their own story with us. Some people like to connect at a very base human level, explore the human condition. These are the people we want around when we are traumatised. One day, we can return the favour. No need for guilt or shame, just discernment. We start sorting through the safe and unsafe people in our lives, and that's okay. We need all the safety we can get when our lives have suddenly become groundless.

Trust Your Instincts

It's not just the judgers, criticisers, and blamers who create a toxic environment for our recovery from narcissistic abuse. A curious and self-compassionate reflection on the brutal realities of betrayal and duplicity will help us identify other things that make us feel unsafe: crowds, parties, locations with no exit, scary movies, whatever. Our own instincts will tell us. Learning to listen to and honour our instincts, to listen to our deep inner voice, is another positive skill to take away from this shocking experience.

Detoxify

Trauma can suddenly turn some people, places and activities in our lives toxic. People change. Nothing is permanent. Trauma brings about sudden and dramatic transformation. We want to cling to our support systems, stay in our comfort zones, but we might now notice that these have become toxic to our health. Some shrinks might say that avoidance is a bad thing, that we need to find the courage to expose ourselves to people and conditions that existed before trauma.

On the contrary; we need to find the courage to let go, detach, detox. Turn inwards and go on a diet from toxic people and influences. Find the courage to seek support validation compassion inside ourselves. Build the resilience to withstand the knee-jerk reactions of the people who have now become toxic to us. Rest in the comfort and safety of our own good hearts. Honour our good intentions. Nurture and nourish the parts of us that have been poisoned by trauma.

Excising toxic people from our lives is not easy. People get hurt and angry about our new boundaries. Admitting to our own faults, our own demons, takes a tremendous amount of courage and honesty. We could choose to avoid them, run from them. But we already know that if we do that again, they will follow us wherever we go. Trauma is an opportunity to detox our lives.

Our physical addictions are what we lean on in times of stress. So choosing this moment to have another go at giving up smoking or drinking or sugary treats might not actually be the best decision for us right now. But *holding less tightly* to the habit might be possible. Find the middle ground.

Have fewer drinks, fewer cigarettes, fewer treats. If the urge to keep our wits about us instead of crying into our beer every night strikes, great! Let's do it! Let's pat ourselves on the back for doing it. Giving up beating ourselves up or punishing ourselves for having toxic addictions is a more important detox at this time. This is self-compassion in action.

Make Room for Positive Influences (Honour Trauma Triggering)
Trauma changes our world view. What were once innocuous, unnoticed influences in our environment can become triggers for anxiety. We can develop acute aversions for certain things: the barrage of violence and fear in newsfeeds, loud or aggressive drunks, nasty mocking humour, noisy claustrophobic crowds, images of cruelty, crazy things we don't want to admit to, whatever. The over-the-top disproportionate emotional triggering of an anxiety condition, whilst unpleasant, has a silver lining: it offers us an acute awareness of the things that offend our souls.

This phase of trauma can be extremely uncomfortable. We learn that people and situations that were once a normal part of our landscape are now off-limits. Panic attacks are best avoided. What feels like loss is actually reclaiming our personal power. Essentially, we are becoming a new person, rebirthing ourselves.

When we start to see our own worth, we find it hard to stay around people who don't. As we create space in the landscape of our lives, we might live for a time, empty. But before too long (it can feel like forever), the healthy mature people and the nourishing experiences we hope for start to miraculously appear. Instead of victim-blamers, criticisers, and frightening circumstances, people and situations that remind us of our value as human beings enter our lives.

Everything is going to be okay.

Cultivate Patience
We can build our capacity to sit on the powder keg of anger when it arises. The anger of trauma can alienate others and create more shame in us. We can build our patience muscle, even in the heat of trauma. By privately listening to, watching or reading radio, television or newspaper

commentators with whom we strongly disagree. This time it *is* exposure therapy. We begin with a few minutes of exposure, then progress to longer periods; whatever we can tolerate. Alone and in private, we approach the opinions of others that we would normally avoid. We can notice the anger as it arises, the sensations in our body, our beliefs and opinions that fight so aggressively with what is being said. And we just allow the anger to be there. We allow the opinions we find offensive to just be there.

We refrain from judging our anger as right or wrong and accept that it just is. The anger is not who we are. Instead of "I am angry" which implies the anger is a part of ourselves, we calmly and mindfully acknowledge, "I have anger". Everybody has anger from time to time. It's not a permanent condition, and it will pass. Each time it arises, we notice it, respect it, refrain from acting out of impulse, tolerate the discomfort, and honour the relief when it passes.

It sounds so simple but is a courageous discipline.

A situation arises. Like a traffic jam or someone cutting us off in traffic. (Road rage is a social problem visitors to Australia notice a lot). We ask ourselves, "Can I do anything about this?" If the answer is yes, then anger is pointless. We just do the thing. Take the side road. If the answer is no, then anger is pointless. We might as well accept the situation and relax into our experience of the present moment.

Slowly Rebuild
Our lives came tumbling down around us, and now we get a choice about the bricks we pick up again to rebuild. Our world collapse is actually filled with ripe potential for a new way of being, starting with looking after ourselves before we take on everybody else's stuff.

Anger Management Meditation Script

It's time to take a break, relax, and deal with anger in a healthy, productive way.

Take a deep breath in. Hold for a moment, and now breathe out.

Breathe in; hold that tension, and then breathe out. Feel the tension release with your breath.

Breathe in ... and out ... in ... out.

Keep breathing like this, slowly ... deeply ... and let your body relax a little.

Anger is a normal and natural emotion. There is nothing wrong with having feelings; you are human, after all. You have the power to handle this anger you are feeling without exploding. So give yourself permission to take this time to deal with your anger.

Anger management doesn't mean you never feel angry. Anger management is managing the behavioural responses that can arise when you feel angry.

All you really need to do right now is take a few moments just to relax. Find some calm. Breathe. Notice your breathing. After you've taken this time out to get calmer and refrain from making things worse than they are, you can proceed with your day.

It's okay to be angry. Just allow yourself to feel however it is you are feeling right now, noticing this feeling but not acting on it just yet. All you're doing is observing. Emotions are neither right nor wrong; they just are.

Breathe in; hold that tension. And now breathe out, feeling the tension release with your breath. Breathe in ... and out ... in ... out.

Keep breathing like this, slowly, deeply, and let your body relax a little. Turn your attention again to how you are feeling. Notice the physical sensation of anger. Where in your body is the anger stored? Is it in your shoulders? Your jaw? Your fists? Your stomach? Between your shoulder blades? These sensations are uncomfortable, but they can be relieved right now by relaxing your muscles.

Tighten your hands into fists. Feel the tension in your hands and arms. Hold, and relax. Let go, allowing your hands and arms to be loose and limp. Notice the difference between tension and relaxation.

Now see if you can create a feeling of relaxation in your shoulders. Focus next on your face and jaw. Clench your teeth and then let it go. Let your jaw go slack. Let all the tension leave your face and neck.

Scan your body now for remaining areas of tension. Relax each area that feels tense. Keep scanning and relaxing, up and down.

Take note of how you are feeling now physically and emotionally. Now ponder these affirmations:

I am feeling angry right now, and I accept the way I feel.
I have the power to control my reactions.
I can fully experience this anger yet wait before I take action.
I can feel angry but calm and in control at the same time.
It's okay to feel angry.

Notice again how you are feeling.

You may feel less angry, just as angry, or more angry now than when you started this relaxation session. To deal with residual anger, you may need a way to express the anger and get it out: physical exercise, journaling, talking to someone you trust. There are many ways to express yourself.

You can let anger out by breathing deeply: breathing in relaxation, and breathing out anger. Let anger go with each breath.

Now that you are calmer, you might want to address the situation that was upsetting by taking action to change the situation or speaking to the person you were upset with. Or you may just choose to let the situation go.

You have the right to feel a range of emotions, including anger, and to express these emotions in healthy, respectful ways that you choose.

Ask the Experts

Levine, Peter A (2008), *Healing Trauma: A Pioneering Program for Restoring the Wisdom of Your Body.* Boulder, CO: Sounds True.

Chapter 6

REFRAMING

We might keep communicating after he leaves, because we are still labouring under the illusion that he cares, that he has a place for us in his heart. This man who vowed to love and cherish us and promised he would have our backs as we let go of our independent lifelines to care for him. We might think we can work it so that we remain friends for life, just like we have with exes past.

We loved and trusted him and placed him at the centre of our universe.

So it can take a while to accept he just doesn't care. He never loved us. We were just a passing obsession, and he only hung around because we were a convenient source of supply, enabling, or cover. His interest in us ended the day he gained our absolute commitment. From then onwards, it was just about what he could get. He only cares about his image, and he loves no one but himself.

Even then, *love*, for him, is just a word that has no real emotional connection. It is a word that can be bandied about willy-nilly to flatter and manipulate people. It's a word to be liberally applied in poetry and seduction. The concept of love, for him, is not the enduring bond of respectful mutual care that we think of, but that ephemeral idealised blip that is the honeymoon phase of a romance.

His urge to live perpetually inside the honeymoon phase is what drives his repetitive compulsion of using and discarding people. Rinse and repeat. Blame the woman for everything, project his own faults and moral shortcomings onto her, and project all his hopes and dreams onto the next one. Every time he marries his mistress, he creates a job vacancy. But he strings his current wife along until she runs out of resources for him to live off, becomes ill, or realises she is being scammed, used. Accepting this foul character-disordered behaviour is a necessary step towards reframing our trauma. It's harsh, I know. But it's also true.

If he can reframe his contempt for us as love, we can reframe things too. His marital vows might have extolled our virtues as being the kindest, most generous person he ever met. Months or years later, he suddenly abandons us, claiming we've done nothing wrong; he just doesn't want to be married anymore. A year after that, his sworn affidavit claims we are a lying, mentally unstable, violent alcoholic who abuses the children and breaks the law. Publicly, he vows that he bears us no malice; he wants to settle amicably, and it's us who is dragging out the settlement process, despite his generous offers.

Essentially, he accuses us of being and doing what he is being and doing. He projects his rejected Mr Hyde self onto us, while we try everything to stand up for ourselves, fight his lies and slander, prove his theft and dishonesty, prove that he has taken the truth of what happened and is reframing it to make himself look like the victim and us the villain.

If the narcopath is able to reframe his abominable intimate partner violence so that he is free of any blame, then how can we reframe his abuse so that it works for us instead of against us? One way to relieve ourselves of the obsessive revisiting of all the broken promises, betrayals, and injustices is to unpack each one and reframe it. His offences are so pervasive that the usual route to forgiveness might not be available this time. Not yet, anyway. Instead of remaining cowed and broken by his cruelty, we have an opportunity to heal from any co-dependency and trauma bonding that snared us, to go beyond the helplessness inherent in, "I can't believe someone I loved and trusted could abuse and discard me in such a cruel, vindictive way."

The pain is so extreme because the narcopath deliberately plunged daggers into old wounds he knew were there. Because we were unconscious of these old wounds, he was able to use them to manipulate us: our fear of abandonment, losing everything, being cast out, not being good enough, being unworthy of love, fundamentally flawed, whatever. His ruthless attack on those core fears, aimed at controlling us, owning us, destroying us, has brought all this suffering of a lifetime out into the light. We can turn our attention from how horrible a demon he is to our own inner demons that have been suppressed, ignored, or that we thought we already dealt with.

With every shameful thought, there is an opportunity to unpack the beliefs behind the shame, to honestly reflect on the best way forward, and to decide whether we want to continue with these old limiting beliefs. Do we want to keep ourselves surrounded by the people who reinforce this old limiting self-image? Are we really so bad that we are unworthy of our own love? Must we really continue to tolerate manipulative and controlling men in order to have a partner or a career, a job, a roof over our heads? Must we really put up with the criticism, scapegoating, and betrayal of our relatives? Must we continue to put the needs of others before our own? Must we continue to laugh along with the tribe every time we witness bad behaviour? Must we stand back and do nothing in the face of cruelty, lies, unkind gossip, barefaced duplicity? Is this who we really want to be?

Unkindness to ourselves often eclipses even that of the narcopath. Lack of support, care, love for ourselves has been reflected back at us for however long we stayed with him. Now is the time to escape the matrix. Now is the time to acknowledge that the reason we feel annihilated when he tells another lie is not just because we are offended, but because underneath that offence, a part of us believes him to be *right*. Part of us believes we are a bad person because we did a bad thing. We lost our temper, drank too much, allowed ourselves to be eroded, trusted him with the bank account, gave up a good job to be his homemaker. We trusted him when we already knew he was a liar. We were foolish. And if we had our way, we would never forgive ourselves for our faults. Forgiving ourselves is Recovery 101. Learning how not to scapegoat ourselves or blame ourselves for everything is way more important than forgiving him or the friends or family who betrayed us in the aftermath.

This can be a Herculean task for those of us who have experienced recurring bullying, domestic abuse, or scapegoating. The likelihood that this is most of us is pretty high, since these unhealed wounds attract narcopaths. Empaths (highly empathic and sensitive people) are human narcopath magnets. The narcopath is a human predator who studies a pack of prey to find the weakest or most vulnerable to exploit. As we grew into adults, we learned to hide this vulnerability as best we could. We long ago abandoned our own inner child. Now is the time to return to that frightened, sad, lonely child and give it the love, kindness, compassion, and support she was deprived of.

Western psychological studies show that a neglectful, undemonstrative, or hypercritical parenting style can create children who internalise this criticism, leading to depression, anxiety, perfectionism, and blaming themselves for everything. Overt parental abuse is not a necessary factor in developing a personality strategy that hides self-loathing or low self-esteem.

It is not just the sad little six-year-old whose mother didn't love her. It is the scared twelve-year-old, relentlessly bullied at school. It is the emancipated twenty-something, sexually exploited and harassed at work. It is the thirty-year-old lied to, cheated on, and unfairly gossiped about by a lover whose name we can't even remember. It is the plethora of small hurts and betrayals that need our attention again so that we can *reframe them*. The lessons we didn't learn at the time because we were too busy; we had things to achieve, a life to carve out. We told ourselves, "Get over it," and we did (or thought we did). Until the most cruel, most vindictive, most manipulative of all our exploiters walked right in and raped our lives. We might even have talked it through with different therapists or counsellors. But the frightened inner child didn't budge from our psyches.

Cognitive processes cannot access the subconscious. Thinking about it isn't going to heal it at the deepest level of our beings. On the contrary; thinking about it, talking about it, only reopens the wounds. Others, impatient with our slow recovery, remind us that we need to stop talking about it. But our incomprehensible emotional pain continues to drive our minds to conjure and re-conjure the betrayals and injustices. The second arrow drives us further from the heart of the recovery matrix.

It is not cognitive but spiritual and energetic *experiential* practices that relieve this deep inner pain. Alternative modalities, which we might be sceptical of: mindfulness (turning our thoughts from internal suffering to a fully embodied experience of the present moment), affirmations (a concentration practice aimed at temporarily inviting positive thoughts to sit alongside the negative ones that continue to arise), meditation (guided concentration meditations make the practice immediately available to novices), visualisations (meditations that transcend the current moment), kinesiology (the body knows), qigong (psychosomatic healing), reiki (energetic healing), chanting (inducing trance-like states in a safe place), self-hypnosis (guided by a trained hypnotherapist to target deep inner beliefs), traditional Chinese medicine or Ayurveda (acknowledging the holistic nature of mind, body, emotions, life force, and spirit), and shamanism. None of these are about stoicism, our culturally preferred coping strategy.

Healing from the trauma of psychopathic and narcissistic abuse is the biggest challenge most of us outside of a war zone will ever face. This is quite apart from rectifying the practical damage of having our homes, bank accounts, careers, and reputations plundered. But it can be done. By re-parenting and re-partnering ourselves. By learning how to be the *first* person to nurture, support, and encourage ourselves. By growing up all over again in a different way. By finding faith in ourselves. As we do all this, the people, circumstances, and opportunities that fit the new adult will start to appear in our lives. By learning to contain our suffering, live in the void, accept the way things are (impermanent, ever-changing, beyond our control), we ironically find more and more balance (and what feels like control and security).

Escaping the Trap of a Victim Mindset

Reconciling narcabuse opens up the opportunity to explore our own beliefs and behaviours around accountability. We have been pushed to the very limits of our own ingrained habit to absorb blame and assume responsibility, by years of conscientious compromise with a narcopath who dodges accountability for everything. Our glue-like loyalty and eager cooperation were exploited to have us pander to his every whim. When blamed, we felt wronged but somehow complicit. When urged to sacrifice in the guise of compromise, we again felt wronged but complicit. We bore the weight of confusing mind-plays by a man who projects his disowned negative qualities onto us: who uses others to supply his needs; who refuses to witness his own wrongdoing; who genuinely believes himself perfect, beyond reproach. This has left us weakened, exhausted, and dreadfully confused, feeling like a victim and not liking the experience one little bit.

But now we, as neurotypical or highly sensitive individuals, are able to use the experience to sort through our own feelings about how accountability works across our personal relationships, our work ethic, our consumer choices, everything. Exactly what are our boundaries for blame and responsibility? How does blame differ from genuine causation? How does personal accountability differ from habituated self-blame? Can we recognise causation but let go of blame? Can we stand accountable for where we are now without beating ourselves up about it?

By and large, the targets of psychological abusers seem to share the qualities of conscientiousness, cooperativeness, loyalty, and a belief in the decency and honesty of others. Those things are shattered after narcabuse. We can withdraw onto our islands of mistrust, violated and isolated. We question everything. And whilst this vast existential questioning can feel groundless and uncomfortable, it also holds within it huge new potential for growth.

Others judge us with accusing phrases that have somehow entered the lexicon as helpful: "Get over it." "Just forget about him and get on with your life." "He's not worth another thought." People for whom kicking people to the kerb is straightforward cannot understand why we can't just do the same. They get frustrated with us when we are still stuck in a victim place after a few weeks. After a few months, people can get downright aggressive about us "playing the victim". It's victim-blaming again. We hear the theory that to escape our role of victim, helpless and hopeless, we must get over blame and assume responsibility. It makes a lot of sense.

We've done it before, many times. Forgiven infidelity, betrayal, deception, dropped the blame and moved on. But it seems so much harder to do with intimate domestic narcabuse. It's so vast. The longer we stayed loyal to our abuser, the deeper the covert victimisation.

We need to remind ourselves over and over that *we are doing the best we can* with what we have at our disposal. And our best is enough. Just because others can't see or refuse to acknowledge our hard work trying to escape a victim mindset, that doesn't mean we should hop on board and beat ourselves up about it too. A victim mindset is one of many ways people get stuck in a rut. When we look around, we can see people all around us who are stuck, in alcoholism and the denial of it, in workaholism and the justification for it, in greed and ruthless ambition and the cultural validation of it, in poverty consciousness. They are just lucky they haven't been victimised to this extent themselves. We can let ourselves off the hook if we feel trapped in a victim mindset and don't know how to escape. It happens. It's happening to us. We never thought it would. Only when we accept it, acknowledge it, and embrace it can we put it down and climb out of it.

After sustained psychological manipulation during this episode, and perhaps over a lifetime if we grew up in a narcissist-dominated family, we are already in the habit of blaming ourselves. We want more than anything to get out of this victim place. It is extremely uncomfortable. We want to gain closure by sifting through all the mutual agreements, hollow vows, and empty promises and figuring out they were all just meaningless words to him.

The first step out of victimhood after acceptance that these things happened is, I think, in recovering our *personal agency*. That is, essentially, regaining our belief in our own personal power, our faith in ourselves. We had it once, before we were devalued and discarded. We can find it again.

We feed the good wolf, not the bad wolf.

We tell ourselves, "I can cope with this pain. I can find a way out of this devastation. I believe recovery from narcabuse is possible. I am strong and brave enough to make big changes to my outlook on life. I have the courage to start again. I can overcome this anger, this resentment, this bitterness, whatever. I am in charge of me from now on. I will not be handing my power over to anyone ever again. I do not need to depend on anyone to do as they say they'll do, or even do what is honourable and decent. I can cope with abuse, deception, betrayal. I can re-parent myself. It might be too late for some things, like restoring twenty years of life savings or professional and social networks, getting another job, or buying another home, but it's not too late to start again. I can stand on my own two feet again".

"I can take responsibility for my view of the way things are. I can take responsibility for my thoughts, own them, and train my mind so that different thoughts habitually arise. I can take responsibility for my speech and the words I choose, for my actions and the intention behind them. I can take responsibility for the way I do things that need doing, with mindful concentration and joyous effort. I can take responsibility for my own boundaries: what I will and won't tolerate. [This is a huge lesson, especially for victims of fraud or abuse. Our willingness to compromise made us easy to manipulate.] I can be accountable to myself and others for the way I make my living, for conducting myself in an ethical manner, and for surrounding myself with people who live up to my high standards."

It is all this underlying detail that is contained in the phrase, "They go low, we go high." A moral injury requires a moral antidote.

Attending to our own authentic values is a vital part of recuperating from our own loss of self-respect. Instead of kicking ourselves for ignoring the red flags, believing the lies, holding out for some decency and honour in return for that which we invested, we can simply start, right now, right here, to honour ourselves, to trust our instincts again, even as we acknowledge we were conditioned to doubt them, to offer up to ourselves the love and compassion we were so starved of with the narcopath, to stop seeking validation outside ourselves and start believing in our own ability to nourish ourselves and be kind to ourselves, to form a solid, steadfast relationship with our own inner self: our inner child *and* inner adult.

We can stop blaming ourselves and take responsibility for ourselves again. Alone.

Instead of staying stuck in the uncomfortable memories of profound betrayal, we can take responsibility for noticing the thoughts and emotions, honouring them, and watching them pass (as they do when we attend to them). Or turn our minds onto another object of concentration. Over and over again. Just like any training, any practice. We can make these things habit by practising them.

With practice, we can help ourselves feel good about ourselves again. By turning towards our own good hearts, and restoring our own personal agency, we can lift ourselves out of the rut of a victim mindset.

An Anecdote on Learned Helplessness

A baby elephant needs a huge chain around its feet, attached to a pole driven deep into the earth, to restrain it. The baby pulls and strains and tugs against this restraint over and over again, until it learns that trying to escape is futile. By the time that trained elephant is an adult, all that is needed to restrain it is a white string attached to a stick in the ground. It has learned to stop trying, to give up, that resistance is futile. The creature has learned helplessness.

We can be conditioned from an early age to believe we can't cope, to cave in to helplessness when under stress. Living with a narcopath conditions us in this way too. Conditioned behaviour is unconscious behaviour. When we bring it into our consciousness, we can notice it when "I can't cope" arises as a habitual reaction to everything from bringing the washing in before it rains to a seriously challenging life event. And we can make an adult choice to fight or run away, instead of giving up and playing dead, like we were conditioned to do.

The Noble Eightfold Path

The Noble Eightfold Path of Buddhist philosophy is a set of ethical guidelines for turning away from extremes and taking a simpler path, known as the Middle Way. These steps are not sequential, nor are they to be taken as a decree, law, or commandment from a higher being. These eight factors can provide a framework for contemplation and self-discovery, especially when we just don't know what to do to escape our pain. They can help us identify what is creating unnecessary suffering on top of our trauma. They can be integrated into daily life alongside most other religious doctrines. The right they refer to is that inner voice we each have that confirms we have made the correct ethical decision.

Right Understanding (or Right View)

This is about seeing the world as it really is, not as we wish it to be or believe it to be from our current viewpoint. Seeing the nature of reality is an ongoing quest for dedicated practitioners of meditation and spiritual seekers.

Right Intent

Right intent comes from our good heart. With courage and compassion for ourselves and others, we aim to detach from desire, ignorance, and aversion on our journey through life. It is a deeply held commitment to ethical behaviour.

Right Speech

This tackles the human tendencies to gossip or react with harsh, defensive speech we later regret. It asks us to be careful with our words, knowing how criticism can hurt and kindness can encourage and uplift.

Right Action

We undertake not to do to others what we find hurtful ourselves. We don't take what is not given to us, and we respect the rights of other sentient beings. Buddhist ethical vows include no killing, no stealing, no lying, no sexual misconduct, and no excessive use of intoxicants (in case it leads to any of the former).

Right Livelihood

This discourages us from doing work which destroys or disrespects life and encourages us to undertake work which improves lives.

Right Effort

This step refers to a positive attitude. We try to refrain from doing things with anger, resentment, or impatience but rather apply good cheer, steadfastness, and patience to every task.

Right Mindfulness

Forming the basis of meditation, mindfulness refers to a clear and open awareness of the present moment. It includes an awareness of how old habits and patterns control us and how our views may be clouded by fear or aversion.

Right Concentration

In meditation practice, concentration of the mind (with compassion) on a single object can lead to calmness and clarity. Concentration on a single object, such as the breath, can help us let go of the past and planning the future, and experience joy in the present moment.

Gratitude Practice

> Thank you for the pain.
> It made me lift my game.
>
> —Pinterest

We might think of gratitude as something that arises when a good thing happens to us, that gratitude arises out of happiness. Perhaps counter-intuitively, the wisdom traditions teach us that it's the other way around: Happiness arises out of gratitude practice. The Buddha teaches that gratitude is the root of joy.

In the aftermath, it can be pretty hard to find anything in our current experience of trauma to be grateful for. Overwhelmed by loss, we are suffering extreme emotions and swirling confusion. What's to feel grateful about? "You don't seriously expect me to be grateful that he didn't hit me, that he didn't kill me, when he took everything it takes to make a life and left me reeling with trauma, do you?"

Well, yes. Gratitude practice can start by entering a back door, from a place of utter darkness, bitterness, and resentment. It can start with recognising that there are people suffering an even worse fate than ours; especially women. There are women whose husbands have set them alight in their kitchens to get rid of them. There are women who are buried to the neck and stoned by the menfolk of their village for their crime of falling in love with the wrong man. There are women kidnapped and sold as sex slaves or used as comfort women, with whole armies raping them night after night. By contrast, we got off lightly.

But if these extreme contrasts only cause more pain in us and not the relief of gratitude, then we start with the simplest of things for which we are grateful. We enter through the front door of gratitude: chocolate, cheese, trees, grass, the food in our bellies, the roof over our heads, the women's refuge we are staying in, the friend's couch we are surfing, the compassionate people who advocate on our behalf. We write a list of ten things we are grateful for and read it every day. We pinpoint whatever, when we think of it, makes us feel a brief moment of respite from trauma, a flush of gratitude. We allow our minds to take time out to think about our list and feel the tiny bit of nourishment we feel from it. We become more mindful of brief moments of gratitude.

Over time, and in combination with the compassion and loving-kindness practices, our list will grow. Our gratitude will grow and, with it, our moments of happiness. As we regain some equilibrium, our faith in ourselves, and a stronger sense of self-worth, so the things we are grateful for will morph and change. We'll see bigger and more profound reasons for gratitude. We'll see silver linings in our own pain and growth. We'll start noticing unexpected things turning up, which we are instantaneously grateful for and joyous about.

We'll start to look outwards instead of focussing on our pain. We'll start to relate in a healthier way to the people around us. We'll start to feel a part of something instead of apart from everything. We'll start to look up and around us. We'll become aware of how our newly awakened self relates differently to the world. And we'll notice how our attitude to everything is at the root of our own happiness. We can offer compassion in action to the world. We'll notice how very interdependent we humans are. We'll find a new purpose.

Expanding gratitude practice into the arena of social comparison focuses on people who are suffering just like us; we greet them with compassion and understanding instead of aversion and judgement. Every city-dweller around the world encounters homeless people every day. Rather than allow ourselves to sink into the arrogant, self-satisfaction of schadenfreude, or ignore and dehumanise these street people, we witness their common humanity. It could be us in that position. It really could. Gratitude will naturally arise. Paradoxically, such gratitude will relieve our own pain, even if we don't yet have the courage or wisdom to relieve someone else's.

Gratitude practice works to bring happiness back into our lives.

Example of a Reframing Gratitude List

I am grateful for my body that keeps going despite its many flaws, birds that sing in the dark night, warm feather duvets, and chocolate.

I am grateful for rainforests and oceans, wild beasts and farm animals, trees and dirt and rain.

I am grateful for the poets, the playwrights, the musicians, the artists, the novelists and educators, the mathematicians and laboratory technicians, the healers and carers.

I am grateful for the car I drive, the fridge I use, the computer and all the other tools of life.

I am grateful for open fires.

I am grateful for my dog.

I am grateful for the whole catastrophe.

I am grateful to the empathic awakened people of the world, who are brave enough to notice the suffering of others and fight against the selfishness, greed, and cowardice of human predators and parasites.

I am grateful to all those people who quietly go about their business in an ethical way, refusing to give in to the temptation of wrongdoing.

I am grateful for all those people who should have helped but didn't, who should have been kind but weren't, who should have lifted me up instead of kicking me when I was down. Because of them, I finally learned to lift myself up, not kick myself when I am down, to be kind to myself.

I am grateful for the few loyal friends who stood by me in my darkest hour, never wavering in their belief in my kind heart and generous spirit, each one of whom I privately name and thank.

I am grateful to my family for showing me how victim-blaming, scapegoating, antipathy, and conditioning really work. Without their knee-jerk criticism, blame, and betrayals, I might never have learned how to be kind to myself, how to support and empower myself, how to be mother, sister, friend to myself. Without them, I might never have learned the true value of people who are really on my team, the people who remained steadfast and understood that my PTSD was not who I really am, but a temporary and understandable response to the pain of narcissistic abuse.

I am grateful to the psychopath for providing the full depth of the human experience to me. Because of him, I got to experience anguish, despair, rage, terror, hatred, humiliation, the desire for revenge, suicidal thoughts, utter helplessness, and hopelessness. And I learned to spell *narcissist* and *psychopath*.

And without him, I might never have learned how much courage, resilience, self-compassion, kindness, and strength lay deep inside me.

I am grateful to the psychopath for giving me a new sense of purpose. From the shocking trauma of narcissistic abuse emerged a compassionate drive to support and empower other sufferers in whatever way I can.

Ask the Experts

Chödrön, Thubten (2001), *Buddhism for Beginners*. Snow Lion.

Chapter 7

HOW LONG WILL THIS RECOVERY TAKE?

I don't think there is really a definitive answer about how long recovery takes. The shortest answer is that it takes way longer than any break-ups in the past. It is not a normal break-up. Recovering from trauma, narcabuse, PTSD, complex PTSD, generalised anxiety disorder, depression or any other mental health disorder can take years, decades, generations. Shrinks will only tell you it takes as long as it takes. Some people are more resilient than others. Some people grew up taking the hard knocks or living on the mean streets. Others grew up shielded from hardship, cloaked in privilege. Some were more awake to bad people or fake people. Still others were just lucky enough to avoid a lot of trouble and strife until they met their abuser.

If I report on my own recovery, people I know personally, people discussed in books or blogs, personal stories told online, then there is some evidence of a pattern. Four-year and seven-year recoveries are often mentioned (mine was four). Testimonials left on the site of my fellow Aussie, Melanie Tonia Evans, proclaim recovery within a year in some cases, by applying the spiritual healing method it took her ten years to devise (her own healing took seven). Time and stoicism alone do not heal trauma. It just sits there, under the surface, waiting to explode when life becomes overwhelming.

Author Shannon Thomas, who has counselled victims of spiritual, psychological, emotional, and other hidden abuse, outlines distinct stages of recovery, a pathway that she has noticed:

1. Despair: The realisation that life has become unmanageable.
2. Education: Learning the specific methods of psychological abuse.
3. Awakening: Awareness that other people have had similar experiences and recovery is possible.
4. Boundaries: Implementing emotional and/or physical distance with an abuser.
5. Restoration: Living purposefully to restore what was lost during the abuse.
6. Maintenance: Returning to earlier stages to heal at a deeper level and maintain recovery from abuse.

—Shannon Thomas, Pinterest

Opening the heart begins by opening to a lifetime's accumulation of suppressed or unrecognised sorrow.

To me, this is the very definition of why the journey of narcabuse recovery can take so long. It's exactly the opposite of being knocked down and getting straight back up again (which is what our culture demands of us). It's about being willing to develop the patience and self-compassion in the face of other people demanding that we get over it, to lean inwards towards our darker impulses, our disowned dark sides, and accept them. It is about peeling the layers of our own onion. Recovery takes time.

Sometimes, your heart needs more time to
accept what your mind already knows.

—Pinterest

Blame, Causation, Accountability, and Responsibility

Quenching the out-of-control fires in one's life takes enormous energy, commitment and perseverance. Perhaps the best step any of us can take in this direction is to try to be as realistic as possible about what we are doing with our lives. If we want to honour the hero within, we have to stop applauding delusion and denial. We have to be honest about our negative habits and attitudes … we have to relinquish and renounce our egocentric, self-serving, and self-referential tendencies.

—Lama Surya Das, *Letting Go of the Person You Used to Be*

In the last few generations, our shared cultural approach to personal responsibility has shifted. From high government, corporations, and service industries to a bingle in a car park. The ideal model has shifted from "I accept responsibility because I am the person responsible" to "I never admit liability." Along with the rise of personal narcissism, our paradigms seem to have moved. Are there more and more people behaving as unethically as they can get away with, or is it just my imagination? Are there equal and opposite movements gathering momentum that are calling people out, holding people to account, or is it just wishful thinking on my part? Is it secularism or patriarchy that have shifted the ethical bedrock of our culture towards rapacious individualism and away from the values of respect and inclusiveness?

These wider existential questions become more conscious for us in the aftermath of narcabuse. The question, "Who am I?" is another pattern that appears in the narcabuse online community. Gaslighting, shifting goalposts, and pathological lying can do that to a person, creating massive insecurity and self-doubt.

The antidote lies in courage and accountability. We can't solve the world's problems or change the people around us, but we can decide one simple thing, step by step, day by day: What kind of person do I want to be now? Shift our focus from the suffering of betrayal and loss to our own personal authenticity.

"Stop playing the blame game." "Stop playing the victim." "Get over it." In my experience over a lifetime, these are phrases used by people who have just wronged us in some way. Refusing accountability for their part in a dilemma, they are shifting blame and shame onto the wronged party. The cause of the issue then remains completely unexamined.

It might be as simple as them asking, "No, how are you really?" Pushing, needling for an honest, articulate answer beyond the polite, "I'm fine, thank you," that you first gave. Then reeling with shock and aversion when you mistake their needling as an invitation to share. Turns out they only asked because of their self-image as a good listener or a kind person. But they didn't genuinely want to hear you say, "Well, he did everything in his power to destroy me, and now I am staying on my friend's couch, applying for jobs and getting nowhere, living on welfare and trying to sort out the debts he left me with." Nobody, almost nobody wants to hear that, except other survivors or healers devoted to psychological and emotional abuse. And we find them online. We find our recovery tribe online, more so than in our community.

Anyone who says the taboo around mental health conditions has lifted in 2018 is expressing wishful thinking, certainly in Australia. As much as the odd footballer or celebrity or public figure might bravely resign, announcing their struggle with PTSD or mental health issues, there is still a great deal of suspicion, disapproval, and judgement out there in the community, especially conservative, stoic, rural communities. There is an undercurrent of distaste for people who succumb to mental illness, as if it were contagious or a choice. And there is an entrenched attitude that people with physical illness are more worthy of compassion. Fraudsters, abusers, and drunk drivers now claim PTSD as mitigating circumstances for their misdemeanours. That doesn't really help with perceptions of either the condition or those of us struggling with it.

In the early aftermath, many survivors experience an overwhelming need to express their pain. We temporarily become oversharers. We are simply incredulous that the man we would have given our life for on Monday turns and attacks us, steals from us, lies about us on Tuesday (and every day thereafter for a long as we stay in contact). We are trying to put into words the complicated matrix of manipulation that has us trapped and disempowered, and we discover a whole new vernacular that is not widely shared: gaslighting, triangulation, love-bombing, goading, blame-shifting, projection, psychopath. Who knew the meaning of any of these terms before they were victimised?

It's an awful lot to integrate alone. Narcissistic abuse syndrome is not yet a thing, so we are suddenly faced with misunderstanding and disbelief, just when we need to be heard. Like autism, postnatal depression, and veteran's PTSD once were, our condition is not yet recognised as a syndrome that is causal in nature. People think it's about us, when it's really about *what happened to us*.

Scepticism was overwhelmingly the response of the people around me in my aftermath, family, friends (with precious few exceptions). Hundreds of other covert abuse victims report the same experience: victim-blaming while we desperately try to find ways to take personal responsibility and find the middle ground of mutual causation. "It just didn't work out" cannot satisfy the moral injury of comprehensive betrayal by a conscienceless individual. Normal avenues to closure aren't available to us. It's simply not possible to shrug it off as just one of those things or to forgive and forget (or "consciously uncouple").

It is not so much the fact that we won't be accountable for our mistakes, but that we don't wish to accept that we've been used and disposed of. As much as being heard is the first tiny step towards recovery, figuring out blame and accountability is the most pressing confusion after sudden abandonment and years or months of hidden power and control.

While we are busy figuring out what the hell just happened and who is really to blame, we can miss the fact that it is the residual rage, fear, grief, and other strong emotions that we now need to be accountable for, not what happened to bring them about. Accountability goes beyond blame or justification. It goes right to the heart of honesty. It requires us to face the things we'd rather turn our gaze from. Personal responsibility is what brings closure, not the apology, confession, or contrition we crave from our abuser. Personal responsibility is the middle way between blaming ourselves for everything and staying stuck in denial of the way things really are.

Abusive relationships have too much one-sided manipulation and deception involved for us to take 50 percent responsibility for our part in what happened. We can do that next time, whilst we take personal responsibility for there never being a next time. We have to face the unbearable truths of psychological manipulation, parasitic behaviour, trickery, and duplicity, all under the guise of love. We have to identify what is love and what isn't.

First up, we recognise that it is not so much his love that seduced and bonded us, but our own experience of loving and feeling loved. We must accept that we loved a false persona: the person he pretended to be, the person he really wanted to be and be seen to be. He hid the person he really was underneath, until his mask dropped. He didn't *have* an evil twin. He *was* the evil twin. We were never loved. We were used.

I challenge any mentally healthy person to deal with that one in a few months. Two, ten, twenty years of our lives, our kindness, our money, our energy were given to someone who attached no value to us beyond that of a vending machine, who used words of love and commitment that should never be used dishonestly, who took everything we had to give and then demanded more. "So *you* get over it, then!"

We can actively turn towards the love and compassion in our good hearts every time anger or hatred arises towards our abuser. We have no control over what arises. Thinking and feeling are automatic behaviours. But with training in mindful awareness, we can notice unpleasant thoughts and emotions and shift our concentration to the loving-kindness that still resides in our good hearts.

We are already experts at blaming ourselves. But personal responsibility is less about absorbing blame and punishing ourselves and more about accepting that this thing happened and figuring out how to take the sting out of it. It's very easy to collapse into aversion for the suffering we are now experiencing, to reel against it, to not want it, to avoid it, suppress it, and pretend it isn't there. This is the stoic "Keep calm and carry on" model most of us grew up with. Ignore it, and it will go away. Or try to shift the burden by oversharing with others. That's what shrinks are for, since most family and friend relationships these days don't provide this service like they once did.

Allowing the devastation to our personal circumstances and the suffering of heightened emotional states to just be there is what taking personal responsibility means. This takes courage, patience, and honesty. It's not something that is modelled very much in our culture. Blame, criticism, and revenge is more the norm, throwing the second punch, an eye for an eye, never admit liability. Or the Christian value of turning the other cheek, passively absorbing the next insult. There is nowhere else to go but forward. When we are going through hell, we just have to keep going.

There is a teaching in Buddhist philosophy to remind us how to transform bad circumstances into a path out of suffering. Counter-intuitively, it asks us to see things quite differently from the way we normally do. In each instance, the practice and growth of patience (in particular, refraining from knee-jerk reactions) support and inform the philosophy.

1.   Turn all mishaps into the path.

We strive to welcome suffering with strength, endurance, compassion, and dignity rather than anxiety, anger, or avoidance. This can be a massive undertaking when we are overwhelmed by PTSD. We hold this intention, and don't beat ourselves up when we fail. As we move deeper into recovery, this resilience becomes possible.

2.   Drive all blames into one.

Even if what happened is actually someone's fault, we can only take responsibility for how we move forward from here. Mindfulness of body and breathing is a good place to start this practice whenever unbearable emotions arise.

3. Be grateful.

Gratitude is the root of joy. Mindful concentration on gratitude for even the tiniest things left on our scorched-earth landscape leads us out of pain and towards the light.

4. See confusion as Buddha (a teacher), and practice emptiness.

The Buddhist concept of emptiness is difficult to grasp and even harder to explain. It is an experiential concept that arises from meditation practice. In meditation, we learn to slip below the confusion and to notice the moment-by-moment, impermanent nature of existence. Even in our misery and confusion, we can notice and accept that everything is just as it is here and now.

5. Do good, avoid evil, appreciate your craziness, pray for help.

Doing good means practicing daily from the authentic goodness of our hearts, going beyond normal politeness and actively experiencing the joy that doing good brings us (without hoping for reward or acclaim).

Avoiding evil means paying close attention to the ways we might do or say unkind things, taking greater care in our interactions with others (also staying away from bad influences, our abusers, difficult people, and bad habits).

Self-acceptance is perhaps the best description of this intention. Welcome in our own selfishness, resentment, and anger with kindness instead of judgement, allowing instead of aversion. We can begin to see our frailties and stupidities with good humour and forgive ourselves for having them.

Prayer, even if we don't believe in an omnipotent being, is a way of spending time with our deepest hopes and wishes for ourselves, others, and the world. Prayer cultivates goodwill. We pray to whatever we believe in for help, not to escape from personal responsibility. No man is an island. There are many more forces than we can control. As Shakespeare wrote, "There is more in Heaven and Earth, Horatio, than are dreamt of in your philosophy."

6. Whatever you meet is the path.

It is our responsibility to take everything that happens, that which is within our control and that which isn't, and transform it into acceptance that this is the path we are on. Even if it's not what we planned, it's what *is*. It's not that everything happens for a reason, but that we make reason from everything that happens to us.

> God, grant me the serenity to accept the things I cannot change,
> courage to change the things I can, and wisdom to know the difference.
>
> —Reinhold Niebuhr, *The Serenity Prayer*

Post-Traumatic Growth, Midterm Recovery

The Life-Changing Legacy of Loving a Narcopath: Life Rape

The deep moral injury of victimisation by an amoral predator changes a survivor's psyche forever. The psychological abuser undermines a survivor's sense of self. We no longer recognise ourselves. We can feel utterly broken, a shell of our former selves. The victim must journey into hell, hit rock bottom, and climb out the other side in a way that simply isn't present in a normal break-up. By the time the mask of a narcopath drops, the damage to every sphere of a victim's life becomes apparent. Victims of narcissistic abuse syndrome must come to terms with life rape. Recovery is an opportunity for complete transformation.

Psychopaths, protected by their extraordinarily charming public masks, covertly undermine the victim's core values, the fundamental principles upon which a personality is built from around age four, by violating the moral codes that create a peaceful, sustainable, and successful society. Humans depend on cooperation in our interdependent, mutually beneficial interpersonal relationships. It's what drives society. So living with a deeply duplicitous person who has already established themselves as a soulmate but who lies, slanders, manipulates, triangulates, and gaslights cuts deeper and deeper wounds into the soul of the victim. The legacy for victims is a shake-up of their core values. This ultimately leads to a new and precious awareness of just how central and important our moral code is. Often, this is all we can hold onto, as everything around us is eroded by the psychopath. We must hold tight to our own moral and ethical principles.

Ancient cultures labelled psychopaths soul thieves, and shamanic healing was aimed at restoring the soul of the victim.

Living with a Vow

Living with ethical vows is a choice that provides security and safety for many people. Religious, marital, and secular vows provide a safety net, a framework for living, not to mention happiness. Most of us feel good when we do good. The very brave among us can feel good about being honest even when it does us harm. The foolish among us (that's most of us folks) can feel secure in the belief that others mean us no harm, particularly those who proclaim to love us the most.

But narcopaths have callous disregard or take gratification from the pain they cause others. Coming to terms with the devastation a psychopath leaves in his path means coming to terms with the fact that evil exists, that we can love people who actively harm others. Not all others, just their intimate others. This can be extraordinarily hard to accept for those raised in close-knit, cooperative families or communities, where psychopathic traits are suppressed by the pressure to conform. Most of us can understand that we can love someone who doesn't love us back. But to love someone who hates us? Despises us? Has nothing but contempt for us as human beings? That can blow your mind.

Buddhist ethics—discerning right from wrong—is based on the simplest of principles. If it hurts when someone else does it to us, then we vow to refrain from doing this to others. Like medical ethics, our first aim is to do no harm. Whilst we have learned that doing no harm does not necessarily mean others will not harm us, it is a simple vow to live by, as thoughts of revenge or retaliation arise.

We might prefer to develop our own personal vow to replace those annihilated by the narcopath, to provide a lantern in our passage through darkness.

Do No Harm: The Balm of Good Intention

The aftermath of narcabuse can be the very definition of groundlessness. We feel as if nothing makes any sense any more. Our world collapsed and turned upside down, leaving us struggling to figure out which way is up. Even as we struggle with our composure and limiting our maladaptive coping responses, the knowledge that our intentions are pure can make us feel better about ourselves.

Early in the trauma, we were rendered powerless by the damage to our safety, security, and self-love; we were battered by the storm. But once we strengthen our personal agency, build our courage, find our safety again, regain some self-love, and learn to live with groundlessness a bit better, the urge towards rectification strikes. From the fruitless undermining process of damage control, through *no contact*, we can begin to restore what has been lost to the narcopath; we begin to heal our wounded souls.

The intention to do no harm is a good place to start, if for no other reason than that it reacquaints us with our own good hearts. We start in our own backyard. If we can't change the world in one go, we can simply attend to our own little lives, from the inside out. I think we all know that small gestures of kindness or generosity towards others give us a warm glow inside.

Our new habit of being kind and generous to ourselves first—applying our own oxygen mask before we try to help others—has hopefully become more comfortable by now. We reduced our tendency to beat ourselves up for failing, learnt that other people's happiness is not our responsibility, and accepted that no one is responsible for our happiness, either. We're moving well in the direction of standing on our own two feet after abandonment. We are starting to see tiny green shoots in the scorched earth left around us.

We now have very personal and intimate experience of the deep damage that psychological abuse can do. So now more than ever, we can appreciate the personal contribution we make to a peaceful world by refraining from doing these things ourselves. Hopefully by now, we also realise how a reduction in our own aggression, confusion, self-blame, and fear changes the dynamic of our day-to-day lives. Our growing awareness—mindfulness—helps us create the internal space and energy to venture out into the world with greater confidence. By now, we have also accepted the hard truth that we just aren't the same person we were before our trauma. And that's okay.

Most people are blithely unaware of the harm they do. The truth is, in this life, there will be times when people harm us and times when we harm others. What matters most is our intention.

Harmful intent = harmful outcome.

Never apologise for having high standards.
People who really want to be in your life will rise up to meet them.

—Pinterest

Ethical Guidelines for Good Character: The Ten Paramitas

Talking about good character is always going to end up sounding like moralising from a pulpit (at least, when I try to do it), and modern individualists sometimes have a huge aversion to any references to ethical behaviour as being "telling me how to live my life." And yet, thousands upon thousands of people raised in a secular culture are out there searching for ways to feel better about themselves and fill the hole of dissatisfaction at the core of their being. Thousands more have become disillusioned with their churches due to a series of scandals and hypocrisy. Psychologists are trained not to give advice but rather provide tools for their clients to find their own way in the dark. So if we've done the best we can all our lives and still end up lonely, lost and miserable, what then?

Being a good person is a motivator for only a very few. The bullies now occupying the pulpits of our press, politics, and corporations are in the habit of nipping the work of do-gooders in the bud with mocking comments about "playing the violin" or just "mwah mwah." The meek amongst us are likely to duck away from the battle and bury our light under a bushel. Most often, doing the right thing is also doing the hardest thing and then bearing the harsh consequences. It takes courage to do what our conscience dictates, vote for kindness and compassion, admit it when we get things wrong, and experience growth through the hard knocks that come with it, especially when the world now seems to be very confused about what is right and what is wrong.

It is people of good character who get trodden underfoot by people of bad character; people with a character disorder. Perhaps it was ever thus. And it is my observation that it is people of good character (but with unresolved insecurities) who are most at risk of narcabuse. People of good character usually don't end up at the top of the tree. Dr Hare estimates that psychopaths occupy around 45 percent of top layers of corporations. When he first brought out his checklist for assessing psychopathy, he was actively approached by numerous corporations in the hope of recruiting these zero-empathy, amoral people. I found no statistics about the number of narcissists at the top of the showbiz tree or the number of sociopaths amongst wealthy property developers, but I think we can guess.

My contention throughout this book is that the antidote to personal annihilation and character assassination by a narcopath is to turn away from the abuse and back towards our own good heart, our own good character. Building a post-traumatic life, behaviours and reputation for ourselves as people of good character fills the void left by narcabuse and creates a solid new foundation. At its simplest, it is refraining from lying, stealing, cheating on our partners, and spreading gossip, since we now know how much pain and dysfunction this can cause. This implies giving up any number of bad habits that we have unconsciously acquired because we think everybody is doing it. Everybody lies; seventeen times a day on average, according to psychological research. Everybody steals the office stationery. Everybody has affairs with married people. Everybody gossips. Everybody judges, criticises, and indulges in nasty dehumanising humour.

So how good does it feel to catch yourself about to do any of those things that "everybody does" and make a healthier choice? It feels great is how it feels. It feels like we are contributing to a happier, more peaceful, and cooperative world. And as narcabuse victims, we love to cooperate, to please people. So now, we shift focus and learn to please ourselves. It's not about anyone else. It's about our own souls, our own character-building. As long as we're not offering unsolicited advice left, right, and centre and using our good character as a bludgeon, as long as we're not preaching from the high moral ground but just quietly choosing to take it, as long as we're treading the middle way every step we take, the cultivation of our good character will rescue us from the pit of despair our abuse sent us into.

Additionally, we find that this quest towards cultivating good character makes some people extremely uncomfortable, even when we refrain from advertising it. People whose bad behaviour we have formerly tolerated, saying, "Oh, that's just the way they are," will fall away. The bad influences will fall away. And if those people are in our families, their bad behaviour will begin to change as our quiet example seeps into our everyday lives. Instead of choosing to lie to us because we are gullible, people will make different choices in the face of our authenticity. Because we are authentically standing inside our own power, we are moment-to-moment more powerful than those who are not. How about that for a concept? The difference between our preabuse good character that attracted the manipulators and exploiters and our fledgling post-traumatic good character is our own awareness. Our mindfulness training has us noticing what we previously took for granted.

When we return to our own basic decency, our own good heart, and are mindful of our own good character, the people, circumstances, and conditions around us slowly start to look more like the safety and solid ground we so crave after narcabuse. Again, it's not about adopting radical moralism. It's not about making others wrong and us right. It's about adopting radical self-care. Because it relieves our own suffering.

The Buddhist guidelines for the practices that lead to liberation from suffering are no doubt similar to many ancient traditions. When you sit in a Buddhist meditation room, you can rest assured that you are surrounded by people who understand the benefits of building good character so as to liberate themselves and those around them from suffering.

These are the Ten Paramitas:

1. Generosity
2. Moral conduct
3. Renunciation (leading a simple life)

4. Wisdom
5. Energy
6. Patience
7. Truthfulness
8. Determination (perseverance)
9. Loving-kindness
10. Equanimity (greeting triumph and disaster just the same)

Think about it.

When you read these words, do they nourish your soul?

Or do they make you go, "Mwah, mwah"?

Note: Rudyard Kipling has been discredited in the modern age. The fact that he is now considered a pariah is not sufficient for me to leave out this seminal poem, which has served to inspire so many before us and most of which is surprisingly relevant to survivors of narcabuse.

> If you can keep your head when all about you
> Are losing theirs and blaming it on you,
> If you can trust yourself when all men doubt you,
> But make allowance for their doubting too;
> If you can wait and not be tired by waiting,
> Or being lied about, don't deal in lies,
> Or being hated, don't give way to hating,
> And yet don't look too good, nor talk too wise:
>
> If you can dream—and not make dreams your master;
> If you can think—and not make thoughts your aim;
> If you can meet with Triumph and Disaster
> And treat those two impostors just the same;
> If you can bear to hear the truth you've spoken
> Twisted by knaves to make a trap for fools,
> Or watch the things you gave your life to, broken,
> And stoop and build 'em up with worn-out tools:

If you can make one heap of all your winnings
And risk it on one turn of pitch-and-toss,
And lose, and start again at your beginnings
And never breathe a word about your loss;
If you can force your heart and nerve and sinew
To serve your turn long after they are gone,
And so hold on when there is nothing in you
Except the Will which says to them: "Hold on!"

If you can talk with crowds and keep your virtue,
Or walk with Kings—nor lose the common touch,
If neither foes nor loving friends can hurt you,
If all men count with you, but none too much;
If you can fill the unforgiving minute
With sixty seconds' worth of distance run,
Yours is the Earth and everything that's in it,
And—which is more—you'll be a Man, my son!

—Rudyard Kipling, *If*

Ask the Experts

Brach, Tara (2003), *Radical Acceptance: Embracing Your Life with the Heart of a Buddha.* Bantam Books.

Mackenzie, Jackson (2015), *Psychopath Free (Expanded Edition): Recovering from Emotionally Abusive Relationships with Narcissists, Sociopaths, and Other Toxic People.* Berkeley.

The Self-Acceptance Project. (n.d.)
http://live.soundstrue.com/selfacceptance/

McLeod, Melvin, *The Wisdom of Anger.*
https://www.lionsroar.com/the-wisdom-of-anger

Chapter 8

BOUNDARIES: BEFORE AND AFTER

A lot of CBT counsellors want us to address the issues of boundaries and assertiveness. There is a strong push in Western psychology that inherently blames the victim, that assumes that we victims of narcabuse are weak, co-dependent, malleable figures. Rendered exhausted and disempowered by our ordeal, we might go along with this theory and blame ourselves too.

A tiny assumption in this logical theory is that our weak boundaries were entirely to blame for our devaluation and abuse by the narcopath. If we had somehow stood up for ourselves, none of this would have happened.

Nothing could be further from the whole story. Whilst it may be true that if we had stood up for ourselves earlier, he might have discarded us sooner, we were being manipulated, so it was never us setting the agenda. Our boundary-setting and assertiveness were simply ignored.

For the theoretical application of assertiveness and boundary training to work, there must also be the underlying fact that the other party cares about how their behaviour affects us. Not only does a narcopath not care, but his profound narcissism means that he instantaneously interprets disagreement, unhappiness, or expressing opinions that differ from his as *abusive to him*. The narcissist is so deeply embedded in his inflated ego that he can only tolerate sycophants (pocket pissers and arse-lickers in Aussie lingo) within his orbit. And it's not just a male ego thing (you know, the egos we are conditioned to protect from a young age). It's not normal.

He simply does not understand compromise. Like a child, he *must* have his own way in every interaction. The only methods he understands are the unhealthy ones he uses: stonewalling, ghosting, triangulation, slander, lies, and deception. And who wants to use all that in defence of ourselves? We couldn't, even if we tried. It is not possible to outmanipulate a manipulator, though you will find advice to this effect online. It only leads to vindictive attacks by the narcopath, who is prepared to stoop lower than any good-hearted person would stoop.

The thing about compromise and boundary-setting with a narcopath is that he doesn't give a damn about our point of view because he knows he can manipulate us and everyone around us to get what he wants, anyway. He will say whatever we want to hear, make any verbal commitment we like, agree to any compromise plan that makes him look like an angel, but then totally disregard the deal, deny the conversation ever took place, and whitewash over the whole issue with blame, insult, and emotional blackmail that might continue in subtle and not-so-subtle ways until the end of days.

Sure, we all like to surround ourselves with people who share our values, our ideas of common sense, our faith, our addictions, or our politics. But a narcopath believes he should have our total obedience, our complete submission, our absolute agreement, and loyalty to the point of adulation. He demands it. Anything less, he deems abusive, vile, vicious, or calculated to upset him. Not only does he disrespect us; he feels contempt for us. The only compromise he will settle for is one in which he wins and we lose. No compromise at all. You're fired! It's not normal.

Living with this kind of behaviour from someone to whom we are bonded by love and loyalty is incrementally destructive. It creates deep moral wounds in the victim, who has learned to tolerate more and more wounding over time. We are not, in fact, weak like we beat ourselves up for being, but incredibly strong, having learned to bear more and more weight until it finally broke us (or we woke up and got out before it did). Once we recover from exhaustion, it is this very strength that will drive us to recovery.

Our job moving forward from abusive manipulation is not so much to work out how we could have asserted clearer boundaries or been more skilled negotiators with the narcopath, but to decide what behaviour we will and won't tolerate from everyone around us moving forward. The people around us can keep us trapped in a snare of our own making.

We might recognise that we have wasted a lot of energy over a lifetime, trying to appease and please others, reinforcing our own negative self-image as a doormat or positive self-image as a compromiser. But rather than allow ourselves to be consumed by negative self-talk about our weak boundaries or co-dependency, we need to meet ourselves midway. We simply acknowledge that we have more to learn about how to set strong yet flexible boundaries in order to prevent others riding roughshod over us again.

So moving forward with assertiveness and boundary-setting, what *is* normal?

As we rehearse the setting of new boundaries in all our relationships in the aftermath, we learn that many people are deeply in denial about their own behaviour. Their own ego-bound self-image gets in the way of an honest assessment of how their behaviour really affects others. It is a common human affliction. When we assert new rules to our relationships, people can kick like mules.

There are some, of course, who welcome honest feedback and strive towards being steadfast friends.

Many people are slack at accountability, not just narcopaths. Many people will stonewall or attack the messenger, rather than acknowledge their own part and engage in a respectful exchange about compromise. Setting boundaries reveals the true colours of the people around us. For many people, change is intolerable. And their ego or self-image is the armour they wear to protect themselves against life's difficulties. The most skilful negotiating language in the world will not stop them digging into their trenches and fortifying their rightness. And it is these kinds of confrontations that we might have avoided throughout our lives. This, we can take responsibility for now, alongside a very deep responsibility for our own accountability and integrity.

A moral dilemma requires a moral antidote.

Observe.
Refrain.
Abstain.
Decline.
Wait.
Listen.
Be still.
Be in silence.
Be alone.

—narcissisticsociopath.net

How to Restore Boundaries Annihilated by Narcabuse

Every narcabuse writer talks about building better personal boundaries in the aftermath. The bottom line about boundaries is the word *personal*. Boundaries are for inviting in what is good for us and keeping out what hurts us. Boundaries are about what we do and don't want, moving forward in our lives. Boundaries are about how we allow ourselves to be treated: what we will and won't tolerate from other people. Boundaries are about standing up for ourselves, claiming our own power, asserting our right to choose.

There is an assumption floating around out there in shrink-land that the victims of psychological abuse were all subservient co-dependents so desperate for approval that they allowed themselves to be pushed around; this is not something we have to take on-board. In the early aftermath, we might allow ourselves to be convinced that if only we'd had stronger boundaries, we would never have been bullied or abused: something else for us to beat ourselves up about.

Please don't get caught up in the pervasive online rhetoric that labels us "co-dependent," as if it were a permanent fundamental trait that stains our character, rather than an understandable response to psychological manipulation from which we will recover. Please don't get stuck in self-blaming rumination about "self-love deficit" being the reason you were targeted. Every second Westerner suffers from self-love deficit. Mindful self-compassion training is the antidote to this pervasive condition.

The narcopath treats the personal needs and boundaries of others with callous disregard. They simply don't matter to him, unlike a person of normal empathy. When our boundaries were ignored, we might have naturally allowed some slack here and there. Every inch we gave him, he took a mile, at first covertly and eventually overtly. He just didn't care. Every incidence of having our boundaries overlooked slowly chipped away at our safety net. We might have fought back at being disregarded with any number of tactics, from negotiation to aggression, none of which can work, because none of that matters to a narcopath. Only getting his own way, winning, and being seen to be a hero does.

I believe we need to drop this story. Drop it by accepting it. Reject the "You have nobody to blame but yourself" rhetoric and settle for the fact that we were manipulated. Again, it's not about blame, it's about *causation*. I believe the most patient, assertive, competent, and independent people can be beaten down by psychological abuse and manipulation. The military knows this. Espionage organisations know this. Cambridge Analytica (propagandists and misinformation specialists) know this. I believe we need to focus on building ourselves up again to be that confident, assertive person, free from the newfound rage and shame of trauma, and the bitterness and resentment at allowing our boundaries to be eroded in the name of loving compromise. Now is the time to build new boundaries to protect the wounds the narcopath inflicted on us.

It is time to honour the wounds we now carry until they heal. It is a time to notice our new over-the-top emotional triggers and respect our need for avoidance. If we now have man-fear, or drunk-fear, or authority-fear, or fear of crowds or locations with no way out, or being stolen from or lied to, why shouldn't we plan ahead and avoid these things? It's not permanent. Who cares if it makes us look neurotic? We *are* neurotic. We are traumatised. We feel things very deeply, and now our nerves are jangling 24/7. It's our job to find refuge and lick our wounds. We don't have to beat ourselves up about being an antisocial loser or a [insert your preferred derogatory term here]. This stage will pass. One day, this great journey of loss will feel like liberation.

Here are a few boundary considerations for a new post-traumatic landscape:

- Do we fail to speak up when we feel bullied, mistreated, or overlooked?
- Do we give way more time or effort than we'd really prefer?
- Do we exhaust ourselves trying to impress or please others?
- Subsequent to the above, do we feel used or taken for granted by others?
- Do we attract people (in addition to narcopaths) who try to dominate or control us?
- Do we stay silent when we see someone else being mistreated?
- Do we pretend to agree with someone we actually disagree with?
- Are we surrounded by energy vampires (people who suck us dry emotionally, physically, or psychologically)?
- Do we pick up the slack of our co-workers and do their work for them?
- Do we overshare with others even after we've recovered from narcabuse?
- Do we have a close working awareness of our own needs for rest, self-care, and stress mitigation?
- Do we capitulate to the demands of others to the point of exhaustion, just to avoid possible conflict?
- Do we feel selfish if we assert our own needs?
- Do we fear losing friends if we are open and honest about our needs?
- Do we fear being labelled a nasty bitch (or some other misogynistic term) if we don't allow others to boss us around?
- Do we fear the backlash if we hold others to account for their poor behaviour?

If the answer to any of the above is yes, then there's room to consider finding the courage to set new boundaries moving forward out of narcabuse. Change is not easy. The truth is, we *will* lose friends over new boundaries. There will be backlash. But the fear that we will hurt others cannot hold us back any longer from the urgent and pressing need to rid ourselves of people who drag us down, hold us back, make us feel small and worthless. By doing this as respectfully and fairly as we can, we make room for quality people who lift us up, encourage us, inspire us, role model a better way of being for us, teach us, help us grow.

The Suffering of Change

The suffering of change is one of the three basic forms of suffering, according to Buddhist philosophy (the other two are the suffering of pain, old age, and death; and existential suffering). Fear of change is what drives conservatism, xenophobia, nationalism, and most other "-isms." Change requires courage, patience, and faith that what we are doing is right, every step of the way.

Mindfulness practice is about identifying our own individual sufferings and their causes. Changing our behaviour will ease our suffering. Tweaking our personal boundaries as we notice them violated will help us regain our personal agency. How do we recognise boundary violations when our boundary antennae have been badly damaged by narcabuse? We start by recognising our own strong emotions.

Sadness tells us we have already lost something and asks us to retreat. Fear also alerts us to danger, acting as an early warning system. Anger is a sign that a boundary has been violated; it screams, "Tread carefully!"

We might be shocked by the amount of rage we feel when we start to set boundaries. A lot of this rage is old anger, anger that has accumulated from the multiple boundary violations in our past, years of nos that were never respected. Like an iceberg, the anger we feel at a new boundary violation is just the tip sitting on a huge mass of previous violations. The thing is, it is *our* iceberg. We can either continue to sit on it, suppress it, or we can face it, unpack it, deal with it, unravel it, endure the suffering of change.

It is fair to say that new boundary setters can carry an energy of anger that is quite off-putting to others for a while. Our anger can be set on a hair trigger, set off by the slightest offence. But this is temporary. We need to expect this reactive period and endure it. Effective boundaries do not attack or harm anyone. They simply prevent the violation of our precious good hearts. It is important to stick with our newfound commitment to boundaries and not submit to our internal or external critics, who would shame us back into their comfort zones. If we are careful about defending our boundaries in non-violent language, we may still offend. We may make people uncomfortable or defensive, but our new boundaries will not seriously injure anyone.

Those who accept our boundaries will love our opinions, our differentness, our otherness, our separateness. Those who arc up at our boundaries are telling us they will only accept our compliance, our yes but not our no. We will either end up with greater intimacy and respect in our relationships or find that there was little there to begin with.

Social Stocktake

One of the universally reported repercussions of narcabuse is the devastation of losing family and friends, either by pushing people away or being dumped. If you thought it was only you, your family, your friends, it isn't. It's a thing. Just like narcissistic abuse syndrome is a thing, not yet fully recognised by our shrinks and our culture in 2018.

This readjustment of networks and communities is also a factor in the pursuit of spiritual enlightenment. That has been a thing for thousands of years. Dedicated practitioners of meditation also find the entire landscape of their lives shifting, perhaps by more gentle and gradual choice, a gradual awakening. For many narcabuse victims, the shift is sudden; it can feel out of control and traumatising. And it can also make us look like the bad guy, especially with the aid of the narcopath's smear campaign. And especially when we unskilfully try to set boundaries with harsh, aggressive language while we are in the highly reactive stage of recovery.

We will make mistakes. None of us is perfect. Rather than wallow in shame at having used the wrong words and caused offence, we can let ourselves off the hook here. Forgive ourselves for our fumbling attempts at boundary-setting. Narcabuse is the perfect storm, and we are right in the middle of it, trying to figure out how to get out. Others don't see the matrix of abuse. It is our private matrix, shared only with the abuser who created it. We have been metaphorically bound and gagged. Anyone would struggle and cry out.

I can only reassure you from my lived experience that getting through that pain leads to enormous freedom, a greater sense of self-determination, and autonomy. The meme "I am losing everybody while I find myself" applies. At first, it feels like social isolation (and it is), but with time, it begins to feel like liberation. Burning bridges is one way we can stop the past following us over the vast chasm we must cross in our hero's journey. Very few are going to want to take that journey with us. And there will be many we simply don't want by our side as we take it. It is essentially a solitary journey.

Accepting this is a great place from which to start the journey.

I firmly believe that one day, everybody will understand that narcissistic abuse syndrome (as coined by the online recovery community) is a thing, that it is the death of a thousand cuts. We already know this because we have experienced it. But it's invisible to the outside eye. Covert abuse is hidden, obviously. Emotional, psychological, moral, social, and spiritual abuse cannot be proved in the same way financial or physical abuse can, like rape in marriage: one person's word against another's. Victim-blaming and women-blaming are deep undercurrents in Western culture, as we soon discover for ourselves. Narcabuse is a spiritual and feminist awakening. We are brutally shaken out of our denial and stunned into a rebirth.

A rebirth is an opportunity for us to start again as resilient, mature adults. The potential for post-traumatic growth is huge. This time, it is about personal choice and responsibility. As much as narcabuse leaves us feeling hopeless and helpless —utterly disempowered—it also levels our playing field. The horror of feeling our lives plundered and our souls raped will eventually give way to relief and the joy of having a tribe who stand shoulder to shoulder with us, a tribe who appreciate us just as we are, offer us love without condition, whose values resonate with our own, and who are fully grown adults capable of honesty, integrity, and accountability.

Have faith that this rebirth will happen in time. The narcabuse online community is too big to be ignored by our culture much longer, and there are too many testimonials from survivors who are now thriving for us to ignore them. If they can do it, we can. We can find a way. We can recover.

Soon after the abandonment (or our flight from narcabuse), some of us are faced with victim-blaming, comprehensive criticism, and minor betrayals by those around us. The shock and trauma of victim-blaming alone is enough to force anyone to armour up and build temporary walls of self-protection to keep the enemy out. For those from narcissistic or scapegoating families, this painful necessity can prevent us from turning our attention to compassionate self-care; we may stumble into the pitfall of self-blame. Many of us find ourselves fighting battles on every front as the vultures descend to pick over the carcass of the relationship. There are demands from lawyers, Realtors, children, parents, siblings, the narcopath, and his enablers. The pressure-cooker can be so overwhelming as to tip even the strongest of us into trauma.

Because we have to adjust to living with "I don't know" as the answer to just about everything soon after the abandonment, we can be overly susceptible to bad advice at this time. We grasp at straws. We desperately want to know why. Why did he leave with no warning, just when we achieved a long-awaited goal, or just when I got sick with cancer and needed him most? Why does he say he loves me, when everything he does proclaims the opposite? Why does he hate me so much, when I have been so loving, understanding, and supportive? Why did he lie about his life story, his financial situation, his plans for the future? Why are his friends and family treating me like I'm the bad guy? There will be plenty of advice about revenge, warning the next host, or exposing the narcissist on Facebook. These are all bad ideas because they lead to vicious covert retribution from the narcopath.

There are the rats who desert the sinking ship immediately. People to whom we were kind, generous, hospitable are suddenly shunning us in the street and the supermarket. The phone stops ringing and our cries for help go unanswered. Just when we feel we cannot save ourselves from drowning, there are people who keep their feet firmly on our heads to keep us under. People imagine themselves expert because they have been through a normal divorce, or they believe themselves wise, or simply because they believe we should take their advice since they are our elders or betters. In the early aftermath, whilst still in shock and grief, most of us are bombarded with conflicting advice in the same way a pregnant woman is.

In my experience of total world collapse, it's not the rats we need to be wary of as we strive to restore a life utterly devastated by betrayal. They've already gone. It's the people who put themselves forward as listeners, helpers, advice-givers. Some of these people are more invested in being seen to be a good person than in genuine and patient compassion (including professional counsellors). They can become pushy and patriarchal, stepping into the breach with insistent intensity (borderline bullying) and get very angry if we don't follow their ignorant advice. They soon tire of our post-traumatic symptoms and start demanding that we return to our happy outgoing selves or else: "Daily floggings will end when morale improves."

They judge us according to cultural ideals of the resilient pioneer who loses everything in a bushfire, stoically refuses to break down, and then bounces back by getting a menial job and living in a tent for ten years, refusing help from anyone. We Aussies love those underdog stories, those pioneering myths. These judgers want to get on with their lives and have everything return to the way it was before: after a month, six months, a year, three years. If we are still suffering anxiety symptoms, nightmares, and panic attacks after a few years, they convince themselves we are refusing to heal, that we are wilfully ignoring the unhelpful help and unsupportive support they have so magnanimously given us. Sadly, it is these people we need to get out of our lives too, because they are never going to get it.

I was surprised to discover that it wasn't just me who experienced a deluge of chaotic and disastrous happenings in the year after the abandonment.

It was not all the result of the smear campaign, which had far-reaching consequences to my social and professional lives, nor entirely the result of being left homeless, crippled, broke, and struggling to contain symptoms of PTSD. More like an extraordinary rip in the fabric of the universe, where we have fallen into hell and everything that could go wrong does go wrong. Utter chaos. It was this phenomenon that led me finally to overcome my scepticism about human energy or spirit.

The darker my world became after narcabuse, the more dark experiences seemed to flood my existence. The more life crises I had to handle, the more appeared on my horizon. The greater weight I had to bear, the more weight was heaped upon me, long after the straw had already broken the camel's back. These happenings went far beyond logical explanation, and coincidence became too unsatisfactory an explanation to accept any longer. The more doors I knocked on, the more were slammed in my face. The more effort I made to recover, the deeper the wounds cut. It was uncanny. It seemed to be about something we can't see, we are sceptical about, we deny even. It seemed to be about *energy*.

There is absolutely nothing normal about a narcopathic break-up.

Backlash

> No man is more hated than he who tells the truth.
>
> —Plato, Pinterest

The really great takeaway from the existential threats an intimate relationship with a narcopath presents is the impetus for a thorough stocktake of our own core values and habitual patterns. Whilst none of us may want to become saints, a shift in focus to cultivating our own good hearts is a step in the right direction. Who could argue otherwise? We are morally wounded because our goodness and innocence were plundered: twisted around and used against us. But if we shift our focus, little by little, day by day, from those wounds, from how extensively we have been wronged, and back to nurturing those core values, a shift begins to happen.

Facing our own demons and changing our habitual behaviour takes an enormous amount of courage. As Yeats said, "It takes more courage to examine the dark corners of your own soul than it does for a soldier to fight on the battlefield." A journey through the dark night of the soul is a hero's journey. Dealing with the backlash we experience when we set new boundaries with people—when we make clear by our words and actions what we will and won't tolerate from them—also takes courage. The result can be extremely painful.

Backlash is to be expected in gigantic proportions from the narcopath, who will use a sledgehammer to crack a walnut, but also from other friends and associates, who are used to us being a certain way and are deeply invested in the status quo, in things being as they always were, in us being the agreeable, compliant doormat who lets things slide. They didn't befriend the person who is now morphing into a stronger, more authentic version of herself. They attached themselves to the person we were before narcabuse, and that person has been annihilated, at least on the surface. That person is inevitably rearranged, put back together differently, stronger, more resilient, more compassionate. That person can be very threatening to people who liked the old version of you.

Take the most banal of examples. If a friend never returns our calls or continually cancels at the last minute because something better has come up, and it pisses us off, we can give ourselves permission to stop communicating. Even though we know these behaviours are normalised in a world where everybody is too busy for everybody else. We can stop making excuses for other people and start looking after *ourselves*. We can give ourselves permission not to go to the concert with everybody else or to skip the family lunch with a racist homophobic old uncle. The world is not going to end if we avoid things for a while. If we cancel our Facebook account, don't check our emails for days, screen our phone calls, don't watch the TV news, nothing is going to happen, except greater peace and calm in our post-traumatic lives.

You never know. You might find you like it and keep some of these new boundaries, moving out of surviving and into thriving again. They might become the foundations for your new life. Because as we start to honour our own needs and our own worth again, we find less need for validation and approval from other people. We won't need others to accept us because we've learned to accept ourselves, warts and all. We've been honest, opened up our good hearts, faced our demons, and have learned to like ourselves again (or for the first time in our lives). We can erect whatever weird and wonderful boundaries we like.

Take, as an example, that friend who never returns calls and frequently cancels at the last minute. We might express how this hurts us and bring about a change in their behaviour. Or we might simply stop calling and making plans with this friend, in the hope that they will miss us and start taking the initiative. If they don't, and the friendship wains and slips away, we will have gained. We'll now know for sure that it wasn't a mutual connection. We can grieve the loss, get over it, and create the space for real friendships to enter our lives.

If, when we try to express how our friend's behaviour hurts us, that same friend retaliates with personal attack, a long list of complaints against us, and victim-shaming about how they are fed up with our PTSD and they refuse to accommodate our trauma sensitivity any longer, then we know for sure that this person belongs in our past. We are already expert at blaming and shaming ourselves for our trauma. We don't need a team who applauds us for it.

Perhaps the most important but painful changes are the ones we crave in our families. It is extremely important in early recovery to avoid those who have controlled, scapegoated, or abused us in the past. We cannot expect them to change. We might have tried every form of communication, healthy and unhealthy, to overcome the dysfunction of a lifetime. Dealing with that dysfunction on a regular basis while we are traumatised is going to inhibit, if not prevent, our recovery. It is not DNA that defines family when we are struggling with narcabuse recovery. Rather, it is the people who stand by us, shoulder to shoulder, steadfast and unwavering, as we walk through hell.

True belonging is the spiritual practice of believing in and belonging to yourself so deeply that you can share your most authentic self with the world and find sacredness in both being a part of something and standing alone in the wilderness. True belonging doesn't require you to change who you are; it requires you to be who you are.

—Brené Brown, *Braving the Wilderness*

Warrior Path Affirmations Script

This is a time for moral courage.
This is a time for cutting away the old.
This is a time for letting go of regrets.
I cultivate self-respect.
I develop confidence in my new self.
I can cope with abuse because I believe in myself.
I can cope with betrayal.
I can see through deception.
I am sparing with my trust.
I balance instinct with critical thinking in assessing a situation or a person.
I trust my new knowledge and awareness.
I believe in myself.
I stand alone from now on.
I don't have to retreat from difficult situations.
I know when to fight and when to retreat.
I do the right thing, the honourable thing.
I am self-contained.
I face challenges with the strength of steel.
There will always be people who like me and people who don't.
What matters is my own behaviour, my own intention, my own heart and mind.
The right people gather round me.
I am my own hero.
I outmanoeuvre deceit.
I will survive and flourish.
I am honest and self-reliant.

I am brave and disciplined.
My willpower is stronger by the day.
From now on, I can.
I stand on my own two feet.
I stand my ground.
I am not a victim. I am in control.
Suffering is not permanent.
I rise above intrusive thoughts.
I believe in my honesty and goodness.
I am motivated, not manipulated.
I choose self-worth, not self-pity.
I protect myself, and then I help others.
I invoke the strength of body, mind, and spirit.
We all suffer. I persevere.
I believe in my courage and strength.
I rise above destructive emotions.

Ask the Experts

Brown, Brené (2017), *Braving the Wilderness: The Quest for True Belonging and the Courage to Stand Alone.* Penguin Random House.

Cloud, Dr Henry, and Townsend, Dr John (2017), *Boundaries: When to Say Yes, How to Say No to Take Control of Your Life.* Harper Collins.

Das, Lama Surya (2003), *Letting Go of the Person You Used to Be.* Broadway Books.

Chapter 9

HOW TO FACE OUR DEMONS

There are two kinds of suffering.
There is the suffering you run away from, which follows you everywhere.
And there is the suffering you face directly, and so become free.

—Ajahn Chah, Pinterest

Reminder: I am a lived-experience author and researcher. This is what I have learned. It is popular psychology, not clinical psychological advice. This chapter is intended to stimulate thought, not provide answers to the reader's individual circumstances.

Peeling the Onion

A man who lies to himself, and believes his own lies, becomes
unable to recognize truth, either in himself or in anyone else,
and he ends up losing respect for himself and for others. When
he has no respect for anyone, he can no longer love, and in
him, he yields to his impulses, indulges in the lowest form of
pleasure, and behaves in the end like an animal in satisfying his
vices. And it all comes from lying to others and to yourself.

—Fyodor Dostoyevsky, *The Brothers Karamazov*

I wouldn't have believed it if I hadn't seen it with my own eyes.

How often have you said that or heard it said? Is it true for you? Can you believe a thing if you haven't seen it with your own eyes? Can you believe the story of a woman's abuse if you can't see the black eye? Can you believe that celebrity is a kiddie fiddler, when you never saw it happen? But you saw him be harmless and daggy a million times. You think you know that guy. Easier to believe he's been wrongfully imprisoned. Can you believe that comedian lured women for meetings and then drugged them, raped them, and laughed at them when they threatened to tell? But you saw him be that funny adorable guy a thousand times. You think you know that guy. Easier to believe that fifty women over forty years are lying.

That way, we don't shatter our nice neat packaged impression of the world. We get to stay comfortable. Whatever media we were exposed to, whatever source we prefer and trust—particularly our own eyes—helps us package our beliefs into a tidy whole. Packing that belief away and layering proof upon proof over it as more evidence proves our position, and next thing, it's fact for us, truth for us. Discovering that our beliefs were founded on lies or false impressions to begin with is very unsettling. We'll hold tenaciously to the proof we believe we already have to shore up our position. This is how the world is according to me, myself, and I.

Some of those layered beliefs are buried deep in our unconscious now. We don't even know we have them. They underlie other beliefs and influence other decisions all our lives. Some of those beliefs are based on decisions we made at a time we can't even remember. When we were babies, crawlers, toddlers. Daddy came back from work angry, and we decide his anger was our fault for throwing our food from our high chair. Then we layer proof upon proof that we are to blame for men's anger. Mummy didn't come when we cried out from our cot. The parenting book told her not to pick us up every time we cried. So we decided that the person central to our world doesn't love us. And we unconsciously replace her time and time again with a central person who doesn't love us, just to prove our unconscious beliefs right. We get picked on and bullied at school because we are fat, bright, beautiful, gay, coloured, disabled, different. So we decide there is something fundamentally wrong with us, we'll never fit in, we don't belong. It makes us angry, sad, lonely, and depressed. Years later, all our lives, in fact, things happen at work, on a train, in the supermarket that echo those beliefs, and we feel the anger, sadness, loneliness all over again and don't even know why, thus proving there is something fundamentally wrong with us. Better hide it. Better pretend we are normal like everyone else.

That's (partly) how we build up our private picture of ourselves, our secret self-image, our personality strategy.

Or we build up a false public image that is more comfortable, a Facebook image. We all want to think of ourselves as loving, loveable, generous, humorous, kind. We all want others to think of us in that way. So we suppress the bits of ourselves we judge to be ugly, unacceptable, or inappropriate. We suppress our grief at funerals. We suppress our anger at work. We suppress our bitterness at Christmas lunch (until the wine kicks in). We hide our dislike of women, gays, disabled, homeless, other ethnicities, other religions. We look the other way, ignore them, both outside us and inside us. If we do the wrong thing—something that doesn't fit in to our ideal self-image—we find every way possible to justify our action to ourselves rather than atone and change. It makes it much easier next time we do the wrong thing. Instantaneous.

And then there is the extreme version, like the narcopath.

They tell a lie. They believe it. They deceive themselves. They attack the person they lied to. They set their own rules about what constitutes a bad lie and what is just a naughty fib. One is wrong, bad, harmful. The other justifiable, kind, thoughtful. Your bum doesn't look big in that. I never said that. I never forged your signature; you must be crazy. Nobody caught them out in the bad lie, so they're okay. They're fine. They're not a bad person for telling it. In fact, that bad lie can move across into the good lie column. Before they know it, they are a habitual liar. They lie. They justify it. They believe it. It happens in a nanosecond. Automatic. And nobody knows they lied, until eventually, one day, they get caught. But so many more never get caught out, and now each of us can see this with our very own eyes. Because it happened to us. Because they lied to us about everything, and then to everyone else about us.

We blame ourselves because we sometimes lie too. But while we can honestly admit this, the narcopath never can and never will. We can unpack our own habitual deceit and self-deceit. With self-compassion, we can honestly and courageously investigate these things and bring them up to consciousness, where we greet them with kindness, gentleness, and humour. We embrace our own shortcomings and accept that we are only human. At the same time, we come to see clearly that we are nothing like a narcopath. We can drop the self-blame and self-doubt. We recognise that we are conscientious about honesty, and we choose truth. When we turn to our good hearts and make honesty and the elimination of denial and self-deceit our intention, we experience phenomenal growth as human beings. We find courage and strength we never knew we had. We bravely take the strength and honesty that were used against us and stand, at last, solidly in our own power as women.

> Whatever we practice we will become. In this
> way we must rely on ourselves.
>
> —Jack Kornfield, *A Path with Heart*

So how do we get past our own ego and self-image, down to the person we really are under all that?

As we let go of old family expectations and pressures to conform to a certain way of being; as we start over like a child; as we purify our intentions and practice mindful self-compassion; as we stop running from truths we have been unable to accept; as we strengthen our loving-kindness, courage, and good character; as we simplify our lives and find refuge in our new boundaries, so we come into wholeness.

> The greatest achievement is selflessness.
> The greatest worth is self-mastery.
> The greatest purpose is seeking to serve others.
> The greatest precept is continual awareness.
> The greatest action is not conforming with the world's ways.

The greatest goodness is a peaceful mind.
The greatest effort is unattached to outcomes.
The greatest meditation is letting go.
The greatest wisdom is seeing through appearances.

—The Greatest Way, sayingimages.com

Healing the Soul

I love you, I am there for you, I will never leave you
are words that should never be lies.
Because that is how you tear a soul apart.

—narcissisticsociopath.net, Pinterest

There is a resounding cry throughout the narcissistic abuse online community that mostly resonates in an echo chamber: "My soul. Oh, my soul!" There is also something uniquely ridiculous (in my considered opinion) in only pursuing medically or scientifically based trauma-recovery methods. That is, trying to apply cognitive theory and happy pills alone to heal a damaged soul, the idea that victims will eventually talk or think their way out of the matrix of abuse. Or explaining the unbearable pain of narcabuse solely by the somatic discoveries of neuro-science or endocrinology. And yet it is the talk therapies and science that we naturally reach for in the West, ignoring the fact that people believe they have a soul which has been irreparably damaged, evidenced by stories of victims who take decades to recover, trying to locate their own souls so they can heal them.

Maybe it's because of the seemingly lunatic ideas that pepper the discourse, that narcopaths are vampires that suck out our souls and infect us with their own disease, the ancient superstitions that narcopaths are soul thieves or possessed by demons. It could be the lingering exhaustion from struggling with nagging psychological and emotional symptoms of PTSD on top of the burnout already present from trying to wrangle a relationship with someone incapable of empathy or understanding, the sheer enormity of life rape, or the fact that we try to squeeze the aftermath into the mold of normal non-pathological relationships. Others who have not suffered in the same way cannot even begin to understand, leaving us out in the cold, searching alone for our lost souls, feeling foolish and careless for having lost them in the first place.

We Westerners, busily attending to the cultural expectations that drive us—most of which are to do with social comparison in a secular society—have long since forgotten how to attend to our deep, inner spiritual selves. Our time gets filled up with questions of are we good enough, do we measure up, are we earning enough, doing enough, having enough? If we just keep trying harder, working harder, making more money, we can one day achieve the shared cultural ideal of happiness, a happy life. When we get the next thing, then we'll be happy. When we are acknowledged and validated by our community, then we will be worthy of our own love, respect, and admiration. When we lose the ten kilos, wear the right clothes, live in the right neighbourhood, get a thousand Instagram followers or Facebook friends, feed our own narcissism and greed. That's how it is for many of us. And we're kept in this straight jacket by those around us, who are stuck on similar hamster wheels, also peddling as fast as they can go.

So when a narcopath invades and strips us of all we strove for all our lives, we can fall into an abyss. It can feel like there is nothing and no one to support us, as we desperately try to prevent our own fall. Many women never learned how to support themselves, conditioned as we were to perpetually look outwards, to subserviently overlook our own needs in service to men, children, elders, everybody else. We hear the cliché that we cannot love others until we learn to love ourselves, but we have no idea how to do that when we've already learned the opposite. We are expert at being hard on ourselves, blaming ourselves, beating ourselves up. Most of us have deeply ingrained, harsh inner critics that speak silently to us when we make a mistake or take a fall. We berate ourselves in terms and tones we would rarely adopt towards other people.

For many of us, these harsh methods are also outwardly manifested in our families. How can we hope to recover our lost souls when people who claim to love us are actually victim-blaming, criticising, scolding, and betraying us? We desperately want change but don't know how to make even the slightest adjustment, because we still look outwards to try to change our external circumstances and conditions. The massive trauma of covert narcissistic life rape might be the first opportunity any of us have had to wake up, to recognise the cyclic nature of our existence, the patterns of abuse we have grown used to and feel powerless to prevent. We know we need to let go, get over it, keep calm, and carry on. But this seems like an impossible dream from inside the snare of strong emotions. For many of us, turning inwards is a last resort, one we only choose when we have exhausted every other option and still suffer unbearable pain.

The damage is in our minds, our energy bodies, our physical bodies, *and* our souls, however we define *soul*; let's just say that part of us that is deeply buried, that part that feels beyond reach, that part that is crying out to be healed, that part we feel we have no control over, but which seems to rule our lives, that part we now feel is hideously wounded. Let's call it our core beliefs, our core values, our consciousness, our spirit. Even if talk therapy has helped us recognise that we have limiting childhood beliefs that keep us stuck, how do we root them out and change them? How can we possibly address, say, our fear of abandonment by just thinking about it? How can we change a belief that we don't belong, will never be good enough, are unworthy of love, or are imposters?

Through spiritual practices. Through cultivating mindfulness of body, emotion, thought, and the way things really are.

Through meditation, mindfulness, prayer, visualisation, opening our hearts, making ourselves vulnerable. By entering into the wounded place voluntarily, courageously, with kindness, curiosity, and honesty. By owning our dark side and nurturing our innocent inner child. By introducing beingness into our daily lives. By choosing to sit and be with our deep inner selves instead of eating that whole cake, or bingeing on *Game of Thrones*, or drinking the whole bottle, or connecting on anti-social media for hours on end, or running a marathon. It can feel ridiculous to begin with, even a bit embarrassing. It can feel like laziness or aimlessness or wasting time. We can easily drown it with scepticism or dismiss it as masochism.

211

But it is these practices that will help us find our souls so we can heal them.

It takes discipline; *that* we can probably relate to: mindfulness boot camp. If we have to make half an hour to sit with ourselves, learn to overcome unhealthy rumination, and nourish ourselves from within, we might just give ourselves permission to do this, especially if we think it might work, when we can see this not as a heavy weight but as a gradually liberating practice.

The bottom line is, keep trying everything until you find the key to your own recovery. It's in your mind, your body, your energy body, and that deep inner part of you that we call the soul.

> Go back and take care of yourself. Your body needs you, your feelings need you, your perceptions need you. The wounded child in you needs you. Your suffering needs you to acknowledge it. Go home and be there for all these things. Practice mindful walking and mindful breathing. Do everything in mindfulness so you can really be there, so you can love.
>
> - Thich Nhat Hanh, www.lionsroar.com

Healing the Inner Child

The causes of ancient wounds to the subconscious mind that create unhealthy guiding belief systems are a bit more complicated than just an unhappy childhood.

Why is this even relevant in recovering from life rape by a narcopath? Because it is these deep core wounds and beliefs that he identifies during the idealise phase, manipulates during the devalue phase, and rips open in the discard phase. He recognises the innocent child in us, promises to take care of her, holds her hostage, then uses her for his own sick gratification. The lies he chooses for his smear campaign are deliberately pinpointed at these vulnerabilities (the things we don't like about ourselves) in the hope that we will never recover. His proud legacy.

But we *can* recover when we shift focus from the story of what he did to us and what we don't like about ourselves to re-parenting our own authentic selves.

> Ambition, self-criticism, shame, self-judgement, and so forth are rife in our culture.… There are inevitably hard times in which we face our deepest fears and confusions, our pain and demons. We have to tend and heal the traumas and sorrows that human life brings us with compassion. But this is not a grim duty. It's a step-by-step journey of freedom and liberation.… The Puritan ethic and sense of original sin underlying much of our cultural history can feed into this. What's beautiful to discover in meditation practice is that this painful cultural conditioning is not true.
>
> —Jack Kornfield, www.lionsroar.com

These culturally conditioned beliefs can be formed at a young and vulnerable age by events or occurrences even good parenting cannot prevent, such as

- a culture of patriarchy (where women and girls are not valued as highly as men and boys);
- a culture of racism (where the colour of our skin determines the opportunities and life path open to us);
- cultural xenophobia (where the religion or geographical background of our family is feared, disrespected, or unwanted);
- an entrenched class system (where moving between classes is frowned upon);
- an environment of stoicism (where discussing life's difficulties is taboo);
- family scapegoating (where one child is continually singled out for blame);
- time-poor parents (where parenting is farmed out to teachers, child-carers, or others);
- emotionally unavailable or avoidant parents (who, for whatever reason, continually allow children to parent themselves at crucial life moments);

- narcissistic parents (who are incapable of prioritising a child's concerns or needs over their own);
- strict social conformity (where childish experimentation or behaviour that values differentness is quashed);
- neglect (actual parental absence due to substance abuse, other toxic parental behaviour, or unmanageable external circumstances);
- bullying (undisclosed by the child or unaddressed by parental figures);
- verbal, physical, or sexual abuse (particularly by a loved, respected, or trusted other); and
- normal trauma (including hospitalisations, illnesses, and accidents).

We might respond with our childish minds by forming beliefs about ourselves and the world that continue to inform our actions even as adults, hidden in our subconscious and rarely brought into awareness. I think of these beliefs as being unparented beliefs. Addressing them is not about blaming our parents but about re-parenting ourselves. Some of the beliefs we find when we peel the layers of the onion might even seem crazy to us, as they are contrary to what our adult self *wants* to believe.

- I am inferior. My purpose is to serve men. Men are to be respected and obeyed. Men are always right and never to be challenged. My opinions don't matter compared to men's. A husband's career is more important than a wife's.
- I'm not one of the cool kids because I am inferior. I am unlikeable. I am not good enough. I need to keep my head down so I don't get bullied.
- I will never escape from poverty. There is no point in trying to escape my fate. I'm a loser. I'm not okay but you are. I'm okay but you aren't.
- I must keep my problems to myself. I am a problem. I must not be a burden on others. I am a burden. I am an inconvenience. I need to stand on my own two feet, so I never ask for help.
- Everything is my fault. I am fundamentally flawed. I am weird and different. I don't fit in anywhere. My sexuality is wrong.
- My mother/father doesn't love me. My sibling hates me. I am unworthy of love. I don't want to get a big head, so I'll never congratulate myself for anything. I always fail, so I'll never try.

- I want people to like me, so I must always put others before myself. I am unlovable. No matter how hard I try, I will never be good enough. I don't deserve to be loved or emotionally supported.
- I don't belong. I'm a freak. People hate me for being me. I'm too sensitive. I need to toughen up. I need to be cruel to be kind.
- I am a mistake. I should never have been born. Nobody loves me. I don't belong anywhere. I'm unwanted. Everybody I love abandons me.
- I have no power in my life. I am helpless in the face of abuse. I am worthless.
- The world is a dangerous place. I expect bad things to happen to me. Men/authority figures/priests/people cannot be trusted. All men are bastards. All women are bitches.
- Truth will always win out. Good will triumph over evil. The justice system will protect the innocent. Others will treat me the way I treat them. Ethical behaviour will keep me safe from harm. God will keep me safe from harm. If I am loyal to others, they will be loyal to me. Everything happens for a reason. Bad things don't happen to good people. What goes around comes around, so I must have done something to deserve this punishment.

In a sense, these beliefs can keep a part of our emotional selves trapped in childhood and cast a shadow over our adult lives. Additionally, it is these vulnerable beliefs that can fuel repetition compulsion: the habit of continually revisiting or recreating painful or disappointing relationships in an attempt to rewrite our codes and achieve a positive outcome the next time. As much as we try to paper over or hide these damaged foundations, or even when we are willing to address them, finding and shifting them is not something we are taught how to do.

In recovery, we come up against a plethora of cultural myths that we didn't even realise we had subscribed to. A lot of people refer to these cultural myths as common sense. Unsubscribing from common sense is not so easy. It can add insult to injury and take us into very dark, solitary, and painful places. Facing these demons is not for everybody, that's for sure. Peeling the layers of the onion opens us further and further into vulnerability and sorrow. It can have an addictive push-through cruel-to-be-kind quality that drives us too far out of our own comfort zones and leaves us feeling more and more alone and traumatised.

Self-regulation becomes incredibly important, so that we don't find ourselves completely overloaded with pain. A therapist or teacher who recognises when we are heading towards this kind of burnout and interrupts the escalation is also essential if we choose the therapy path. Recovery from abuse has an energy all of its own that might push us into a great internal scream of "I just want it to end." We can feel overwhelmed and fail to recognise that we are holding the steering wheel. We can back off, take a break, go easy, and shift the focus back to kindness, gentleness, tenderness, and warmth, offer ourselves the encouragement and validation we most need to hear when we come up against a buried false belief.

Let me give an example of one such *common-sense* belief that some of us encounter: "All mothers love their children."

Facing the fact that this simply isn't true can leave us out in the wilderness again, struggling to come to terms with another unquestionable foundational belief we now see might not apply in our case. That's a really big one. That requires us to be radically kind and compassionate towards our own pain. That may even be a myth we'd prefer to hold onto—just like believing our abuser loved us once too—and that's okay. There is no trauma recovery rulebook that stipulates we must drag the bottom of our own ocean of pain, dredging up every tiny fragment of delusion and myth and setting it straight. Only we can know how much pain we can take. Only we can learn how to make meaning and growth from our own suffering.

Our commitment from here on in is to be *kind* to ourselves.

Why Does This Keep Happening to Me?

Narcissistic parents teach us that we need to be perfect and successful, but that you should never be rewarded for it or feel "enough." Narcissists are masters of moving the goal posts so that nothing their victims do is ever enough. Our accomplishments are rarely acknowledged unless they meet an arbitrary criteria for "what looks best to society," or confirms the narcissistic parent's own grandiose fantasies. Our abusive parent is never genuinely proud of us unless he or she can claim credit for that particular success ... "My parents are rarely proud of me no matter what I do. For them, it was never enough. For the most part, I raised myself and accomplished this in spite of what they did."

—Shahida Arabi, *Power: Surviving and Thriving after Narcissistic Abuse*

Our magnetic attraction to the narcopath might have been the result of our childhood conditioning if we had a narcissistic parent or primary caregiver. The reason we feel like we fit together like puzzle pieces, have known each other for ever, or are soulmates can be due to the echoes of hidden toxicity in our family of origin or early caregivers.

- Love-bombing provides us with the external validation we sought and never received from our parents. Loved at last (not).
- Intermittent reinforcement from a loved one feels natural and normal. If we were praised for behaviour that served our parents, and our own unique achievements were undervalued or ignored, we became used to conditional love.
- Being emotionally abandoned when our parents withdraw their conditional love and support can breed a deep fear of abandonment by loved ones.
- We normalise controlling, extremely selfish, or dominating behaviour from a loved one. We develop coping techniques, and they become our comfort zone.
- We learn to equate the appearance of having it all together with having worth.
- We become dependent on external validation to feel good about ourselves.
- A narcissistic parent can teach us to hide our true feelings, opinions, moods, or reactions in order to avoid conflict and hypercriticism. Over time, we can hide them even from ourselves and only feel confusion instead of a healthy recognition of toxicity.

- We learn that no matter what we do, we are never good enough.
- If we were scapegoated as children, we learn to blame ourselves and think we don't deserve better treatment from people around us.
- We learn to undervalue ourselves.
- Catering to a self-centred parent can teach us to be fixers, pleasers, rescuers, or martyrs.
- We can repeatedly go with toxic relationship dynamics driven by a subconscious urge to heal the original toxicity this time around.
- Our pain threshold for toxic behaviour is much higher than those who have never been abused, so we hang on to a toxic relationship way longer than is healthy for us.
- We're trying to make a toxic person the family we never had, when in reality, they are exactly like the family we did have.

Here's a method for finding and transforming wounds we might not even know we have:

Notes on This Inner Child Guided Meditation

Guided imagery of our inner child can help us activate our emotional memories and connect directly with our subconscious mind. Picturing ourselves as children stimulates the brain to access things that we usually keep filed deep in the dusty archives.

There is no wrong way to do this. Even if we think of ourselves as not very visual or imaginative, we can recall things from memory. We might use an old photograph as a place to start. Relaxed, open, and grounded, we can use our imagination to replay the movies of our past. We are not aiming to transport ourselves back in time—to *be* that child again—but to observe ourselves as children from our adult place now, to take that child into our own loving embrace, to soothe, comfort, encourage, validate, uplift, nurture, and nourish her.

We can recognise the innocence, goodness, and purity of this child. We can connect with the child who is, as yet, unaffected by harmful or painful events or to the child who is acting out, crying out for support and understanding at any age. Opening to this vulnerable child will make us stronger over time, not weaker. The practice will strengthen our own protective instincts. Offering our adult love and protection to our remembered inner child will grow our capacity to nourish and protect ourselves in the future and support the conscious process of building better boundaries.

Inner Child Visualisation Meditation

Relaxed, centred and grounded, allow your memory to access an image of you as a child, teenager, or younger adult. Recall the room or the outdoor space, the temperature, the aromas, any detail that comes back to you. It might have been a time and place when you needed help, support, comfort, love, or companionship, or a time when you were deeply hurt, afraid, or traumatised.

As your adult self, approach this dear young one slowly and carefully, with kindness and gentleness. Ask the child in words (or in another way) how you can help her now, and allow the answer to come in whatever way it comes. If there is something or someone preventing you from helping the child, stand firm, and with right on your side, create a force field of safety around you and your child. Allow a safe, impenetrable, invisible dome just big enough to contain you and your child to descend around you, wrapping you up in comfort and safety.

If your child will let you, take her in your arms, hold her hand, or stroke her hair, whatever gesture feels right and good at this moment. If the child is too afraid or hurt to let you come that close, then reassure her. Tell her she is safe, you aren't going to hurt her, and you are never going to leave her again. You are sorry she is going through such a hard time. Tell her you're sorry you weren't there for her the first time, and you'll always be there for her from now on.

Spend time with your precious little child. Notice the tenderness and love you feel for this girl. Tell her how much you love and care for her. If she has physical wounds, tend to them. Soothe and comfort her. If she is angry or afraid, be patient with her. Stay with her as long as feels right.

Undertake to visit your inner child again. When it is safe to do so, return to your adult self in this room and this time.

Revisiting your dear child self, you may find that she is a different age every time you visit, facing different challenges and circumstances. Or you might replay the same scenario every time you commit to the practice. Every time you do this, you are helping to heal and integrate any part of your past that is wounded. Your child now has an adult who will always be there for her.

Healing the Past and Embracing Change Affirmations

Grounding and Centring Introduction

I am learning a new way of life.
It is safe for me to let go of old habits.
I forgive myself. I release the past hurts that are keeping me stuck.
I am letting go and staying open.
I now love and accept myself exactly as I am.

I enjoy my own company.
Within me is a special place of serenity and power.
With every breath, I release the old and receive the new.
As I allow myself to feel my sadness, I open up to my joy.

I reclaim my natural ability to follow my intuition.
The creative power of the universe is now flowing through me.
I am now creating my life the way I want it to be.
As I relax and let go, I flow towards my greatest good.
I surrender to life. Through surrender, I find the light within me.

I am expressing more and more of my potential.
I am creating balanced, harmonious prosperity in my life.
I open my eyes to goodness, beauty, and abundance.
Day by day, I am being filled from the source within me.

I trust the wisdom inside of me.
I trust that my heart will guide my footsteps in light.
I trust the flow of life.
I relax and let myself be.
I am open and willing to change.

As I follow my intuition, creative energy flows through me.
By being myself and doing what I love, I make a significant contribution to life.
I find fulfilment in everything I do.
I allow myself to be. I do what feels right. I have everything I truly want.

In my own time and in my own way, I am creating miracles in my life.
New goals and new dreams come to me as I need them.
My new life is filled with endless possibilities.
As the flow of life changes, I change.
I accept all the feelings that come with change and growth.

I appreciate, love, and respect my body.
As I trust and assert my feelings, I create a healthy, beautiful body.
I love and appreciate myself as I am now.
I deserve the best in life.

I deserve to be loved.
I deserve harmonious relationships.
As I cultivate harmony within myself, so harmonious relationships come to me.
The qualities I admire in others, I cultivate in myself.

I am attractive, desirable, and loveable.
The more I love myself, the more others love me.
I treat myself exactly the way I want to be treated.
I support and appreciate myself.

I accept perfect health now.
I am open to new possibilities.
I have everything I need in life.
I am loved and loveable.

I am good enough, I am good enough, I am good enough.

I release my sensitivity to criticism and my need to judge or criticise others.
I am confident in my own ability to be successful at work and with people.
I rejoice in even the smallest accomplishment.
I am my own best friend.

I did the best I could as I was then.
That was then, and this is now.
I love myself. I forgive myself.
I rejoice in the new me that is growing in strength and joy every day.

I nourish my inner child with love, support, and kindness every day.
I no longer need to look for love outside myself.
I release my tendency to sabotage myself and allow my light to shine from within.
I am talented, gifted, and accomplished, and that's okay by me.
I am intelligent, powerful, and strong, and that's okay too.

Other people's cruelty, nastiness, and anger do not affect my love for myself.
I am safe. I am secure. I am fine, even when I make mistakes.
I am loveable. I am good enough. I no longer doubt myself.
I am my own best friend.
I have my inner child for company when I feel lonely.

I handle conflict with grace, dignity, and kindness.
I now have a happy, peaceful life, filled with happy, peaceful people.

I support and appreciate myself.
I am not a mistake. I am a unique being, surrounded by divine light.
There is nothing drastically wrong with me.
My past has gone, and I accept the future with adult strength and maturity and the eagerness of a child.

My personal likes and dislikes are okay. I accept myself just as I am.
I trust the flow of life.
I relax and let myself be.

As I open to new possibilities, my intuition guides me to people, places, and experiences that are perfect for me.
As my new path becomes illuminated, so my confidence in moving forward grows.

I am safe. I am supported. I am valuable.
I deserve to be loved. I was never at fault for anyone's inability to love me.
I now attract loving, kind, caring people who will never use, abuse, or abandon me.

Energetic Healing: The Final Frontier for Sceptics

Western surgeons established centuries ago that we have a number of systems cooperating in our bodies, including the skeletal, blood, nervous, and hormone systems. Eastern medicine would also contend that there is another system, a system of energy flow, a pathway for the flow of life force in a living body. Managing this flow of energy is the basis of a number of martial arts and healing modalities, like yoga, tai chi, qigong, and reiki. The energy is called kundalini or chi. The system works through seven energy centres, called chakras.

Indigenous cultures throughout the world include shamans in their community. Shamanic practices have been around for tens of thousands of years. Stories of shamanic healing for PTSD and other ailments are trickling into online forums and mainstream psychology. Ancient initiation rites, many of which were potentially traumatising, were a pathway to adulthood, to growing up, standing alone in the wilderness, passing through darkness, and coming out into the light wiser, braver, and more whole. Shamans see trauma as a growth experience. When plunged into darkness, no one can see how there can be anything positive to come from a trip through hell, but it is here that we find the light of our spirit.

When the mind says, "I give up and surrender to not knowing," and the body says, "I am exhausted and weak," that is when the spirit takes over. We find spiritual practices that awaken the *fire* of our inner spirit. Emerging from the fire of trauma, we become whole, spiritually as well as emotionally and psychologically. Sandra Ingerman, a shaman and psychotherapist, describes a trauma recovery pathway I inadvertently discovered for myself:

1. Talk it through (in therapy) until the need to talk it through passes.
2. Process and integrate the trauma over time.
3. Quiet the mind.
4. Rediscover the life force or spirit.
5. Invite a spiritual helper and spiritual practices or rituals into your life.

Until I experienced it for myself, I would tune right out once people started talking about dark energy and the like, putting it firmly in the science fiction/scepticism/far-out-hippie/witch-doctor compartments. Despite practising yoga for twenty years and regular visits to a traditional Chinese medicine doctor to restore a sense of balance, certain aspects of spiritual healing, like crystals, faith healing, and indeed shamanism, were all a bridge too far for my level of scepticism. Early in the aftermath, my old practices helped towards balancing mind and body to cope with the swirling vortex of the psychological trauma. And training in mindfulness as described in this book slowly generated positive thoughts and emotions alongside the negative ones that naturally arise when traumatised.

It took a profound spiritual experience with an expert qigong (a Chinese martial art) teacher and "healing space-holder" (her words) for me to finally take energetic healing out of its box and open to the idea. Like mindfulness, take it as my working hypothesis for a while and see where it took me. It took me right into full remission from CPTSD.

Rather than try to describe how it works, let me describe the experiences that proved to be the final piece of my healing jigsaw.

I often choose sound as the object of my concentration in meditation, to descend beneath the swirling surface waters of the mind and down into the still depths of witnessing my own thoughts. Since training in mindfulness is training in concentration, I would rest my attention on the sounds in my current environment. Broadening focus from the sounds inside the room, to the near distance, then the far distance, until the full landscape (or cityscape) of sound is held in curious, compassionate awareness.

Since I loved sound and music (doesn't everybody?), I thought I would attend a qigong sound meditation group, just for the experience. The meditation leader gently and skilfully led us on a sound journey, using a weird and wonderful selection of bells, bowls, pipes, and gongs. The sound resonated through our bodies, and the teacher guided us through visualisations of light and energy in each of our chakras. Looking around the sea of faces after that experience, I could not only feel the balance and recent memory of transcendence in myself but see the radiance, calm, clarity, and balance in the people around me.

So I booked myself in for a sound massage. The combination sounded pretty nice. Once there, all I had to do was lie on a massage table and relax. The healer used sound rather than pressure to reverberate in the natural resonating chambers of the body by placing Tibetan singing bowls over each chakra centre (base of the spine, pelvis, solar plexus, heart, throat, third eye). It was soothing, calming, and relaxing, and the sensation of a bell ringing through my chest cavity and pelvic girdle was delightful. So I settled for enjoying the experience while it lasted, doing nothing, concentrating on the somatic sensations. Then an extraordinary thing happened.

Just as the sound massage was coming to completion, the healer began to ring high-pitched bells around the top of my head: the area of the crown chakra. I suddenly felt as if the top of my head had opened up, allowing a mass of dark fizzy energy to pour out like Coke out of a shaken bottle. I felt like a vessel opened up and emptying its contents, accompanied by the soft, unintelligible whispering and gentle tinkling bells of the healer.

As she continued, the vessel emptied itself, and the flow reversed, with pure white, clean light gently flowing into the opening at the top of my head. The warm white energy filtered into all the nooks and crannies of my body and settled into my torso and limbs like water settles in a pond. I saw and felt it all happen to me, as clear as day, a vision, a profound spiritual experience.

When I left, my centre of gravity had completely changed. I felt as if I was connected with the earth for the first time in four years. I also felt an extraordinary connection with other people, as if I were flowing as one with every being around me, somehow sharing our struggles and joys, our basic humanness, with an acute awareness of how we are all in this life business together.

That night, I attended an event that might previously have triggered me into an early departure: crowds of people, alcohol, noise, screaming kids, performers trying to drag audience participation out of each of us. I was consumed with joy at the human condition. Despite a fellow narcabuse companion sharing her potentially triggering abuse stories all night, I remained joyful, calm, centred, and grounded.

Gone was the constant burble of anxiety in the pit of my stomach. Gone was the feeling of imminent threat, and the jumpiness at sudden and unexpected stimuli. Gone was the anxious background hum of hurt and shame and the broken record of thoughts I had already thought a million times before. That night, I slept through without a nightmare, and I woke not in fright, but in calm, deep peace. The relief was indescribable.

That day, I developed a migraine headache, complete with strobe lighting, excruciating pain, and nausea. I'd not had one of those since my teenage years. When I finally pulled my head out of the toilet bowl, a strange calm descended. The purge left me feeling as if the trauma had finally left my body, as if my walk through hell was finally over. I was back to normal. And it has been that way ever since.

This was no doubt the shamanic healing that so many in the PTSD and narcabuse communities reach for as a last resort. There are stories of people (including some known to me personally) who travel to Tibet or Peru to visit shamans of ancient cultures in order to purge themselves of the lingering symptoms of PTSD. All that is needed is a willingness to put our scepticism to one side and take it as our working hypothesis for a while, just like mindfulness, visualisation, and other spiritual practices.

I had conscientiously done the work of figuring out what the hell just happened with my rational mind; built up a toolkit of tactics to cope with constant anxiety and socially inappropriate triggering; and devoted myself wholeheartedly to healing my own wound, re-birthing myself, and re-parenting myself. I slowly got a handle on living with PTSD without giving up hope of liberation from it. In so doing, I had finally overcome old habits of self-loathing, self-blame, and spiralling bouts of depression. I had left a whole lot of toxic influences behind me and learnt to stand on my own two feet. I was absolutely ready for the final piece of the jigsaw to come along. And it did.

Each of us has our own unique story. We each have to find our own way in the dark for a while, travel through the underworld in our hero's journey. There are naturally times when we lose hope or feel like we've tried everything to cure ourselves of this moral injury. We reach our wit's end over and over again. But we just keep going, one step at a time. Along the way, we find our tribe, and we learn to stand alone in the wilderness. Our compassion, wisdom, and courage grow. We regain our faith in ourselves and humankind. We now see and accept the darkness of the human condition. We have woken up, grown up, and learned to stand inside our personal power. We are kinder and more patient. We listen more. We see what is really going on. We trust life again. We lost our innocence and naivety, and gained equilibrium in the face of adversity. We walked through hell and came out into the light.

We did it.

Endnote: Tell your story. Nobody else can see a domestic abuser who doesn't leave bruises and broken bones except his victims. And people who believe us when we tell our story. Be brave. Tell your story. It might help someone else.

Ask the Experts

Miller, Alice (1995), *The Drama of Being a Child: The Search for the True Self.* Virago.

Forward, Susan, and Buck, Craig (2002), *Toxic Parents.* Random House Books.

Kornfield, Jack (1993), *A Path with Heart.* Bantam Books.

Downloadable Inner Child Meditations and Affirmations
http://defoore.com

Hanh, Thich Nhat (2010), *Reconciliation: Healing the Child Within.* Berkeley, CA: Parallax Press.
https://www.lionsroar.com/healing-the-child-within/

Kornfield, Jack, "De-Conditioning Cultural Beliefs."
https://www.lionsroar.com/be-free-now-an-interview-with-jack-kornfield/

Arabi, Shahida, "Narcissistic Parents."
https://selfcarehaven.wordpress.com/2017/12/16/the-psychological-war-zone-the-children-of-narcissists-face-these-5-consequences-in-adulthood/

Kornfield, Jack, and Goodman, Trudy, *Exploring the Shadow.*
https://www.youtube.com/watch?v=woHkEBBJDM8

Shamanic Teachers
http://shamanicteachers.com/practitioners.html

Healing Space Holder and Qigong Teacher
https://qigongmelbourne.com.au/

Survivor-Derived Spiritual Healing Method
https://www.melanietoniaevans.com/

About the Author

Margot MacCallum (a nom de plum) has a Diploma of Dramatic Arts, a Master of Business (Human Resources), and is studying towards a Diploma of Counselling. She had a successful career in film, television, voiceovers, and stage productions for twenty years. She also worked as a corporate group facilitator and administrator, and ran her own small service and retail business.

She was raised in a rural setting and privately educated at a Christian women's college. She has lived and worked in Australia's two largest cities and in London. She now leads a simple, solitary life in a country cottage, surviving on very little and relishing it.

She has experienced comprehensive intimate partner abuse twice. On both occasions, she lost everything, including the support of her family. Training in mindfulness led to transformation of her inner world and a commitment to support and empower other women who experience lingering trauma from profound psychological, emotional, and financial abuse.